Opening Doors in the Heartlands:
A History of the University of Wolverhampton

Mike Haynes and Lib Meakin

First published by the University of Wolverhampton 2013
University of Wolverhampton,
Wulfruna Street,
Wolverhampton,
WV1 1LY
www.wlv.ac.uk

ISBN: 978-0-9576636-0-2

Copyright © Michael Haynes and Susan Elizabeth Meakin 2013

Contents

Acknowledgements

The Growth of the University

Foreword
Chapter 1 Roots – the Early Years 01
Chapter 2 Towards the Modern University 29
Chapter 3 The Workforce – Students 65
Chapter 4 The Workforce – Staff 89
Chapter 5 A Small Town in a Big Conurbation 109
Chapter 6 The World Beyond the Open Doors 153
Index 175

The University of Wolverhampton and the Wider World

About the Authors

Foreword

I have great pleasure in introducing this book. This is not just a history of the University of Wolverhampton but a story of its growth and the times in which it grew. It is both a history and a social chronicle. Mike Haynes and Lib Meakin have told the story well and it is a very proud story.

Any university that has a history dating back 180 years and has had 25 different names clearly has a story to tell. It is a story that shows how the University, right from its very first development, was focused on providing opportunity - opportunity to engage in learning as a means of improving and enhancing both individual and collective life chances.

In the Robbins Report of 1963 and the Dearing Report of 1997, higher education was defined as being a vehicle to enable individuals to push at the frontiers of knowledge and discovery; to encourage individual academic excellence; to develop the skills and knowledge needed for the world of work and to help to create and shape a democratic and inclusive society. The University of Wolverhampton has been at the forefront of these challenges since 1827 and continues to be so today.

Working across Wolverhampton, Walsall, Telford, Staffordshire, Shropshire, Sandwell and Dudley, the University is immensely grateful for the civic pride that has contributed to investment in the institution. Going forward we are now delivering in 13 countries and in three continents as we contribute not just to regional economic development but also to the global economy.

Today we are at the heart of economic regeneration and pursuing a form of social mobility that focuses on both economic and societal change whilst also investing in intellectual development. We are committed to being the Opportunity University and to making a real difference to all those we work with.

Professor Geoff Layer
Vice-Chancellor

Chapter one

Roots – the Early Years

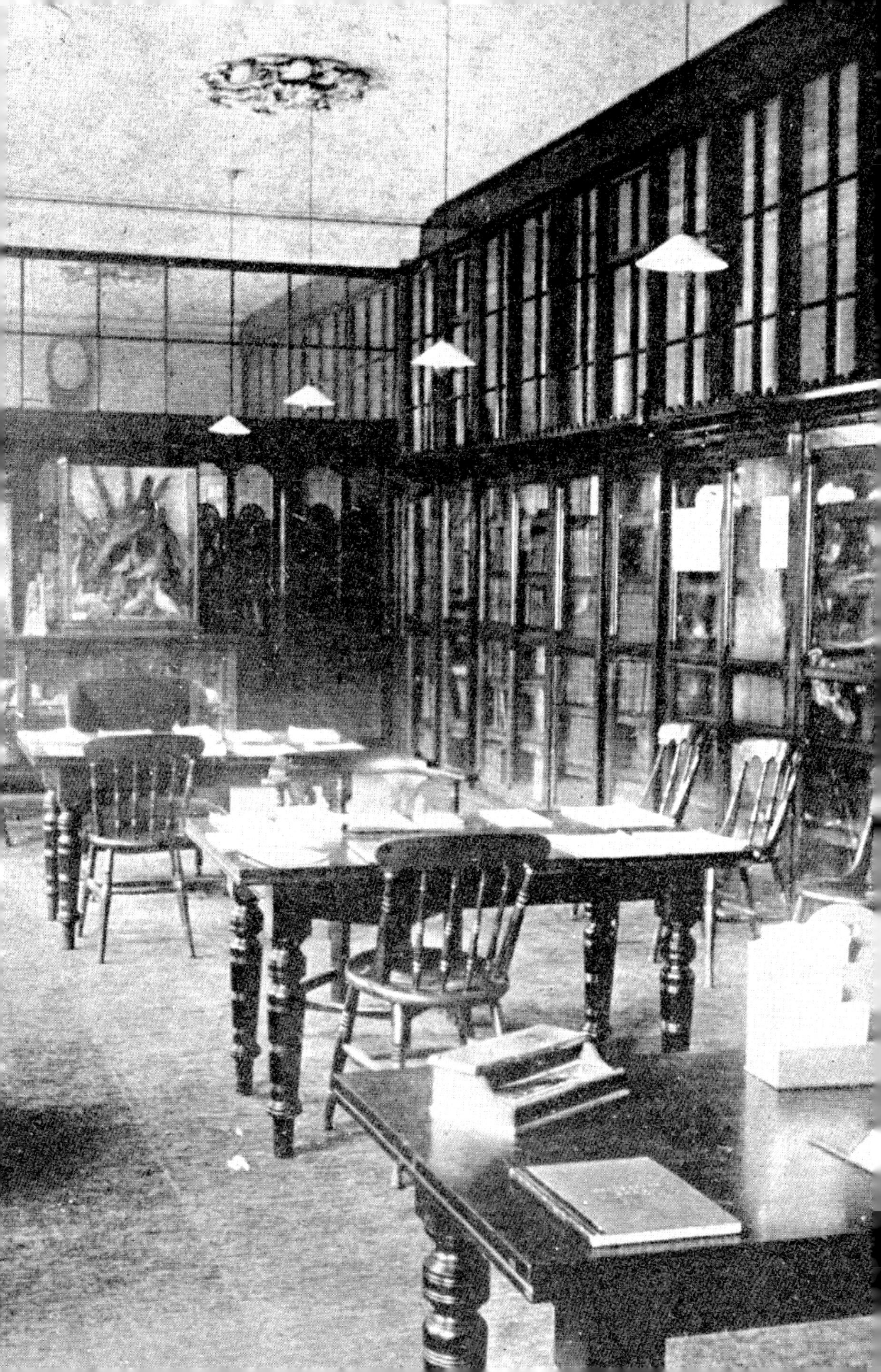

In one hundred and eighty years a small, local workers' library and meeting room has become one of the largest national higher education providers in the country with 23,000 students and nearly 3,000 staff occupying large estates in a city and two nearby towns. To make sense of how the University of Wolverhampton grew from its nineteenth century roots we have to join a local to a national story and that national story to an international one. What is striking in this story is that at each stage people were striving for more. At first the battle was to obtain any access to education, then to higher levels of study. Successful institutions then sought the highest status available. People involved had no greater foresight than any of us do, so the story of this striving often involves twists and turns and unexpected outcomes. Apparent victories and defeats could be overwhelmed by forces that people did not anticipate or at best only half foresaw. With the benefit of hindsight, five big themes can be identified running through the history of higher education in England and of the University of Wolverhampton.

The first of these is the struggle to develop universal education – first at the elementary level; then at the secondary; and finally the higher level. The second theme is the battle over the purpose of education, the extent to which it is limited by the requirement for a workforce to be educated for economic competitiveness. The third is the growing role of the State in educational provision. The fourth, the growth of professionalisation, associated with the rise of credentialism – the imperative for individuals to gain formal qualifications in the labour market. Although these themes are common to much of higher education across the world, the fifth theme is arguably rooted in the particular social conditions of England. This is the continuing role of social inequality and social class.

All societies are affected by social division but the strength of that division in Britain has been a constant presence in the development of its education system. In 1931, R.H.Tawney famously wrote that 'the hereditary curse upon English education is its organisation upon lines of social class'.[1] At first it dictated that the masses did not

Artist's impression of Wolverhampton and Staffordshire Technical college

[1] R.H.Tawney, Equality, London, 1931, p. 142.

Educated to your Class

> *Elementary education was the education of a special class which could obtain no other ... and secondary education that of their masters.*

This was how R.H.Tawney described nineteenth century education in his 1922 plea for 'secondary education for all'.

Before 1870, parents paid for their children to be educated in voluntary schools. The task of these schools was to teach the four Rs – reading, writing, arithmetic and religion. State money was used to police their 'efficiency'. 'Education should be suited to the condition of workmen and servants' it was said in 1833. Work would begin from the age of 10 or 11, with, for the more skilled, further learning through apprenticeships. Schools were also intended to re-enforce the moral and political order. In 1843, shortly after a huge general strike, perhaps the first in the world, Sir James Graham, the Home Secretary said 'the police and the soldiers have done their duty, the time has arrived when moral and religious instructors must go forth to reclaim the people from the errors of their ways'. In 1867, with the franchise being slightly extended, Robert Lowe made a similar argument. 'If the lower classes must now be educated ... they must be educated that they may appreciate and defer to a higher civilisation when they meet it'.

In 1870, The Elementary Education Act (Forster's Act) created 2,000 local school boards which had an input into the existing 8,800 voluntary schools and the authority to build their own 'Board' schools. State aid had provided only 30% of income to supported schools in 1870 but this rose to 60% in 1887 and 90% by 1902. In 1880, elementary education was made compulsory for 5 to 10 year olds but was not free for most people until 1891. The school leaving age was raised to 11 in 1894 and 12 in 1899. By 1900 near universal elementary education existed, the numbers in elementary schooling rose from 1.2 million in 1860 to 4.7 million in 1900.

But there was little chance of going beyond this. Secondary education was, as Tawney said, for another class. Some elementary schools began to develop higher level classes for those aged 13 and 14 but before 1902 these had an uncertain status as 'higher grade schools'. The best that could be hoped for was some additional part-time education in a technical college or institute.

need any education. Then, throughout the nineteenth century, a limited elementary education was thought sufficient. For much of the twentieth century secondary education was divided by class, sex, school and function. Today this curse is still a factor, debates concerning early and secondary education have been joined by another about who can access higher education and what kind of higher education do they need?

It is within this historical framework that social processes developed which led, in the late twentieth century, to pressure for a mass higher education system. Many of today's universities developed, in an inconsistent and idiosyncratic way, out of a patchwork of diverse institutions founded for specific tasks. Seeking a way to describe the evolution of the higher education system Alan Matterson once reached for a line of G.K.Chesterton, 'the rolling English drunkard made the rolling English road.'[2] The history of higher education in general, and universities in particular, is chaotic – halting development gives way to lurches forward and balance and stability rarely last for long. The Robbins Report of 1963 made this point more bluntly, 'higher education has not been planned as a whole or developed within a framework consciously devised to promote harmonious evolution'.[3]

The front-sheet to this book shows this evolution for the University of Wolverhampton. We see its roots in a patchwork of independent institutions, some formed in the 1800s and others as late as the 1960s. The physical locations of the University derive from this patchwork. It now occupies sites in three urban areas several miles apart – the City of Wolverhampton, the Black Country town of Walsall and the Shropshire town of Telford. Wolverhampton lies twelve and a half miles (19.5 kilometres) north west of Birmingham. Walsall, four miles (6.44 kilometres) to the east of Wolverhampton merges into the conurbation linking Wolverhampton with Birmingham.

Telford, sixteen miles (25.74 kilometres) to the north west of Wolverhampton is a new town developed from the 1960s.

Here we look at the beginnings of this development – from the nineteenth century to the 1960s. This story is part of the heritage of the University and the wider society of which it is a part. But 'heritage' is an ambiguous term in a world in which selling the past is itself an industry. 'Heritage' gives us a sense of the past but it can also be a distorting prism. This chapter therefore draws on surviving records and on the work of historians, some of whom have been based in the University, particularly in its early Polytechnic years when they saw it as part of their task to record and unravel the past of the Black Country and the wider West Midlands.[4]

The Nineteenth Century Black Country

The modern story of higher education in the Black Country is rooted in the industrial revolution. Why and how this began in Britain in the late eighteenth century remains debated, but by the mid-nineteenth century Britain was the first industrial capitalist state. With a population of only 27 million in 1851 it was producing a huge share of world industrial output. The census of that year showed it to be the first urban society with half of its population living in the towns – a figure no other society would achieve for another half century. Industrialisation gave rise to new centres and conurbations – mining settlements, textile, iron and, later, steel towns. In the middle of Britain it helped to create the Birmingham conurbation with the Black Country to its west, emerging around a small coalfield. Here in 1838 Charles Dickens found 'miles of cinder paths and blazing furnaces, and roaring steam engines…such a mass of dirt, gloom and misery as I never witnessed.'[5]

---

[2] *A.Matterson, Polytechnics and Colleges, London, 1981.*
[3] *Report of the Committee appointed by the Prime Minister under the Chairmanship of Lord Robbins, London, 1963, p. 5.*
[4] *The Journal of West Midlands Regional Studies began to be published by the Wolverhampton College of Technology. It became West Midlands Studies and ran to 18 volumes. A full set is in the Wolverhampton City archives along with Master's dissertations done by Wolverhampton students. Several websites also contain useful material.*
[5] *C. Dickens, The Letters of Charles Dickens. vol. 1 1820-1939, 1965, Oxford.*

A Class Act

For the upper classes and the richer middle classes, school education either involved personal tutoring or the fee paying 'public' school. In the early nineteenth century some thought that these schools were made worse by the arrival of the children of the new class of manufacturers. In 1806, one clergymen lamented that,

'Rugby school is also on a bad footing. In it are many of the Sons of Gentlemen, but more of those who are the sons of Manufacturers at Birmingham, Wolverhampton, etc, who having little sentiment of the disgrace of anything dishonourable, act as their inclination lead them ...'

From the 1830s the 'public' schools were reformed and began to consciously try to mould a new upper class irrespective of its sources of wealth.

Beyond them, were the grammar schools. The older grammar schools had charitable roots (like some 'public' schools) but they were reformed and turned into fee paying schools for the sons of the comfortably off. There were very few such schools for girls. A Schools Inquiry Commission, dismayed at their scarcity and poor quality, recommended that a girls school should be established in any town that had a grammar school. While the working classes would start work at 11 or 12 middle and upper class children – with their access to secondary education – would move on at 16 or 17 or, perhaps, by 1914 aged 18.

The majority of those leaving the public and grammar schools went straight into work. Even for the groups at the top of British society university attendance was unusual. While graduation was necessary to reach the top in the church, law and, increasingly, the civil service it would not be until the 1950s that half the élite industrialists would have degrees. In the late nineteenth century only a quarter of the boys from the top public schools went on to study at Oxford and Cambridge.

The universities of Oxford and Cambridge were rescued by reformers from aristocratic and clerical decline and supplemented at the top of a hierarchy by the University of London. This was established by Dissenters in response to religious exclusion from Oxbridge, it gained the right to award degrees to students studying elsewhere. They continued to overshadow the rest of the system and, like the public schools, helped link together Britain's rulers. Oxford led the way over Cambridge, reducing the share of sons of the aristocracy and clergy from 68% to 32% between 1870 and 1910. Concerns over the restricted curriculum were addressed by the addition of five red brick (civic) universities between 1900 and 1910 developing from existing colleges in major towns and cities, awarding University of London degrees, concentrating on the sciences. Expansion then slowed with one further university opening between 1910 and 1945. These were a product of industrialisation and local initiatives, drawing on more regional recruitment and expressing a degree of regional pride. In this period the numbers going to university rose slightly and the share of the age group increased from 0.8% in 1900 to 1.5% in 1924 and 1.7% in 1938. But the chances of a son of a worker's family making it were slim and calculated to be around 1 in 1,000 on the eve of the First World War.

The term 'Black Country' is an unofficial one. Covering roughly an area of 100 square miles, the Black Country was said in 1843, to be 'a mere speck on the map of England... [but]...its enormous stores of mineral wealth, and consequent density of its population, give it an importance in an economic and moral point of view, to which...no other tract of equal extent can lay claim'. In the mid eighteenth century some specialisation was already evident amongst the market towns and industrial villages of the area. Walsall was known for its saddlery and the villages between it, Wolverhampton and Dudley, produced different types of metal goods. When ironmasters like Dud Dudley, the Darbys and John Wilkinson worked out how to smelt iron with coke in nearby Shropshire, in and around what is now the World Heritage site of Ironbridge, they helped to free iron making from its dependence on wood and charcoal. Iron could now be produced in greater quantities and production shifted to places like the Black Country where iron and coal were found together in a ten yard coal seam that came out from the Dudley Hills.

Villages became towns and towns merged into one another, linked by a dense network of roads, canals and then railways in which the blackness of the coal dust mixed with the blackness of the atmosphere. By 1900 the population of the Black Country was 700,000.[6] Wolverhampton developed as the unofficial capital, though local purists argued that the true Black Country finished on the outskirts of the town. Its population grew to 15,000 in 1811, quadrupled to 61,000 in 1861 and reached some 95,000 in 1901.

'Muck and brass' went together and the modern patterns of inequality, the class and social divisions that structure society and its education systems, were shaped by this process of industrialisation. The old aristocracy survived partly by reconfiguring the basis of its wealth away from farming and exploiting the resources under the land and rents from the industry and towns built on it, including those in the Black Country where the Earls of Dudley were prominent. Challenging them for influence were new middle classes, the businessmen, large and small, whose wealth came from running and serving the coal, iron, tin plate, lock making, leather industries etc as well as becoming involved in building and services.

Below them were the mass of the population – the workers and the poor. Many were migrants, drawn into the area by its new industries, living in social conditions as bad as anywhere in England. Houses were packed, jumbled together with mines, furnaces and workshops, waste heaps and spoil tips. Wolverhampton itself, said an 1862 satire designed to shame those doing well out of the bad conditions, was 'smokery, chokery, stenchiness, slum.'[7] The lack of sewage and the contamination of water meant that disease was endemic, including diarrhoea, killing several thousand of the very young every year. Epidemics added to the problem – cholera hit hard in 1832 and 1849 but there were also epidemics of scarlet fever and measles which kept the rate of infant and child mortality high.

This was a place in which there was limited concern about education for most people and in which its development was haphazard. There were divisions over how much mass education was needed. Did workers need, want or deserve much more than they had? Was it safe? Employers in general, but Black Country ones in particular, appreciated drawing on pools of cheap labour. With profits deriving from low wages and slum rents there was little incentive to change.

[6] R. Trainor, *Black Country Élites: The Exercise of Authority in an Industrialized Area, 1830-1900*, Oxford, 1993.
[7] G.Barnsby, *A History of Housing in Wolverhampton 1750 to 1975*, Wolverhampton, 1986.

The Beginnings of Wolverhampton Adult Technical Education

The distant roots of the modern University of Wolverhampton rose from a number of attempts to create a basis for adult technical education in England, in the first part of the nineteenth century.[8] The people involved believed that not only should there be a basic education but some wider possibility of higher learning beyond 11 or 12 years old. The most radical believed that alongside political and economic rights were educational rights. 'Possessors of great wealth', argued the Chartist and working class reformer William Lovett,

> *still consider education their own prerogative, or a boon to be sparingly conferred upon the multitude instead of a universal entitlement for advancing the dignity of man and for gladdening his existence.*[9]

Such ideas of a 'universal entitlement' fed into the mechanics' institute movement – an uneasy combination of working class self help and reform from above. The model mechanics' institute was formed in London in 1823 (becoming the basis later for Birkbeck College). By 1826 a hundred mechanics' institutes had been founded and by 1850 as many as 600. Although formed by, and for men, women were allowed to attend lectures and some developed 'Ladies' lecture programmes.

In Wolverhampton, a town marked by its poverty the, initiative tended to come more from 'the middle layers'. In 1827 a group of reformers and those seeking to bring light into the local darkness formed a 'Wolverhampton Mechanics' Institute' and library which in 1835 became the 'Wolverhampton Tradesmen and Mechanics' Library'. Books could be borrowed and there were rooms where lectures could be heard and classes given. Just over a decade later, in 1847, the Institute was given a new lease of life as the 'Wolverhampton Athenaeum and Mechanics' Library'.

These early initiatives struggled because they were founded in the middle of a period of economic and social turmoil. Many workers lacked the basic literacy to participate. In the 1840s in the county of Staffordshire, which incorporated much of the Black Country, 43% of men and 60% of women still could not sign their names.[10] For those with a basic literacy, the idea of education in what were effectively night schools had to struggle with other demands – work, family and political activity. Middle class support was self interested too, with even those involved wary of an education that might undermine existing society, and the majority hostile or indifferent. But the Athenaeum and Mechanics' Library struggled on until the late 1860s when it was absorbed by a bigger initiative.

Before that, however, a parallel attempt was made to create an adult education college in Wolverhampton. In the 1850s the Christian Socialist F.D. Maurice encouraged a new wave of working men's colleges where men could take classes in the arts, humanities and some technical subjects. In Wolverhampton this initiative led to a new 'Working Men's College' being opened in 1857 with a rising young local liberal politician, Henry Fowler, playing a leading role. Maurice saw such colleges as a way of improving the social position of workers and increasing their skills but also bringing about a better understanding between capital and labour. Fowler shared this view telling the first annual meeting of the new college that 'the aim of adult

---

[8] J. Jones, Historical Sketch of the Art and Literary Institutions of Wolverhampton, from the 1794 to 1897, London, 1897.
[9] Quoted D.Reay, 'The zombie stalking English schools: social class and educational inequality', British Journal of Educational Studies, vol. 54 no.3, 2006, p. 293.
[10] W.O.Henderson, The Origins of Technical Education in Wolverhampton, College Studies in Local History no.1, Wolverhampton, 1948.

education was not to turn working men into scholars, but to improve their competence as craftsmen and their value to the community as citizens. Regard the influence of this education in respect to the relation of the working man and his master'. This venture too had limited success and came to an end in 1865.

Workers in the Black Country remained trapped by their poverty and the low technical standards demanded in the industries of the day. Their employers, and the middle classes more widely, remained suspicious of education beyond the elementary level and its value for the mass of the population. It was a third initiative for local adult education taken in 1870, the year of Forster's Act and the school board system, that was to have more lasting results. In Wolverhampton there was a mass of school board activity with Henry Fowler becoming the first Head. Reformers on the Town Council were also able to belatedly establish a Free Library in the Town. This had been possible earlier, a Free Library Act being passed in 1855 allowing local taxation to be used to create libraries. Proposals to levy a rate for this in Wolverhampton had been shouted down by rate payers. In 1869 and 1870 new proposals were made and it was decided to get around rate payer opposition by taking the campaign into the factories and workshops, something that was done with some success.

The new library for the population was opened in 1870. In 1872 it moved to new premises previously used by the local police and fire brigade. The municipal librarian, John Elliot immediately began a series of evening classes which quickly became the major vehicle for part-time education beyond the elementary level. Normally a person had to be over 14 to attend and 348 registered for classes in 1872. By 1884 the number was 945 and by the 1890s over 1,000. The library classes depended on charitable donations and the fees of those who registered. Ironically, given the debate in education about the balance between self emancipation and social control, one of the first class rooms was created from converted police cells.

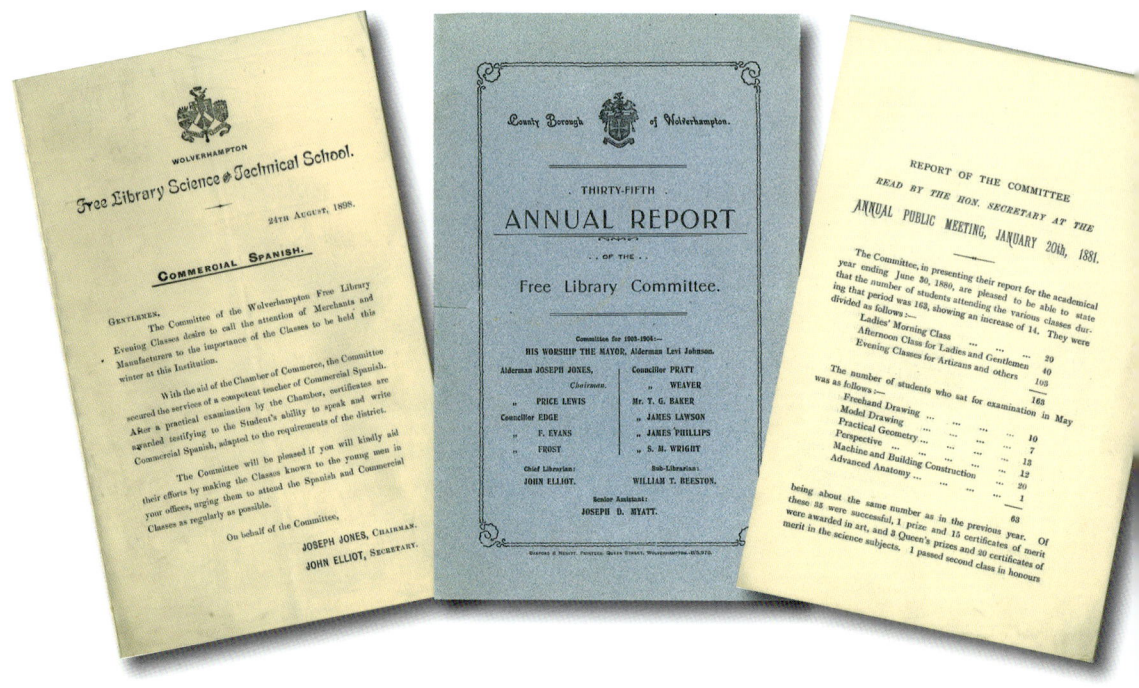

The classes developed and donations enabled laboratories to be financed including a metallurgical laboratory in 1893. In 1894 the first full-time teacher, a science master, was appointed alongside the part-time ones. With the opening of a new town library, the classes gained exclusive use of its premises and became the 'Science, Technical and Commercial School' – overseen by a technical committee of the town council and, after the 1902 Education Act, the new local education committee of the corporation.

People registered for the classes to improve their education, taking evening and Saturday classes in such subjects as natural history, archaeology, the sciences and mathematics. A very small number were even able to use the classes to gain the occasional scholarship to one of the few universities. But they were not typical, when Thomas Hardy's Jude Fawley, writes to enquire about getting into a barely disguised Oxford College he is told 'Sir, I have read your letter with interest; and, judging from your description of yourself as a working-man, I venture to think that you will have a much better chance of success in life by remaining in your own sphere and sticking to your trade than by adopting any other course. That, therefore, is what I advise you to do.'

The classes were also of wider social significance for informed leisure and entertainment. Telephones were demonstrated in 1884, magic lantern shows given and more popular shows put on. Although those attending came from the middle classes and better off working classes this was a slight crack that could be widened in the fight for educational reform. In 1889, perhaps not co-incidentally the year of the centenary of the French Revolution, the classes were described as a 'people's college', reflecting the radicalism of the idea that education should go beyond elementary or the barely developed secondary education to a third and higher level.

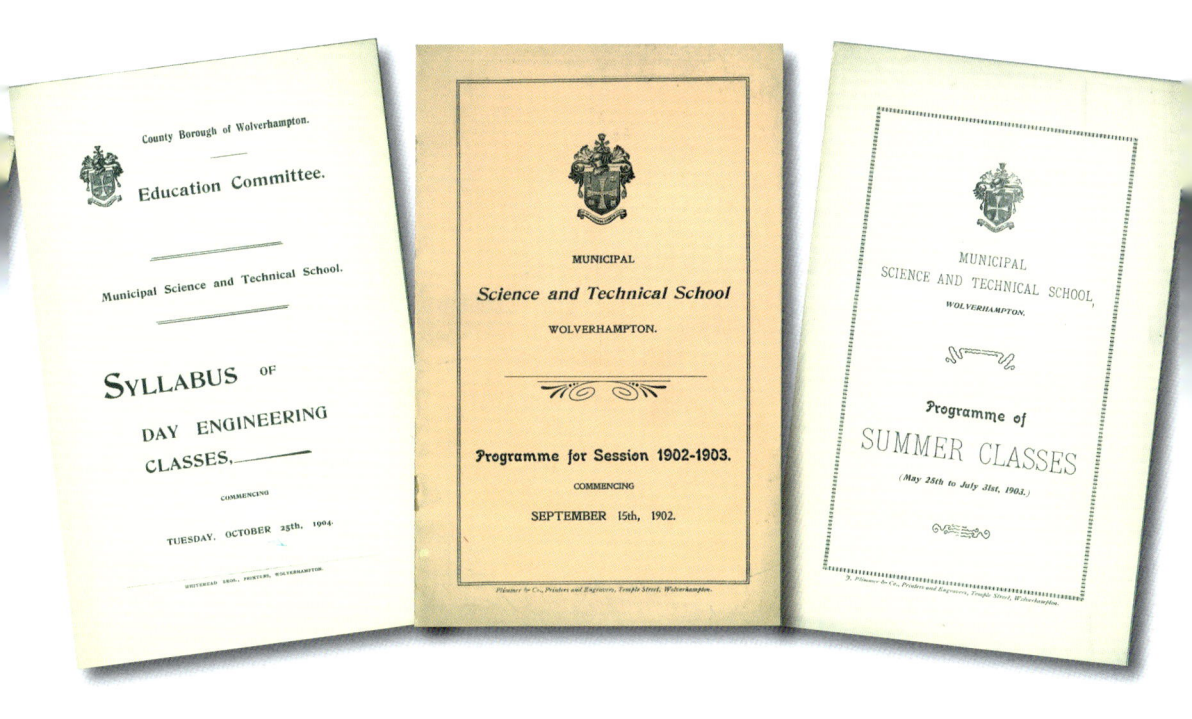

Even with these developments, in the Black Country more generally and Wolverhampton in particular, provision was still limited and relatively backward. When nearby Birmingham University obtained its charter in 1900, it drew on the science college established in 1880 on the basis of a gift of £180,000 by Sir Josiah Mason whose fortune came from his firm's work in the Birmingham hardware trades. Wolverhampton had no such great benefactor, nor the determination to take the opportunities that were available. In 1889 a Technical Instruction Act was passed which allowed councils to levy a small rate for technical education. The next year brought more potential funding. Money controversially set aside to help reduce the number of publicans was diverted to possible support for technical education as the so called 'whiskey money'.[11] But those running Wolverhampton chose not to take up these possibilities.

Amongst local employers there was a lack of interest in paying for more technical 'college' education. Although there were some larger firms in the area, the profile was still one of smaller scale firms who either drew on local craft traditions or depended on their workers' sweat. In 1896, for example, one local report admitted that the premises of the technical classes in Garrick Street were 'perhaps one of the worst Free Library buildings in the country, for a town of this size'. The limited vision of local employers was not encouraged by the economic difficulties in the region as, from the 1870s, it entered a crisis of competitive restructuring of the industries behind its earlier growth.

Despite this leading to some renewed radicalism – not least the development of trade unions and socialist organisations – the political challenge was not enough to break the complacency and narrow mindedness of those who controlled local society. Reforms came but they often involved an uphill struggle. Only after 1900 were there signs of more progressive alliances developing. These in part reflected the emergence of newer industries requiring a stronger engineering base alongside the political rise of social liberalism and the Labour Party. This would help to encourage a step forward in secondary education and a more serious attempt to engage with post secondary possibilities.

'Art Applied to Manufacture' – the Development of Art and Design Education

The second root of the University of Wolverhampton is to be found in the development of provincial schools of art and design. By the 1870s there were over 100 of them and their development seems almost precocious compared to other parts of the nineteenth century education system. But they arose for specific economic and social reasons. In the workshops and factories, self taught workmen and women could copy and make but did not necessarily have the skills or the right 'taste' to design and create the new styles needed in an expanding market. In 1835-36 a Select Committee of the House of Commons on Arts and Manufactures was set up, dominated by followers of the philosopher Jeremy Bentham and economic liberals. Their aim was to find a way to improve design and to help industry work better while supporting the development of 'taste' in a society where the middle classes had cultural aspirations for themselves and others. This is highlighted by the Wolverhampton born artist-teacher, George Wallis.

> *Having seen during a residence in Manchester, 1832 to 1837, and in the Staffordshire Potteries, Wolverhampton and Birmingham, from 1837 to 1841, the utter neglect of everything like artistic principles*

[11] *1890 Taxation (Customs and Excise) Act*

Roots – the Early Years

in the various industries of those places, in 1839-40, I publically lectured on the subject; and subsequently formed an experimental class at Wolverhampton to test certain methods of teaching elementary drawing by black board illustration on a large scale, this satisfying myself of the value of such a method of instruction.

In 1838 Wallis had also organised an exhibition in conjunction with the Mechanics' Institute in Wolverhampton to display local art, manufactures and industry. This was claimed to be the first of its kind and a source of inspiration for the 1851 Great Exhibition, for which Wallis became a Deputy Commissioner. Art and design schools would go one step better, 'the primary purpose' he said 'is to teach art as applied to the manufacture'[12] In the Black Country a small School of Design in this tradition was created in 1849 in Stourbridge, a town where the glass industry had particular needs but where there was also a stronger radical tradition. Two years later, in Wolverhampton, the Great Exhibition was said to have 'provided a profound sensation', encouraging the opening of an art school there, the 'School of Practical Art'. This was transformed by subscriptions for a substantial new building in 1853.

In 1878 there were said to be only 178 students on the books. But by the 1880s economic and social change had created the possibility of developing an institution with a secure and substantial basis.

School of Practical Art

[12] G.James Daichendt, 'The nineteenth-century artist teacher: a case study of George Wallis and the creation of a new identity', *International Journal of Art and Design Education*, 2011, vol 30 no.1, pp. 71-79.

A History of the University of Wolverhampton

Right:
The Municipal School of Arts and Crafts

Below:
The Wolverhampton Art Gallery.

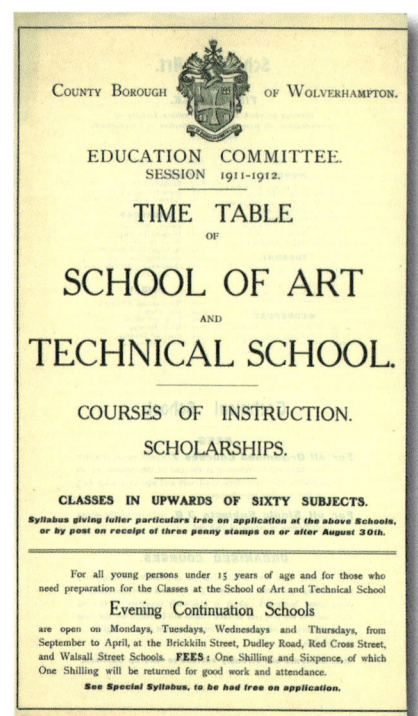

1884 in a building which stands today as a tribute to Victorian municipal pride. Its design captures the attempt to link the perceived values of the ancient world of Greece and Rome with those of the superior classes of late nineteenth century England.

The next year, directly behind it, 'The Municipal School of Art and Craft' was opened. It was financed by donations of over £4,500 and a government grant of £1,000. This time in a red brick building it became a more significant element in the town. By 1896 there were 383 students registered and it was developing in breadth and depth.

Whatever the disdain for technical education amongst the middle classes, there was a growing sense of the importance of municipal pride as well as a recognition of the need to support better design for local industries. This led to support for a new Art Gallery, paid for by a government grant of £1,000 and local subscriptions. It opened in

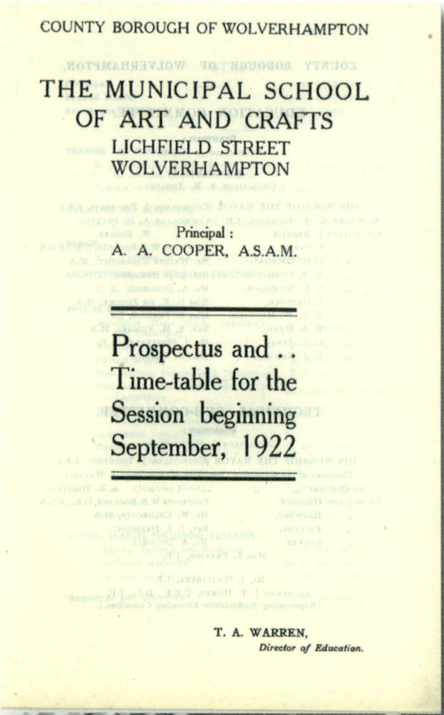

13

The School was overseen by the committee of the Art Gallery expanded to incorporate others and members of the Town Council. After the national education reforms of 1902, the School came under the ultimate control of the new local education authority. In its early years it was run by a succession of headmasters. Students studied a variety of classes beginning with general skills and developing in more specialised directions which fed into local industries and crafts including jewellery, metalwork, ornamental woodwork, stone work, pottery etc. The new wrought iron gates of the School in the 1880s were themselves designed by a student and attracted some national attention.

Training the Teachers

In the first decade of the new century a third root of the modern University of Wolverhampton came into being. This was a new teacher training college in the Black Country situated at Dudley. As a result of educational reforms local education authorities were able to take new initiatives in teacher training. In Dudley, the LEA took the lead in establishing a new training college which would supply teachers to the local region and even beyond. The new Dudley Training College was seen as a means of civic development leading to the 'permanent elevation of the castle borough to a foremost position amongst the leading education centres of the country'. It was built on a hill, on land bought from the Dudley family, enabling it to overlook much of the Black Country as well as the rural lands to the west. It was set in large grounds with playing fields and entered by an impressive gate. Status and hierarchy were important and even the location and building design told a story. The foundation stone was laid by the Countess of Dudley on September 10th 1908 in a major civic ceremony and the substantial building opened less than a year later, on July 10th 1909, by the liberal Minister of Education, Walter Runciman.

The initial aim was an intake of 70 women and 30 men who lived locally. Demand was high and came from farther afield, soon small halls of residence were being planned. Gender was important, school teaching was a route, especially for the women who in their white blouses and black skirts predominated, hoping to 'go up unto the next class'. But in class terms a teacher was 'in between' and so were women teachers. If they were to control they also had to be controlled. Typically the first Principals were men and the Vice-Principals women. As in schools, where boys and girls were separated, so there were separate entrances and separate common rooms. Interaction was to be controlled by the very design of the building with the grand hall the central space where all could come together under the eye of those at the high table.

On the Eve of the 1914-1918 War

The structure for post school education was now in place, the 1902 Education Act had created local education authorities to replace the 2,000 or so school boards. It resolved the issue of who could provide a higher level of education by allowing these LEAs to 'take such steps as seem to them desirable to supply or aid the supply of education other than elementary'. It also led to an increase in funding for education from local rates. The appetite for this education was in place from the traditional sources of young and mature workers and progressively from people emerging from secondary schools. The expansion of secondary education was through scholarship schemes to grammar schools which gave places in exchange for state aid. This was the origin of the working class grammar school boy who could 'get on'. But they were still few – numbers in public supported secondary schooling rose from 60,000 to 230,000 between 1902 and 1913 but this excluded 95% of children, disproportionately girls.

The development of post school 'technical' education now had a firmer footing under local control with new colleges being created. National numbers rose from 120,000 in 1893 to 708,000 in 1911. 95% of those in post school education were part-time, 15% in day courses and 85% in evening courses. The immediate task of those involved in the technical school in Wolverhampton was to take responsibility to organise and develop the patchwork of provision that already existed including the classes of the Free Library and some of the work done in the higher grade elementary and technical schools.

At this point an important role was played by sympathetic Councillors and by George Chell, who had begun to work at the Free Library in 1884 and become assistant librarian and secretary to the many classes. He now became secretary to the Science and Technical School overseeing the old classes and those in a collection of evening schools. From 1905 new classes began to be developed and co-operation between the Art School and the emerging college was reflected in the preface to the 1907-8 School of Art, Science and Technical School and Branch Technical Classes (Higher Grade School) Syllabus.

> *It will be found on perusal of this Syllabus that excellent facilities are offered for all to continue their education after leaving the Day School. By attendance at the various classes set forth therein, a splendid opportunity is afforded for the acquiring of knowledge to fit one for their future career, whether it lie along the pathway of Art, Literature, Science, Technology or Commerce, and the instruction given, will be with a view to enable earnest students to grapple with the difficulties they meet in their daily occupation.*

In 1910 Dr J.D Coates was appointed Principal for what was now to be a college, and Chell became its secretary – a position he would retain until 1936. The appointment of a Principal with a doctorate was a statement of ambition for an institution which, with the Art School, already brought together some 2,000 students.

The longer term issue was to establish a new college out of the constituent parts, with a purpose built physical base in the town. Negotiations began between Wolverhampton Council

Making Teachers

The way that teachers are trained has changed enormously over time.

At the start of the twentieth century there were only 1,000 or so grant aided secondary schools with some 11,000 teachers and a pupil teacher ratio of 1:16. Like teachers in the public schools, these were usually university graduates and therefore men. Having a degree was considered a sufficient basis to be able to teach in state maintained schools until 1973. It still is sufficient in 'public' schools. But where did the teachers for the schools for the mass of the people come from? In the nineteenth century this meant the elementary schools. In 1900 in the 35,000 schools at this level there were some 130,000 teachers – largely female. The teacher pupil ratio was 1:42.

Teaching was initially meant to be cheap and it was thought that anyone could do it. The monitorial system was developed to allow older children to teach younger ones under the supervision of an untrained adult. In the church run schools this evolved into what was called the 'pupil teacher' system – which survived until the inter-war years. Older pupils at 13 might be taken on for a few years as pupil teachers and then, if they were able, they might get scholarships for a two year training course at a church run training college – later supplemented by local authority supported colleges. They would then become officially qualified as elementary school teachers. In 1849 there were only 681 certificated teachers. By 1870 the number had grown to 12,000 certified teachers, 1,000 adult assistant teachers and 14,000 pupil teachers, by 1895 the numbers were 53,000, 28,000 and 34,000 respectively.

Teachers were not especially well paid – in 1900-01 a male certified teacher earned £128 a year and women £86. The fight for pay and status has been a long one and as early as 1870 the National Union of Elementary School Teachers had been formed to promote the interests of teachers, later becoming the National Union of Teachers.

The 1944 educational reforms changed schools but the status and training of teachers was still poor. In 1951 there were 160,000 primary school teachers and 100,000 secondary school teachers in state schools – most of them without degrees and with limited training gained in teacher training colleges. Women teachers did gain equal pay in 1955.

The Deanery and the Staffordshire County Council with a view to a degree of joint provision. It was necessary to agree on the relative weight of the two councils in organisation and finance; the location of the college, the balance of its courses and to find a site. In 1912 the Deanery, a seventeenth century building whose design was reputed to have involved Sir Christopher Wren, was purchased. Debate immediately erupted over whether it should be preserved or cleared away. The secretary to the Society for the Preservation of Ancient Buildings, Earl Ferrers is reported as saying 'when the destruction of this educational asset is threatened in the name of education - strangeness passes into nightmare'.[13]

With these debates on-going, a new college 'for further education' was formally founded 'under an agreement concluded in July, 1914 between the Corporation of Wolverhampton and the County of Stafford. A Joint committee of the two authorities constitutes the Board of Governors'. The College would be managed by a technical sub-committee of the two Councils. It would

[13] *Express and Star, 2 October 1920*

incorporate and build on the technical education traditions that went back to the days of the Free Library and beyond. It would stand, alongside the Art School and the nearby Teacher Training College, in offering something more at a time when, for the majority, 'higher education' still meant the chance to go not to college or university but to a secondary school.

By the second decade of the century three of the roots of the University were in place, continuing education in the technical and in the artistic aspects of manufacturing industry and commerce and in teacher training. Developments had been unsteady but the trend was ever to increase educational opportunity. This endeavour was now to face an unprecedented emergency of war.

War (1914-1918)

In July 1914 no one had any idea of the scale of the catastrophe that was about to occur. Within weeks the world was engulfed in war. In Britain over six million men (in theory aged 18 to 41) volunteered or, from 1916, were conscripted to fight. One in eight were killed, one in four wounded and a smaller percentage captured. The overall casualty rate was over 40%. War therefore took away a generation and stopped the possibility of education for many. It also stopped plans for the new technical college in Wolverhampton.

But the war did not stop the need for technical and other education – even war time propaganda needed artists. War fuelled scientific development, the new Principal of the Technical College was allowed to go and work on war related research for the government, Chell again taking over the running of the College. The war effort also needed skilled workers in the factories including in some of the workshops of the Black Country. Just under half of all men aged 18-41 went off to war, but many skilled men were put into reserved occupations.

Women were encouraged, and drafted in, to replace the men going to the front. There were therefore new opportunities in technical education. Technology was at a premium in the war industries, there was a need for some technical military training and for courses for wounded and demobilised soldiers. In the longer term this would begin to help weaken, but only a little, some of the prejudices that had constrained development before 1914.

The strain of war also led to growing discontent. One response to this was Lloyd George's famous call to build a 'land fit for heroes' which was restated at a huge meeting in the Grand Theatre in Wolverhampton in November 1918. A degree of educational reform was also pushed from below as workers organised into trade unions and struck for better conditions. This organisational wave had begun before the war and it had found its echo in the Black Country not least amongst some women workers. Education reform took a lower place than the fight for better work conditions but some argued that workers' organisation would be a springboard to wider change. R.H.Tawney hoped in 1918 that it would no longer be possible in educational terms to 'keep the workers children in their place'.[14] He was too optimistic but at the height of radicalisation new demands were made including one from the National Union of Women Workers that asked for representation on the governing committee of the new Wolverhampton Technical College – a request that was ignored.

The Inter-war Years (1918-1938)

The dominant story of education in the inter-war years is one of incremental change. In the face of economic difficulties and conservative government policies, educational reforms did not have a high

---

[14] R.H.Tawney, 'Keeping the workers' children in their place', Daily News 14 February 1918 reprinted in The Radical Tradition, Harmondsworth, 1964, p. 49.

priority. The economy was affected by a serious crisis after the war and then again in 1929-1933. There was a prolonged restructuring as old industries declined and new ones, like the car industry, were established. The Black Country had its share of declining industries and unemployment. In 1933 J.B.Priestley described the poverty of Rusty Lane in West Bromwich. While they 'exist in their present foul shape, it is idle to congratulate ourselves about anything.' Delegates to the international economic conference to deal with the economic crisis of the 1930s needed to go not to Mayfair 'in season' but West Bromwich 'out of season.' In a world of material and educational poverty he saw young boys throwing stones at a factory. 'I could not blame them if they threw stones and stones and smashed every pane of glass for miles. No one can blame them if they grow up to smash everything that can be smashed.'[15]

In the first post war cutbacks, national plans for technical education were suspended and the hopes for a technical college in Wolverhampton fell victim to these cuts. In 1919 Dr W.E. Fisher had been appointed as a Principal of the College but his early years were spent trying to work on the basis of accommodation in old buildings that were hardly fit for purpose, to continue to develop technical education, service industry and meet the aspiration of growing numbers of students.

During the Session 1920-21, 1,553 men and women attended for instruction at the Technical School, in addition to 1,082 at the Evening Continuation Schools, which give preliminary training. The Technical School Programme for the forthcoming Session includes 150 Classes, arranged to provide

19 Courses of study (of two to five years' duration) suited for the workers in various local industries of importance, or for those preparing for the professions.[16]

The move to give the new college regional status, planned before the war, was now brought to fruition with the erection of two purpose-built significant buildings at the intersection of Wulfruna and Stafford Streets.

The first was the Engineering Block, opened in 1926:

The coming session will stand out boldly in Wolverhampton history. By taking gradual possession...of the new Workshops and Laboratories

[15] J.B.Priestly, English Journey, London, 1934.
[16] Wolverhampton Technical School Programme 1921-1922, p.6.

Roots – the Early Years

as the Session proceeds, we shall mark the birth of a Technical College which clearly is destined to perform great things for the industrial and social betterment of this neighbourhood… The Wolverhampton and Staffordshire Councils have each resolved to proceed immediately to the erection of the complete College… Here, therefore, are great hopes of our materialising an Institution (at a cost of £150,000) which will be a credit to Wolverhampton and District, an immense emotive power behind the local industries, and a ladder by which the earnest student may ascend to the heights of any fair ambition. The approaching Session offers to everyone the privilege of a first place upon what time will translate into an historic roll. [17]

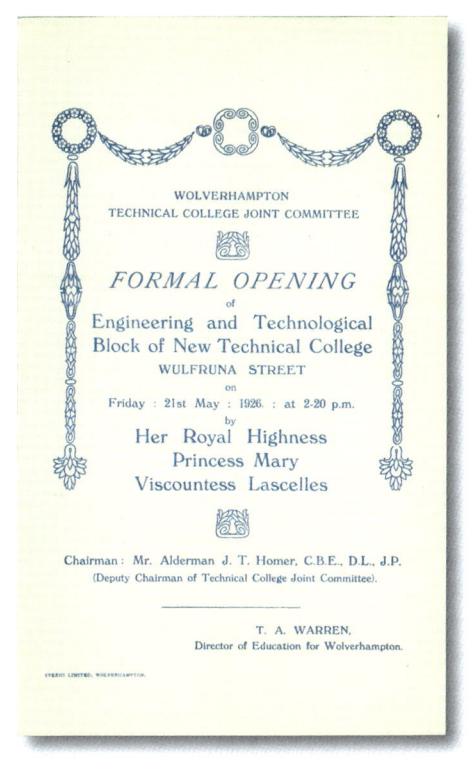

WOLVERHAMPTON
TECHNICAL COLLEGE JOINT COMMITTEE

FORMAL OPENING
of
Engineering and Technological
Block of New Technical College
WULFRUNA STREET
on
Friday : 21st May : 1926. : at 2-20 p.m.
by
Her Royal Highness
Princess Mary
Viscountess Lascelles

Chairman : Mr. Alderman J. T. Homer, C.B.E., D.L., J.P.
(Deputy Chairman of Technical College Joint Committee).

T. A. WARREN,
Director of Education for Wolverhampton.

[17] *Municipal School of Science, Technology and Commerce, Programme 1925-1926, Preface.*

A History of the University of Wolverhampton

*Below right:
'The Marble'
reception under
construction*

*Staircase in
'The Marble'
reception*

*Below left:
The Library*

The second building is known locally as 'The Marble' because of the marble flooring and pillars used in its construction. Much of the curriculum was still taught in various locations around the town but some flavour of the importance of a high status building for technical education is given in the excitement shown as the opening day in 1933 approached. 'Our long-promised College is rapidly rising on its site. Columns and girders in profusion proclaim that of definite certainty we are to possess that temple dedicated to Commerce and Industry for which the Deanery Site was purchased some twenty years ago.'[18]

There was a stirring warning to future staff and students.

> *...in this September of 1933 we take over a great inheritance. Only long years of earnest striving by vigorous predecessors have brought us this great College. The succeeding year is our own. And history again illumines the way. Passivity and sloth have often lost what courage and zeal have earlier won. Whether this fine building is to become a local pride or a mere sufferance will largely be determined by the happenings of the next decade.*[19]

[18] *Wolverhampton and Staffordshire Technical College Programme 1930-1931.*
[19] *Wolverhampton and Staffordshire Technical College Programme 1933-34, Foreword by T A Warren, Clerk to the Governors.*

21

WOLVERHAMPTON TECHNICAL COLLEGE.

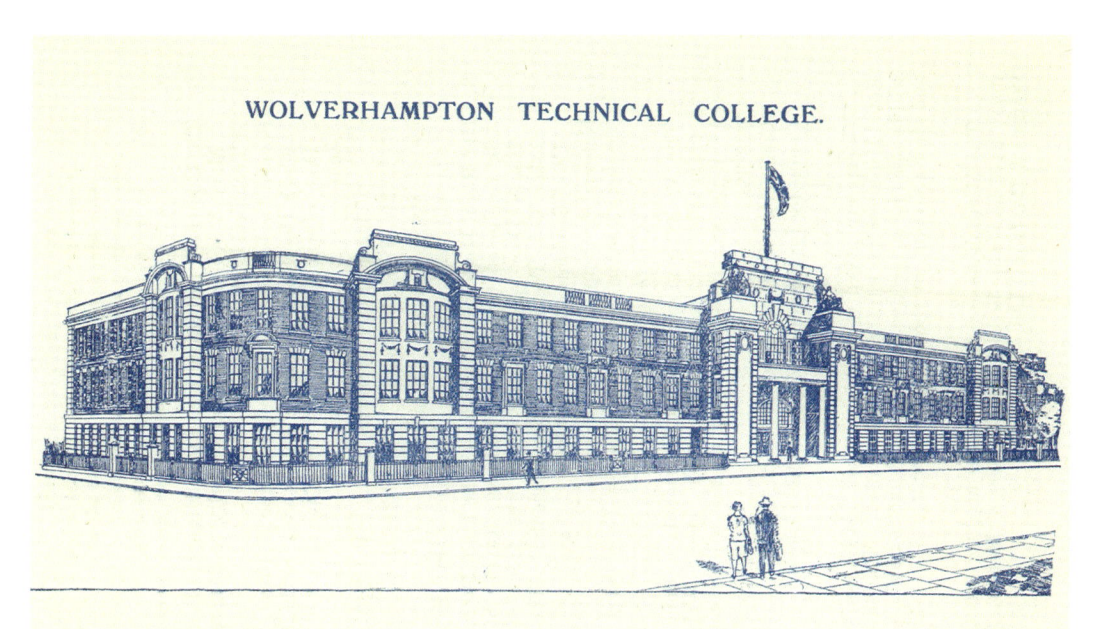

Perspective Sketch of Complete College as ultimately projected.

The College as planned and when built

In 1925, a new Board of Governors had been created and the college became the 'Wolverhampton and Staffordshire Technical College' with Fisher as its Principal – a position he would hold until the 1950s. By the mid 1930s, therefore, the College at last had a central location, buildings and developing programmes. It could take root as one of the variety of institutions that developed in England to try to offer a post-school, more advanced education to the wider population.

It did so from 1929 against a background of deep economic crisis. The College felt the impact of the crisis in terms of recruitment and the need to make other savings. In 1933 a degree of recovery began, led by newer forms of engineering and the car industry as well as house building, all of which benefited Wolverhampton itself and lifted some of the gloom that Priestley saw in nearby Rusty Lane. In the second half of the 1930s numbers rose and Fisher, always a vocal force in defence of technical education, began to talk much more positively about the breadth and depth of the work of the College.

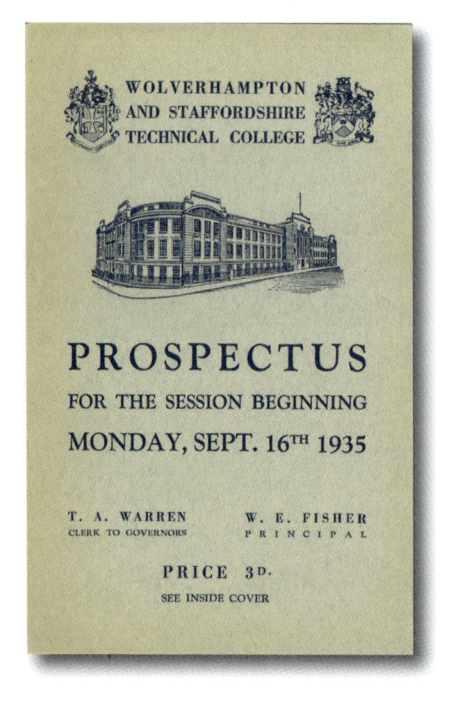

Nationally, on the eve of the next war the education system still looked too much like it had done a generation before. By 1938 only 15% of children were going on to some type of secondary education despite the raising of the school leaving age to 14. Education beyond this was largely part-time, fragmented and predominately the college as night school. There was a limited change too in teacher training colleges. The number of teachers grew and their status was improved by a new pay system but school teaching in state schools was still widely seen as a second rate profession dominated by women who, until 1944, had to leave the job when they married. Training colleges like that at Dudley expanded and lost some of the earlier oppressive intimacy. But training was still a form of institutionalised apprenticeship. Progressive initiatives were present but the bigger picture was a continued emphasis on discipline and a modicum of self improvement.

Schools of Art were also constrained in this era. Reputations grew and not least, for Wolverhampton, because of the work of its most famous local graduate, Sir Charles Wheeler, a student at Wolverhampton Art School 1905-1910, who was developing as one of the leading British sculptors of the mid-century. Expansion was limited partly by national economic conditions and partly by the varying fates of the local industries that they supported.

A Second War (1939-1945)

In 1939 there were still some 1.25 million unemployed. But war soon eliminated unemployment and by May 1940 the government passed the Emergency Powers Act requiring people to put 'themselves, their services and their property' at the disposal of the government. The numbers in the armed forces would rise from 500,000 to over 5 million and the degree of economic mobilisation outdid that of the First War. At its peak, 55% of the workforce was either in the armed forces or directly serving the war effort.

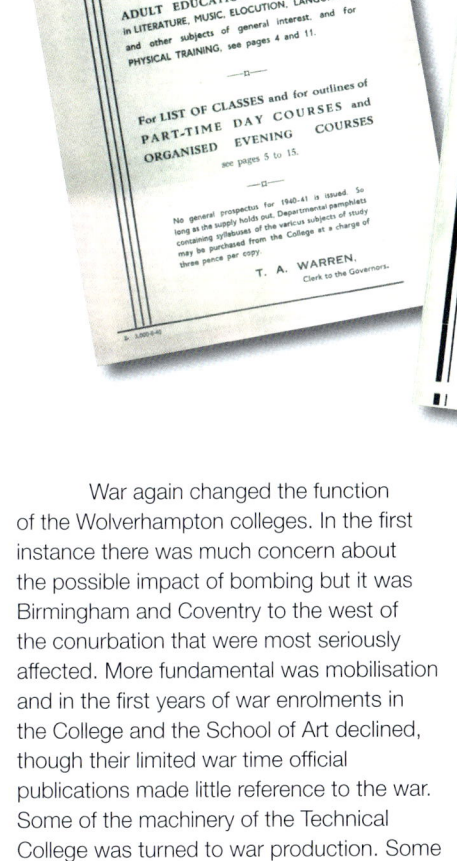

War again changed the function of the Wolverhampton colleges. In the first instance there was much concern about the possible impact of bombing but it was Birmingham and Coventry to the west of the conurbation that were most seriously affected. More fundamental was mobilisation and in the first years of war enrolments in the College and the School of Art declined, though their limited war time official publications made little reference to the war. Some of the machinery of the Technical College was turned to war production. Some courses were suspended but technical training was increased for war industries and some 3,000 armed services personnel, including air crew who did full-time training. Between 1943 and 1948, to escape the Blitz, the Maria Grey Training College was evacuated from London to share Dudley Training College. War also further loosened ties of tradition. Female students, for example, found a new freedom in the crammed College as their world overlapped with men in uniform in the forces canteen, student dances and, in the midst of war time rationing, the delights of pork pie and beetroot on a Sunday.

Technical Education – a Widening Vision in the Long Boom

The Second World War changed the political debate in Britain. People had been promised a degree of reform and social justice during the war. Mobilisation had shown the extent to which the limits of the past were a product of self-imposed blinkers. Even before the end of the war change was beginning and it intensified under the new Labour Government after

1945. The 1944 Education Act finally laid the basis of a free secondary education system for all, but it also led to a new concern for continuing post-school education. This would now have three clearer elements – at the top would be the universities, below them the various colleges with an increasing range of external higher qualifications then, more clearly developing, a further education sector. This was still far from a 'higher education system'. In practice there would continue to be debate about who did what. But there was more logic to the new arrangements. Local Authorities moved quickly as part of reconstruction to develop their provision. In Wolverhampton, Wulfrun College of Education was formed in 1949, initially working from the Wolverhampton and Staffordshire Technical College site. This would adopt provision of the lower levels of courses. The Technical College would then, with the School of Art, concentrate more on 'higher education'. Although this still remained a fuzzy concept, the aspiration was clear, to focus on work at this higher level and with a wider remit.[20]

But nationally some of the older problems and divisions re-emerged in new forms. If the majority now had the right to a secondary education the expectation was still that they did not need or have the capacity to benefit from much more. School reform split children on the basis of the '11 plus' examination into a favoured grammar school elite of around a fifth, a second group who would go to technical schools and the majority whose education would be more vocationally orientated in secondary modern schools. The Further Education College would then be a route forward for those defined as the 'brighter working class kid' with 'higher education' expanding for the children of the middle classes and the most academically orientated working class children. In the event, in most of the country, children were split at 11 between the successful who went to grammar schools and the unsuccessful who went to the secondary modern schools. Britain continued to have what some now began to call a system of 'educational apartheid'.

This 'educational apartheid' came under increasing pressure as England changed and people began to demand more for themselves and their children. After 1945, economic growth was sustained for a quarter of a century. Unemployment all but disappeared in some years. Standards of living rose. Growth in the West Midlands was especially strong - reflecting demand for new goods, not least cars, and a degree of restructuring towards service employment and white collar work. Labour shortages became a problem, new supplies of workers had to be found and soon migrants were attracted from what was called the 'new Commonwealth' – the West Indies, India, and West and East Pakistan (Bangladesh from 1971).

With demand rising the 'in between' parts of the higher education system began to grow. In the Technical College there was expansion in three directions – one was science and technology. Business and commerce also developed from a strong base that had been established in the inter-war years. The third less obvious strand was the development of liberal studies- humanities teaching which was seen as valuable in its own right but also necessary if the status of the College was to be raised and upgraded.

The Municipal School of Art and Crafts had exchanged 'Municipal' for 'Wolverhampton' in its title. In 1950 The 'Wolverhampton School of Art and Crafts' underwent its last name change dropping the word Crafts and becoming a College, the, 'Wolverhampton College of Art'.

During this time there was national recognition of Wolverhampton as a centre of the metals industry. The College had long-standing courses in aspects of foundry work. These were developed into a national

---

[20] *Joint Education Committee of the Wolverhampton and Staffordshire Technical College Minutes, June 20 1949.*

Plan of the Foundry Laboratory

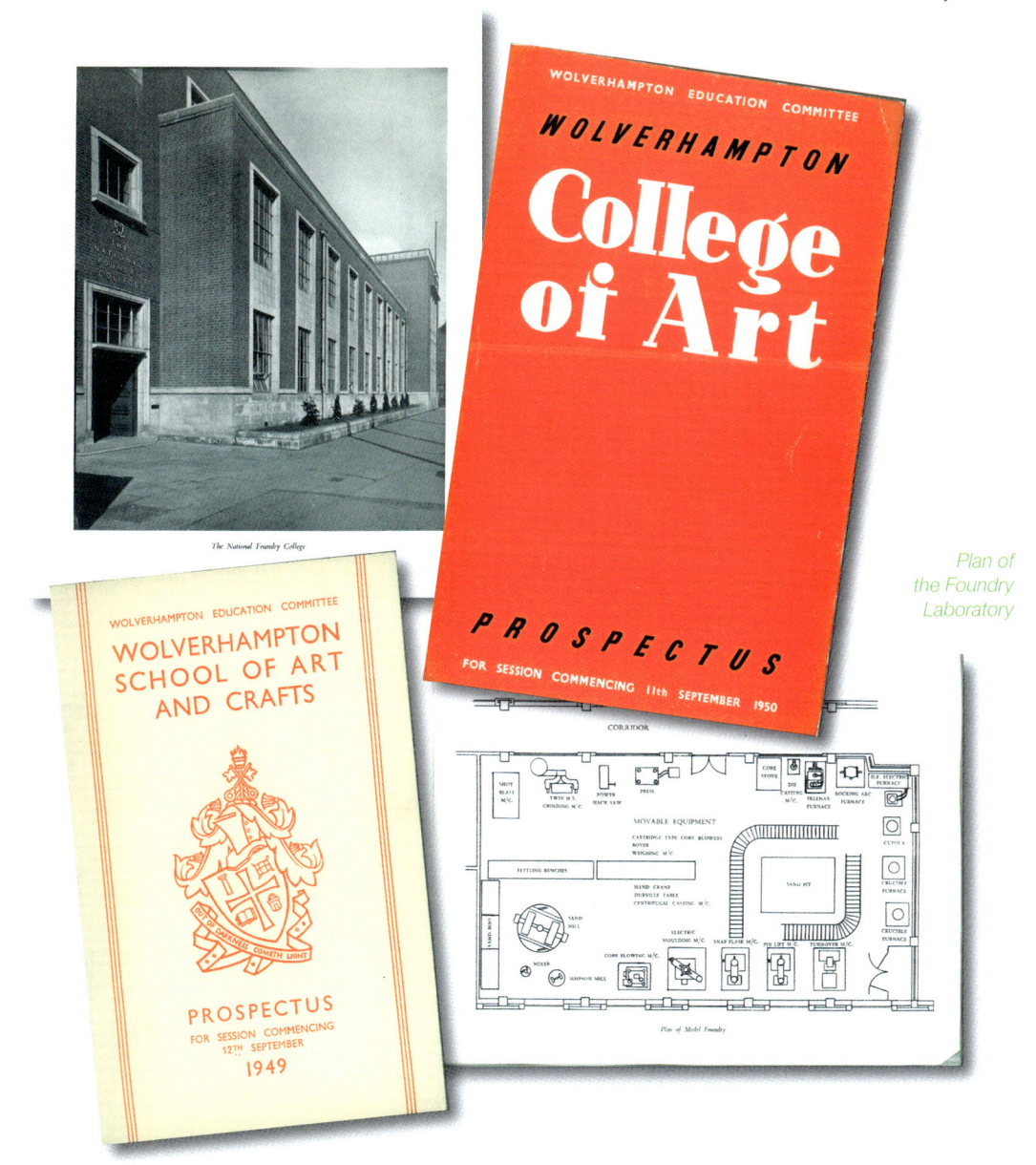

specialist college, 'The National Foundry College' was opened in 1948 occupying five rooms in the Technical College building. It moved into the Engineering Block in 1954.

Expanding Teacher Training

There was also major expansion in teacher training. The 1944 McNair Report had suggested a new structure. Training colleges like that at Dudley were brought under the academic oversight of 19 Area Training Organisations (ATOs). These were based in university schools of education which had developed to teach and research and to give graduates who wanted it some training in teaching after their first degree. The ATO for the Midlands was based at the

University of Birmingham Institute of Education. The university link brought a degree of status but for the universities themselves improving teacher training was not a priority, nevertheless this loose structure lasted for three decades.

By 1958-59 the Dudley training college was part of a national network of 140 teacher training colleges with 31,000 trainees. The focus was still on two year courses to supply 'lower level' teachers in primary schools and the new secondary moderns for children who were themselves seen as 'lower level'. But this was being recognised to be insufficient. There was a demographic bulge developing following a post war boom in births and a sense that old social divisions in education could not be justified.

The 1960s therefore saw a massive expansion which created something of a golden age for teacher training, albeit still with teachers struggling to improve their status. The total numbers in teacher training were increased to 70,000 in 1964 and to 120,000 in 1972. The two year training course was changed to three years and the Robbins Report of 1963 recommended the development of a BEd degree for teachers without the traditional university qualifications.

The 'training college' gave way to 'college of education' and new ideas about child centred development began to be explored. This ferment was evident in the West Midlands too in the existing colleges where it led to new Black Country colleges being established that would later become part of the development of the University of Wolverhampton.

The first initiative was the creation of the Wolverhampton Technical Teachers College opened in May 1961. This had begun as City and Guilds technical teachers evening course and full-time summer courses organised by the Technical College. Its aim was to train students, aged over 25, to teach technical and agricultural subjects in further education colleges. The numbers of further education teachers was growing rapidly – by 1960 there were 17,000 full-time lecturers (and a larger number of part-time ones) and it was estimated some 3,500 new ones would be needed each year. But many again did the job without any specific training.

Immediately after the war three national specialist colleges had been set up to train teachers for further education. It took a long time to establish Wolverhampton as the fourth.[21] This college separated from its parent the Wolverhampton and Staffordshire Technical College in 1961 and soon had its own buildings at Compton Park in the suburbs of Wolverhampton where mixed hostels were also built. Its aim was not to 'train' but to 'educate [people] to teach' in engineering, building, commerce, science and agriculture. Expansion was quick, by September 1966, 216 trainees had enrolled on the one year course and the plans were to take up to 400. Growth was assisted by the new availability of local education authority loans which enabled a larger number to find the means to train.

The second new initiative was the creation of a Day Training College, for male and female teachers, in the centre of Wolverhampton. Wolverhampton Teachers' College for Day Students opened with 95 students in 1961. 'It is one of several colleges, mainly in densely populated areas of the country, which were founded primarily to offer training facilities for students who for domestic reasons prefer a non-residential course.'[22]

Nearby, at Walsall, the largest of these new colleges was created as the West Midlands College of Education in 1963. The College was linked to the Walsall local education authority but had a governing body nominated by a cluster of local authorities. It quickly expanded from its first four-story teaching block and student residences to a site with a substantial number of buildings (study block, library, hostels, refectory, physical education facilities, music centre etc) and over 1,000 teacher trainees by the early 1970s.

[21] J.H.Williams, 'The Wolverhampton training college for technical teachers', The Vocational Aspect of Education , vol. 14, 1962; pp. 3-7; C.L.Heywood, 'Wolverhampton Technical Teachers College', The Vocational Aspect of Education, vol. 14, 1962, pp. 8-14.
[22] Wolverhampton Teachers' College for Day Students Prospectus 1977-78, p.2

The Transition Years

In 1955 the National Council for Technological Awards was established to administer a degree equivalent award for advanced work in technical colleges. One was the Diploma in Technology and Engineering (Dip.Tech) designed to offer national standards with sufficient flexibility to respond to local demand. The Dip.Tech was to be 4 years with a lengthy period of industrial experience in the middle, the 'sandwich' course. In the winter of 1956-57 a new Principal arrived, Robert Scott, who was to oversee the next stages of the College. The DipTech was developed at Wolverhampton and headlined on the 1957-58 prospectus, with a change of name to: 'Wolverhampton and Staffordshire College of Technology'. The arrangement between Wolverhampton and Staffordshire Councils had been adjusted as student intakes and separate developments had changed their requirements of a College. Nationally, attempts were being made to sort out the confusing pattern of 'technical education'. These were noted by the Principal of the Wolverhampton and Staffordshire Technical College in his 1956-57 report:

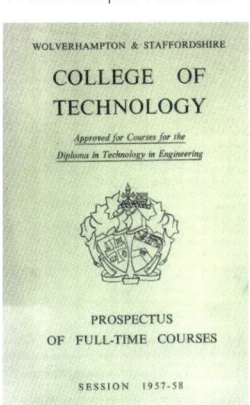

And so it is that probably for the first time in technical education, and rare in any British national institution, a pattern of logical development is becoming recognisable in a system so obviously the child of an industrial revolution whose very watchword was laissez-faire, and whose progenitors placed unbounded faith in the unfettered individualism of men of affairs.

West Midlands College of Education 1963

In 1956-57 ten technical colleges were raised to the status of Colleges of Advanced Technology and a second tier of twenty five regional colleges established. Wolverhampton and Staffordshire missed out on this becoming a large third tier 'area' provider. But this setback was seen as temporary, there was even talk of a University of the West Midlands located to the west of the conurbation centered on Himley Hall. When proposals were made in the mid 1960s to create polytechnics, Wolverhampton and Staffordshire were to argue, successfully, for a polytechnic in each area.

The next half century would see massive growth, unification and the recognition of formal inequality of status in English higher education. It was a journey that would take Wolverhampton and its constituent parts first to polytechnic and then university status in 1992. On 1st April 1966 the College of Technology reverted to single authority status, becoming known as the 'Wolverhampton College of Technology'. The College of Art soon began work on a major new building. An interim Committee of Governors was set up as a sub-committee of the Wolverhampton Education Committee to oversee the transition, including the preparation of the site for the new Polytechnic. On Tuesday 28th January 1969, the Polytechnic Council met for the first time.

Chapter two

Towards the Modern University

WOLVES
POLY:
ANOTHER
DAY IN
PARADISE

First CHOICE

NEWS FROM WOLVERHAMPTON— THE PEOPLE'S POLYTECHNIC

THE POLYTECHNIC WOLVERHAMPTON, MOLINEUX STREET, WOLVERHAMPTON WV1 1SB
CENTRAL REGISTRY TEL 0902 313000

Wolverhampton was one of thirty new polytechnics. Their creation was a significant step forward in higher education in the United Kingdom. A polytechnic in an area like the Black Country would also create a deeper basis for local educational expansion. But why did the government of the day move to expand higher education and, when it did so, why did it take the form of the creation of a group of polytechnics rather than universities?

The rationale for expansion is easy to explain. Economic growth had brought a degree of national and local prosperity. Some of the social barriers of the past had been diluted. In the late 1960s, Britain was a more equal place than it had been before and would be in the future. But higher education had changed less. Student numbers and the breadth of recruitment remained poor compared to many other advanced countries. Even The Economist in 1958 could say 'Everything must change … the varieties of degree, the methods of selection … and [the view] that the universities' main task is producing firsts in arts and science for the top jobs'.[1] The trend was pointing in a new direction and, in the language of the time, there was also the problem of 'the bulge' – the coming of age of those born immediately after 1945. The creation of several new universities in the 1950s and early 1960s was one response to this. Further development of teacher training colleges was another. The creation of new polytechnics and the consolidation of parts of higher education was to be a third.

In 1961, the government of the day established a committee to examine the future of higher education. Led by Lord Robbins, an economist, it reported in October 1963. It was the first high-level investigation of higher education as a whole and the first to think through how more of a system might be created. But the real significance of the Robbins Report lay in the way it consolidated an expansionary and more inclusive view of higher education. The argument was already being put by some educational reformers that, having won the battle for universal primary education and universal secondary education, the issue was now the fight for universal tertiary education.

Robbins did not want comprehensive higher education in this more radical sense. Higher education would be selective at 18 but it should be comprehensive in the sense of being available 'for all those who are qualified by ability and attainment.' – an argument that became known as the 'Robbins principle'.[2] The report also set out an humane vision of the

"objectives essential to any properly balanced system: instruction in skills; the promotion of the general powers of the mind so as to produce not mere specialists but rather cultivated men and women; to maintain research in balance with teaching, since teaching should not be separated from the advancement

---

[1] Quoted A. Briggs, 'Development in higher education in the United Kingdom. Nineteenth and Twentieth centuries', in W.R. Niblett ed., Higher Education. Demand and Response, London, 1969, p.115
[2] Committee on Higher Education, Higher education: report of the Committee appointed by the Prime Minister under the Chairmanship of Lord Robbins 1961-63, London: 1963, p.8.

> *of learning and the search for truth; and to transmit a common culture and common standards of citizenship.*

This would require a huge commitment to expansion, although the figures which seemed bold in 1963 soon proved conservative.

The question was how would this be done? The most radical ideas involved creating a new comprehensive university system that could unite and expand the different forms of higher education. Despite a new Labour Government coming to power in 1964, this seemed too radical a position and in any case most of the government's focus was on the need to create a comprehensive schooling system. However, there was a desire for public control of higher education to use available resources for direct social benefit. There was also a need for technical, work orientated, high level training for young and mature people responding to the economic demands for a competitive workforce. The general approach of the government was to work around, rather than directly challenge, entrenched positions of privilege. The resulting compromise in higher education was called 'the binary system.' Higher education would be expanded by developing two separate and ostensibly different but equal sectors. The existing universities would be allowed to grow as they were but not increase in number. They would remain autonomous and continue to get their funding from the University Grants Committee. Alongside them a new polytechnic sector would be developed, building on existing colleges. This 'polytechnic sector' would have a distinctive and more vocational mission.[3] The new polytechnics would derive their degrees from the Council for National Academic Awards (CNAA).[4] Above all they would be in the 'public sector' controlled and funded by local education authorities even though their aim was to recruit far beyond their borders.

This aspiration, to open up higher education while keeping it rooted locally, was an important, if still halting, step forward. The new polytechnics had their critics, but also their eloquent defenders, arguing that separate might not only be equal but better – offering a more useful peoples' higher education. In a speech at Woolwich in April 1965 the Labour minister of education, Anthony Crosland, gave the case for polytechnics a radical spin saying, 'let us move away from our snobbish, caste-ridden hierarchical obsession with university status'. But saying 'separate but equal' or 'separate and better' was one thing. Getting full recognition for the work done in polytechnics and the quality of their students would prove harder. It would take a generation before it became clear that those working for mass higher education in a unified system were more in line with the pressures of social and economic change in the UK than their critics.

In 1966, a government working paper set out the case for 28 new polytechnics, soon increased to 30, which would be formed from 50 existing colleges. The first new polytechnics were designated in September 1968 with Wolverhampton's to be formed of a merger between the College of Technology and the College of Art. The new 'Polytechnic Wolverhampton' received its formal designation in September 1969 with an inauguration ceremony in January 1970.[5]

> *This has given residents of Wolverhampton and the surrounding area the opportunity of easy access to one of the Country's major technological institutions in which a wide range of full and part-time courses up to degree or equivalent level can be followed.*[6]

---

[3] J.Pratt, The Polytechnic Experiment: 1965-92, Buckingham, 1997.
[4] H.Silver, A Higher Education: Council for National Academic Awards and British Higher Education, 1964-89, Brighton, 1990.
[5] The official title was The Polytechnic Wolverhampton until 1989 when it became Wolverhampton Polytechnic but it was locally always known as Wolverhampton Polytechnic or the Poly- we use the names interchangeably.
[6] Wolverhampton Polytechnic Prospectus 1970.

A History of the University of Wolverhampton

The new Polytechnic and Faculty of Art Buildings formally opened in 1970 by Sir Charles Wheeler

Opening the Doors to the Many

Élite higher education has been defined as allowing less than 5% of those leaving secondary school to go on. Mass higher education takes the figure up to 40% and over 40% might be thought of as moving towards universal higher education. At the start of the twenty-first century some countries have already begun to move into the universal stage and the UK is moving, albeit hesitantly, in the same direction. In each stage of development fears have been expressed: the fear of social destabilisation; the fear this democratisation involves reduced standards of university degrees; the fear that it risks producing an over educated labour force. Education is never simply about the economic, but in a capitalist society the economic is dominant. These fears misunderstand how the continued restructuring of the economy creates new educational demands. In turn this affects forms of study. Apprenticeship and work-based training were never available on a scale sufficient for a modern economy and many employers were reluctant to finance them. Subjects of study also change. At one point higher education in Wolverhampton was dominated by the study of metals and engineering. But these industries have risen and fallen, today the links to art, education, commerce, biology and pharmacy seem to provide as much continuity with the older colleges as its 'technical past'.

Even in manufacturing industry the share of administrative, technical and clerical staff in the workforce rose from 23% in 1963 to 44% by 2003. In the economy as a whole as table 3.1 shows, there have been radical changes in occupational structures.

Table 2.1 Percentage Employment by Occupational Groups in the UK 1921-2010

	1921	1931	1951	1966	1977	2000	2010
Managerial, professional and technical	6.2	6.6	8.2	12.9	26.7	37.4	41.9
Personal services	11.4	12.1	9.4	12.1	11.0	7.3	8.9
Sales	9.1	13.7	9.8	9.7	6.3	8.5	8.6
Clerical	7.3	7.2	11.4	14.0	16.1	14.0	12.1
Skilled, semi-skilled and unskilled manual	46.4	43.1	43.0	47.4	36.8	32.8	28.4
Agricultural	7.7	6.4	5.5	3.5	1.7	-	-
Other	11.8	10.8	12.7	0.3	1.4	-	-

UK Commission for Employment and Skills, (2012), Working Futures 2010-2020, London: UKES p. 91

Changing economies need a more advanced level of general higher education. The development of which has made the UK attractive to overseas students and their governments looking to advance their own economies.[7]

[7] A. Newell, 'Structural change' in N. Crafts, Ian Gazeley and Andrew Newell eds., Work and Pay in Twentieth Century Britain, Oxford: Oxford University Press, 2007, p. 39.

Consolidation and Closures

In the first years of polytechnics the senior management teams were carried over from the old colleges. Former college heads became 'directors' who then came together nationally as the Committee of Polytechnic Directors. At Wolverhampton the Head of the Technical College, Robert Scott, became the new Polytechnic Director, with the Head of the College of Art one of his deputies. Like other first polytechnic directors Scott had a technical-scientific background but as the polytechnics developed so their management structures grew and came to have a slightly more diversified background though still, overwhelmingly white and male.

Scott retired in 1978 to be replaced by George Seabrooke and then Michael (Mick) Harrison who was seen nationally as something of a first having begun his career as a sociologist.[8] His appointment reflected a broadening of the work of polytechnics like Wolverhampton. These Directors oversaw an organisation in transition, with a redefined purpose, new buildings and an expansion in population.

Creating a new institution in name was one thing, creating it in practice was harder. This required bringing together the constituent parts, the creation of a common academic framework and central support units. A management structure appropriate to a higher education institution had to be developed within the local authority. Faculties and Schools were created and reformed. Central services were consolidated and reconfigured. Managerial layers expanded and contracted. These organisational efforts absorbed considerable resources and passions. Staff had their lives changed, with redundancies, re-deployments and transfers to different sites. Longstanding departments were shed as work formerly done in the two colleges was excluded as being of too low a level. The 1970s saw a sometimes painful process of relegation for some activities to the further education sector including catering which had been a part of the Technical College since its foundation. Printing also suffered similarly from a decline in interest and status.

More painful still in the short term – but important to consolidation in the longer term – was the crisis in teacher training in the late 1970s and early 1980s. At first the new teacher training colleges seemed to be booming. They had organisational options.

The new Polytechnic Library named in honour of Robert Scott on his retirement

[8] He was the author of an early sociology textbook

When the old universities as their sponsors proved less than helpful, some like Walsall quickly took advantage of offering a BEd degree validated by the Council for National Academic Awards. However, bigger issues were at play. In schools the passing of the demographic bulge could have been an opportunity to further reduce class sizes and contact time for teachers. But in the late 1970s, with economic difficulties growing, it became the pretext for the opposite – a huge reduction in teacher training numbers to reduce the flow of new teachers. Places were planned to be cut within a decade from 80,000 in 1976 to 18,000. This meant college closures and mergers which fell especially heavily on those colleges linked to the local education authorities. It was this national adjustment that led to the incorporation of local colleges of education into the Polytechnic at Wolverhampton. This enabled it to establish its own Faculty of Education, acquiring new sites and staff in other locations, Dudley and Compton Park in Wolverhampton.[9]

Change was quick, one prospectus contained a slip of paper with 'Additional information for 1977 entry' that 'The Wolverhampton Teachers' College for Day Students, together with the Wolverhampton Technical Teachers' College and Dudley College of Education, will become a Faculty of Education in The Polytechnic, Wolverhampton on 1 September 1977.'[10]

The human impact of the closure programme was mitigated to some extent by an unusually generous (Crombie) redundancy scheme for older lecturers. But those who hoped to be taken on by the Polytechnic were not guaranteed a place. Some felt 'lucky' to be chosen while others were pushed aside. The pain was the greater because the closure of the colleges of education was one of the first examples of the mass redundancy of professionals which, alongside the redundancies in manufacturing, were beginning to become more common. It provided a case study of the problem of 'the redundant professional' by a young lecturer in the polytechnic, Derek Portwood.[11] A further loss was the withdrawal from Himley Hall in 1984, this site had housed the Management Centre but became too expensive to maintain.

[9] Rudi Herbert, A study of educational policy making at local level (sic): A case study of the merger of Dudley College of Education and Wolverhampton Polytechnic 1974-1976, University of Birmingham M.Ed Thesis., 1977.
[10] Wolverhampton Teachers' College for Day Students Prospectus 1977-78, enclosure
[11] D. Portwood, 'Professionals and Redundancy', Journal of Further and Higher Education, vol. 4 no.3, 1980, 3-19; D. Portwood, 'Careers and redundancy', The Sociological Review, vol, 33 no. 3, August 1985, pp. 449-468.

The final mergers in the polytechnic era came in 1989. The West Midlands College of Education in Walsall had escaped the initial cull of teacher training at the end of the 1970s but by the late 1980s the case for the unification of the remaining education colleges seemed overwhelming. The property of the Walsall College was formally transferred to the Polytechnic in April 1989 and this site became the location for the Polytechnic and then University Schools of education and of sports and performing arts. Glass making at the former Stourbridge School of Art was also relocated to Wolverhampton, 'lock, stock and furnace'. In the 1960s degree level work on glass had been developed in Stourbridge as part of the movement to revitalise art education. It broke what Keith Cummings called 'the two hundred year separation between the roles of designer and skilled craftsman'. Stourbridge students learned to explore, and sometimes rediscover, production techniques and even to appreciate the element of public performance on glass making. A government decision to bring the era of the small independent art school to an end coincided with a sharp decline in the local glass making industry by the 1980s.[12]

The Growth of the Polytechnic Wolverhampton

The big story of the polytechnic era is that of an overall expansion in higher education numbers and range. with a shift in distribution between universities and polytechnics.

Beginning in 1969 with 150,000 students, polytechnics grew to become the larger part of higher education in the UK with 450,000 students by 1992. In the mid 1960s only around 5% of school leavers had gone on to higher education, by the early 1990s the figure was one third and many mature students were joining them. It was the new polytechnics like Wolverhampton which opened their doors to make higher education more widely available. The biggest growth was in people studying for full-time degrees which by 1992 made up two thirds of those in polytechnics. The result was that by the turn of the 1990s as many people had a polytechnic degree as a university degree. Polytechnics offered different ways of studying, in 1992 they had 77,000 students studying on 'sandwich' courses (with a period of paid work) compared to only 18,000 in the university sector. They also had twice as many (125,000) part-time students as the then universities. Broadening recruitment meant that polytechnics had to look beyond narrow school based qualifications. More than half of those entering the polytechnics had non-traditional qualifications compared to 30% in the university sector.

Students came from a wider social base than ever before – there were more women, more mature students, and more students from minority populations. In the higher education sector in 1970 there had been some 255,000 students over the age of 21 studying for qualifications but by the mid 1990s the figure was 1.06 million. Some 600,000 of these were part-time – two thirds of those studying for HNC/D type qualifications; one fifth of those studying for undergraduate degrees and most of those studying for postgraduate qualifications. Mature students were more evident too on full-time courses. By the early 1990s over a quarter of those on undergraduate full-time degrees were over 21 and nearly a half of all full-time UK postgraduates were over 25.[13]

Wolverhampton Polytechnic was involved in all these advances describing itself as a 'Peoples' Polytechnic'. At the start of the polytechnic era, in 1970-71 it had 4,924 students, 3,239 of whom were part-time. Its main campus was in the centre of Wolverhampton, split by the ring road with the former Technical College on one side and the former Art College on

[12] C. M. Brown, 'Twentieth Century Growth and Regional Change in the British Glass Industry', Geography, vol. 64, no. 3, July 1979, pp. 196-204; K.Cummings, 'Born in Industry: The First 150 Years of Glass Education in Stourbridge, England', Glass (New York, N.Y.), Spring 2005, no. 98, pp. 40-45.
[13] A. Fuller, 'Credentialism, adults and part-time higher education in the United Kingdom: an account of rising take up and some implications for policy', Journal of Education Policy, vol. 16 no.3, 2001, pp. 234.

Coming From Behind

As higher education expanded and became more familiar, so its attraction as a literary setting grew. Writers like Kingsley Amis, Malcolm Bradbury, David Lodge and Tom Sharpe used post school educational settings ranging from Oxford Colleges to 'local techs'. But it was Howard Jacobson who wrote the polytechnic novel, *Coming From Behind* (1983) set in Wrottesley Polytechnic, a barely disguised version of Wolverhampton, where he taught at the turn of the 1980s.

Most of the characters in *Coming From Behind* were either recognisable from his time or composites including the successful Cora Peck who has elements of Maggie Gee. Gee, another leading novelist of the last four decades, obtained one of the first PhDs in English at Wolverhampton with a study of the role of the artist in contemporary fiction. She then went on to have her first novel published in 1981, ahead of Jacobson.

Jacobson appears in *Coming From Behind* as Sefton Goldberg, struggling with his Jewishness and hormones as well as the indignity of being at Wrottesley. Jacobson jokes that Sefton is writing a book called 'Sefton's Revenge'. When *Coming From Behind* was published (after he had resigned) those caricatured saw it very much as Jacobson's revenge. But it soon became a matter of inverted pride to be 'in' a successful novel and some even made competing claims to be a person being caricatured.

The plot of *Coming From Behind* revolves around a series of real incidents including the temporary acquisition of accommodation in the Molineux football stadium which was used for some two decades for teaching and staff rooms as the Polytechnic expanded. Jacobson also satirises institutional life at this time, including many of the organisational processes which reflected the competing demands, fashions and occasional whims of those at the top.

But the bigger theme is Jacobson's condescension to Wrottesley as a town, its students and his colleagues. Jacobson pokes fun at what he sees as the uncertain role of teaching English in a setting quite different from the traditional university. He also revels in describing the weaknesses and failures of Sefton Goldberg who finally escapes back to Cambridge but only in the most demeaning way. To deliberately confuse the Wrottesley students, even as he sleeps with some of them, Goldberg tells them that the minor but best selling authors of the past had produced the great works of literature. If Jacobson's work escapes this fate and his first novel remains of interest to future generations, Wolverhampton Polytechnic will live on in the sexual, educational and status struggles of Sefton Goldberg and his colleagues during his time at Wrottesley.

the other. Mergers had brought campuses and students at Compton Park, Dudley and Walsall. A small base was started in Shropshire, at Telford. By the end of the polytechnic era, numbers had grown significantly. In 1990/91 12,484 students enrolled, 72% on degree courses and 12.5% for postgraduate work – largely at diploma and Master's levels.

Figure 2.1 - Changing Students Numbers at Wolverhampton in the Polytechnic Era

declined. This was the 'dirty and onerous end' of the metal industry, one of the Black Country's areas of specialisation. This deterioration is reflected in Polytechnic publications, with the dynamism of the area being a marketing attraction in 1979 – 'With its world-famous industries Wolverhampton provides the opportunities of the nation's second largest conurbation.'[14] There was a more hesitant note 10 years later. 'Wolverhampton is a town proud of its Black Country industrial heritage, yet facing up to

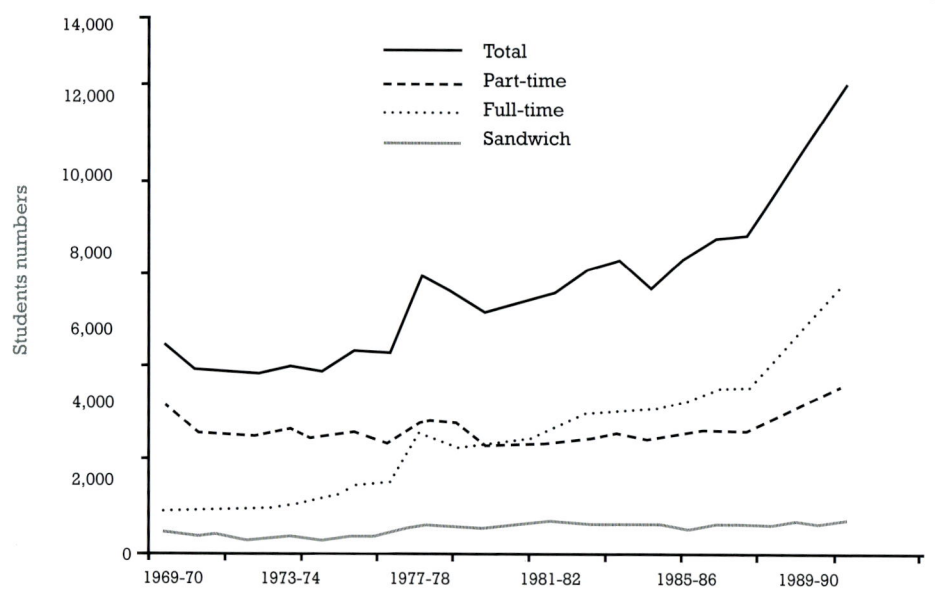

This expansion took place against a background of poorer national economic growth and the re-emergence of a pattern of successive economic crises. This was evident regionally. Manufacturing declined relatively and former growth industries now experienced absolute decline. Output in the car industry fell sooner and more sharply than in most other major economies. The West Midlands was hit and the Black Country, which had tended to do less sophisticated manufacturing work suffered more. Demand for castings and forgings, 80% of which went to the motor industry,

the challenge of the post-industrial high-technology future.'[15]

Although the longer run trend of student numbers was strongly upwards, the atmosphere in the polytechnic years was rather different from the post-war determined enthusiasm. There were cut-backs in some years, the overall mood was less certain and more politically divided, although never as polarised as the national mood during the Conservative Thatcher era (1979-1991). A key issue was resourcing. Government policy makers saw polytechnics as a cheaper way of expanding higher education

[14] *Wolverhampton Polytechnic Prospectus Part-time Courses 1979/1980, p.4*
[15] *Wolverhampton Polytechnic Student Guide 1988/89*

than university growth. The technicalities of the formulas that led to this can be found elsewhere. What is important here is that in the universities the unit of public expenditure on teaching stayed up, in the polytechnics it fell by 25% in the 1980s.[16] At the start of the polytechnic era the student staff ratio had been quite good but it worsened continuously, rising significantly above those in the universities. Even as numbers grew, therefore, so did a sense of dissatisfaction and injustice when the government cut back, as it did, for example, in the early 1980s. This put pressure on staffing and forced redundancies. Wolverhampton Polytechnic had to make its case as a modern, if cash strapped institution.

The lively 1986 Prospectus contrasts with 1971's utilitarian version

> *What is a Polytechnic? About fifteen years ago when Polytechnics were rather new and unknown, many people thought they were just technical colleges, and definitely inferior to universities. These days, the Polytechnics are well-known for their lively and innovative courses. They still receive lower funding from the Government and this means that buildings are sometimes shabbier, but critical inspection by, or on behalf of, the Council for National Academic Awards (CNAA) means that the specialist equipment, accommodation and staff skills, necessary to run high quality courses, are all checked out regularly in Polytechnics. Many students now choose Polytechnic courses in preference to the Universities, because they know they are up-to-date, relevant and geared to living and working in Britain (and Europe) in the 1900s.[17]*

This focus on employment would be strengthened in the following years. Education has always been expected to play an economic role. This had an organic element in the past, with institutions responding idiosyncratically to demand. Now, with higher education more structured and full-time, those who saw education primarily in terms of how it might serve the economy argued for more formal links. At the wider level too the 1980s saw the emergence of ideas that would later be called 'neo-liberal' and which increasingly prioritised an economic agenda over all others. In 1987, for example it was said that:

---

[16] D.Watson. *Whatever happened to the Dearing Report? UK Higher Education 1997-2007*, London 2007, p. 17 for the resource series.
[17] *Wolverhampton Polytechnic Student Guide 1988/89* p.6

> *There is an urgent need in the interests of the nation as a whole, and therefore of universities, polytechnics and colleges themselves for higher education to take increasing account of the economic requirements of the country.*[18]

These changing demands on education had an impact on the structure of courses and teaching.

Organising Education in a Polytechnic Framework

Polytechnics, Wolverhampton amongst them, mapped out a form of higher education that better reflected the world they were in. They widened the traditional subject matter of higher education study; they stressed the linkage across subjects with an emphasis on multi-disciplinarity and inter-disciplinarity. Languages, for example, were combined with the study of society rather than great literature of the past. The sciences, social sciences and the humanities were offered as combined studies. New areas developed, like the growing study of the environment, which could link the sciences and form a bridge to the social sciences and humanities. To make this effective course structures had to be unified and integrated. Polytechnics led the way in the adoption of the modular framework, enabling units of study to be combined. Modularisation required a different form of the traditional academic year. This was divided into two halves with modules usually taught on a half year basis. First year modules continued to be qualifying modules for part two which lasted a further two years for full time students, three for courses with a 'sandwich' year.

Modularisation allowed the adoption of a credit accumulation model. Each module had a standard credit weighting depending on its size. To gain a degree students had to accumulate sufficient credits of the right level. The grade of the degree then reflected the marks gained in a specified range of modules. The importance of this system lies in the word 'accumulation'. This model gave students flexibility. For most full-time students this did not matter, their studies proceeded much as they had always done. But for part-time and mature students credit accumulation helped cope with the disruptions of life. Credits could be more easily transferred between institutions as people moved. They could also be converted into diplomas and certificates if a person was unable to complete a full degree. An important, although temporary, innovation was the Diploma in Higher Education, developed as an intermediate award to attract mature students coming from various access courses.

These initiatives were not planned on sheets of blank paper. Structures already existed. For example, the Polytechnic, like most English higher education institutions, operated its two semester system for teaching within a three term framework. Such inconsistencies, and there are many, make for particular local difficulties which on a day-to-day basis consumed significant time and effort. The important thing is that the logic of what developed in the polytechnic sector (and the Open University which was also pioneering in its approaches to the organisation and delivery of teaching) reflected the forms appearing elsewhere in the world. These forms would become increasingly common, and indeed recommended, in the university sector as a whole from the 1990s.

Innovation also appeared in

[18] Department of Education and Science, Meeting the Challenge, London, .1987.

teaching methods – in part a product of the desire to teach better, in part a product of rising numbers and falling resources. Eric Robinson had suggested that technical college teaching involved too much 'spoon feeding'.[19] This might be unfair but even if true, could not be applied to degree level students who were required to be self-motivated. New times required new approaches. The lecture, the seminar, the practical session continued to dominate but polytechnic staff were finding more innovative teaching and assessment styles, aided by the technology it had early embraced.

Recognition and Status

It soon became apparent that polytechnics and universities were more similar than expected. In fact the logic of the binary divide was a problem from the outset, although in the early years there was a strong commitment to making it work. There were also practical issues in terms of control and funding of Polytechnics by local educational authorities. The question of democratic control of universities in relation to their 'communities' remains open but the idea that local authority control was the solution proved a problem. The polytechnics argued that the link was a constraint on their development rather than a support (what the local authorities thought is still not researched). The polytechnic directors lobbied the government to remove or at least to mitigate what they saw as the unhelpful elements in the local relationship. The result was the 1982 National Advisory Board for Higher Education to advise on funding.

On the political side as early as 1976 the then labour Minister of Education Gerry Fowler had spoken of a future 'when the rigid hierarchical distinction between polytechnics and universities and other institutions would be dissolved'. There was no immediate enthusiasm to do anything about this in the Labour or subsequent Conservative governments. Yet the Polytechnic era did not last. With hindsight there seems to be, as a senior civil servant of the time put it 'an inevitability about the evolution of a single higher education sector'.

What people wanted from a polytechnic education was the same as they wanted from a university, a degree level education. Initiatives to create diplomas of various kinds tended to be seen as stepping stones to the full degree. They also wanted access to a similar range of courses to those in the university sector, especially in the arts, humanities, social sciences, law and business studies as well as science and technology. When the Polytechnic Wolverhampton was founded there had been fears the College of Art would be submerged in an alien environment but this was not the case. The range of subjects offered at Wolverhampton like other polytechnics became, in a joke of the time, 'more poly than technic'.

On the other hand, polytechnics had abandoned some of their earlier diversity of provision, with the majority of non-degree work ended, 'sandwich' courses much reduced. Research activity had increased. Universities too offered more vocational courses while the polytechnics had become 'institutions which increasingly came to look like universities but which lacked the legal status, the funding structures and the public recognition which the universities enjoyed.'[20] Some of the early defenders of the polytechnic ideal saw this as an expression of 'academic drift' and behind 'academic drift' was 'social drift'. Polytechnics were accommodating too much to the middle class few. There was a partial truth in this. Recruitment was still narrow socially, although at Wolverhampton it was much wider than most. What such criticism missed was that people wanted the possibility of the same education and the same qualifications

[19] E.Robinson, The New Polytechnics, Harrnondsworth, 1968.
[20] M. Shattock (ed.), The Creation of a University System, Oxford, 1996, p.11.

A History of the University of Wolverhampton

that previously narrow élites had claimed for themselves. One result of this was that 'drift' was a two way process. If the polytechnics became more like universities then so, over time, did the universities become more like the polytechnics, something the more radical reformers had always argued was necessary. Amongst students, the NUS had at one point even spoken of the need for a 'polyversity' ideal. This merging of practice further weakened the case for separation and divide.

The key change which paved the way for the final evolution in 1992 of a unified sector was made in 1988 with an Education Reform Act giving polytechnics the corporate status that some had wanted from the start. They would now be independent of local authority control. Funding was to come from a National Funding Council while the Act also created a separate University Funding Council (replacing the University Grants Committee). Polytechnics like Wolverhampton now depended on central government for their funding and the differences between their situation and that of the older universities reduced even more. A bolder step, to complete merger, seemed to be one too far in 1988 but almost immediately the 1988 Act appeared to be a mere stop gap.

The result was that very quickly and with remarkably little controversy, more than a century of formal separation in institutions of advanced education gave way to unification in name and key processes. A 1991 White Paper proposed unification and in 1992 the Further and Higher Education Act created 32 new universities from the Polytechnics, with the University of Wolverhampton as one of them.

At this moment of change the last statement from 'the Polytechnic Wolverhampton' summarised what was passing.

Poly students graffiti on the Berlin Wall Autumn 1989

> *What are polytechnics? Polytechnics are equal partners with universities in providing first and higher degree courses. Polytechnics also provide many hundreds of courses outside the degree field including the Higher National Diploma (HND) and numerous professional qualifications. There are more than 300,000 students in every conceivable type of course at Polytechnics, almost half of them women. A further 60,000 study part-time during the day whilst some 30,000 take courses in the evenings.[21]*

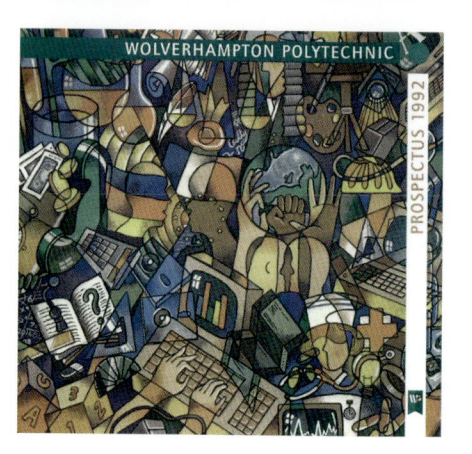

[21] Polytechnic Wolverhampton 1992 prospectus p.4

Art students with their logo design for the new University 1992

The University Era

The new university coat of arms depicts the engineer Thomas Telford and the Lady Wulfrun

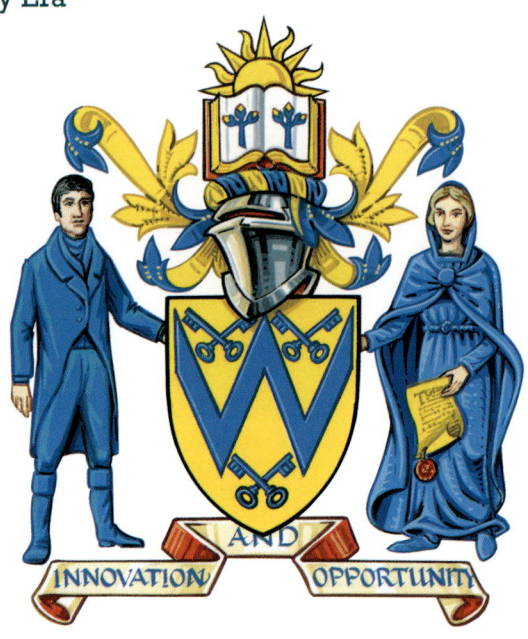

The journey to full university status had been prolonged, progress was and is full of contradictions. Looking back over the decades it is easy to see how socio-economic change played a role. Urbanisation, industrialisation, and then the shift towards a society based more on service work all helped to create new demands that affected higher education. Institutional and bureaucratic logics were at work. Social scientists talk of the way that status had been increasingly tied to credentials, with degrees some of the most prized. Education too has logic of its own and so do people. It is always fashionable to lament decline; and it is certainly true that history does not always move upwards in straight lines. There is a paradox too in education – it can be used for good or ill. But there is no paradox in ignorance and opportunities denied. Today education is rightly seen as a human right and the widening of opportunities for education, whatever qualifications we may wish to make about the adequacy of its forms, is a major advance. This applies no less to an advanced society than a poor one and the fact that in the United Kingdom today we have mass higher education in institutions like Wolverhampton is a sign of the progress.

Since 1992 the new university sector continued to grow, outnumbering the older one. Figure 2.2 shows the continuing rise in student numbers since 1995, with undergraduate numbers rising most steeply.

Distribution has been uneven, creating universities with widely different student populations ranging from 5,000 to 35,000. The rate of expansion has not been constant. Between 1980 and 1993, full-time equivalent student places rose by around 77%, from 638,250 to 1,128,000. This expansion was frozen in the 1990s, with a spike in growth following the removal of the cap on student numbers following the 'Dearing' recommendations in 1997.

The Jump to Mass University Education

Sometimes things happen in quite unexpected ways. When the Conservatives came to power in 1979 they saw the expansion of higher education as a problem and looked to contain long term growth. This was because of concerns about costs, the state of the economy, political discontent and a traditional conservative sense that higher education should be the privilege of the few. One minister even proposed to 'demote' universities which were unresponsive to government initiatives to 'polytechnics'. Yet when the Conservatives left office in 1997 they had presided over a higher education revolution which had brought together most provision into universities and massively increased access. This revolution began late and took everyone by surprise. It was even said that it was done 'in a fit of absence of mind'.

Looking back, a number of factors help explain how this happened. There was an element of catching up with some competitor countries whose higher education systems were more widely based. The changing pattern of the economy was making people more aware of the need for a highly educated workforce and weakening old distinctions. As the anomalies of the binary division became clearer, so too the bureaucratic case for unification become stronger. The Conservatives were adept at recognising and engaging with a sense of aspiration amongst their potential voters. The fact that such radical changes were being introduced by 'reliable conservatives' weakened opposition until it was too late. It may also be important that the changes were completed under John Major, a Prime Minster who had not gone to university himself and who seemed less concerned with traditional higher education status battles.

Historians will continue to argue about the balance of these and other factors. But this will take second place to the bigger issue, analysing the scale of the social shift that mass higher education involved and its consequences.

University status for polytechnics left a series of questions unresolved. One of these was the purpose of mass higher education. Related to this are debates about institutional status. Behind these stands the question of how universities are to be financed. In the next decades these all became the subject of sharp debate and a succession of policy initiatives from the governments of the day.

A History of the University of Wolverhampton

Figure 2.2 - Higher Education Students in England 1995 to 2009[22]

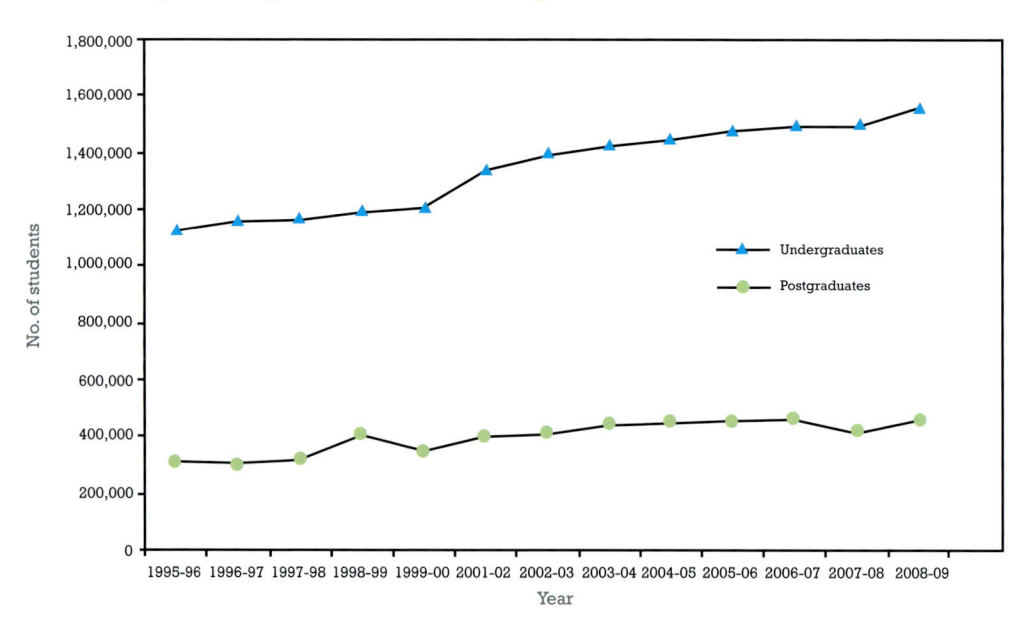

[22] Authors' calculations from HESA publications (various)

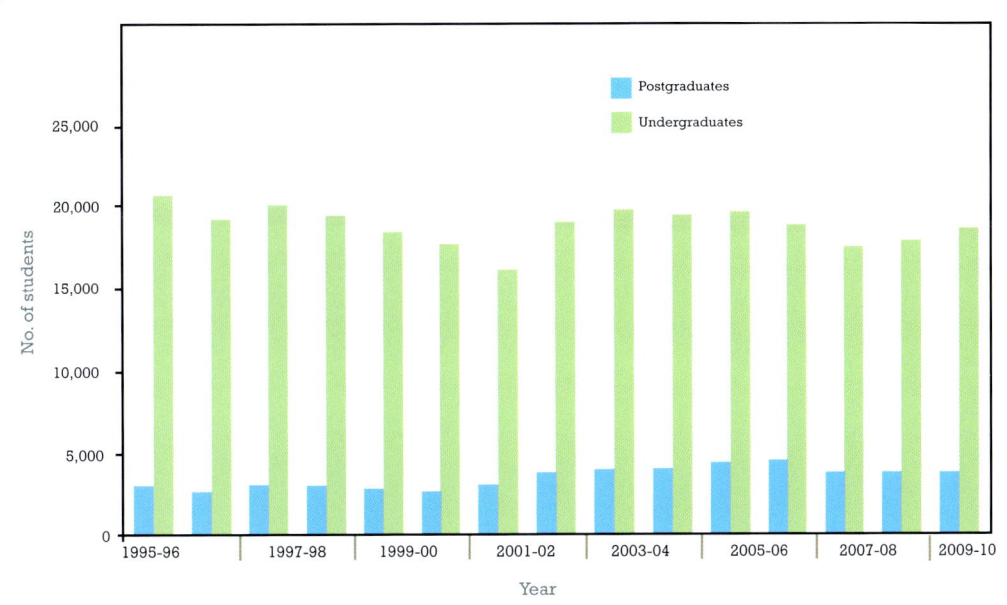

Figure 2.3 University of Wolverhampton Undergraduate and Postgraduate Students 1995-2010

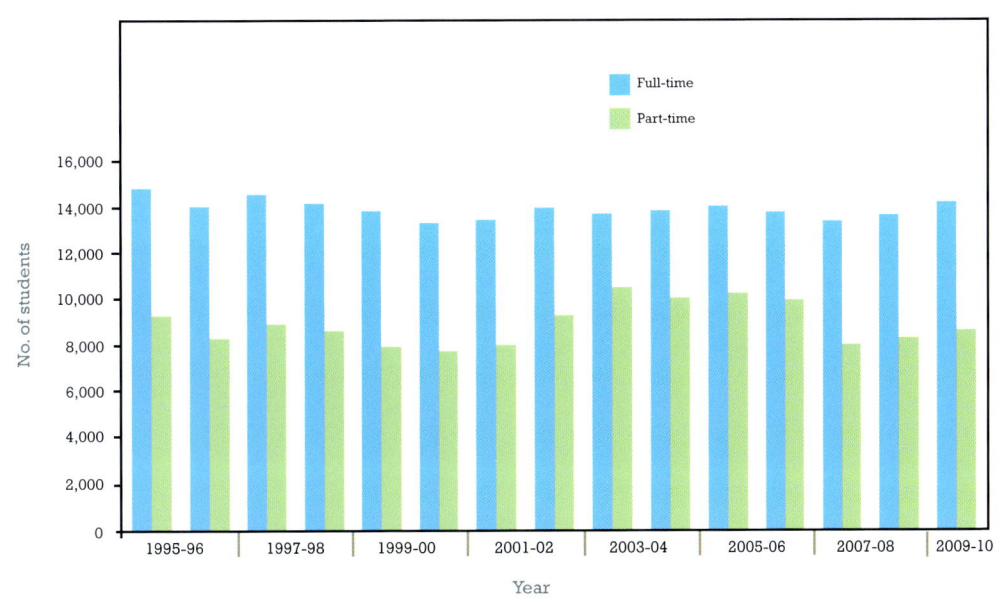

Figure 2.4 – University of Wolverhampton Full-time and Part-time Students 1995-2010

A History of the University of Wolverhampton

Student nurse uniform badges

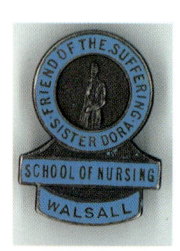

At Wolverhampton in the university era there have been fluctuations in student numbers but within a fairly narrow range within 4,000 places.

The long standing links between the institution and its local economy are reflected in the student body. There was a high level of part-time, mature and local students. Figure 2.4 shows the distribution between full-time and part-time students as a whole, since 1995.

By 2013 there were 23,207 students, 58% women and 42% men. 18,880 were undergraduates (15,237 full-time, 7,970 part-time) 4,330 postgraduates (1,937 full-time, 2,400 part-time).

The university era saw one further significant step in the integration of higher education provision. This was the decision to make nursing a degree level profession with the disbanding of traditional nursing schools and the creation of a nurse training, predominately in the new universities. Universities would now combine with local hospitals to offer higher level nurse education. In Wolverhampton this led to the development of the School of Nursing and Midwifery. This has since become the School of Health and Wellbeing, one of the larger schools, with a footprint in Wolverhampton, at Walsall and much further away at Burton-on-Trent.

School of Health and Wellbeing building

Expansion required a huge campus development to provide more and better teaching accommodation. Overall in the two decades after 1992 more than £150 million was invested in new capital projects in terms of building and equipment. The city site in Wolverhampton was redeveloped to create new buildings for teaching, academic and administrative staff with further developments continuing to be planned.

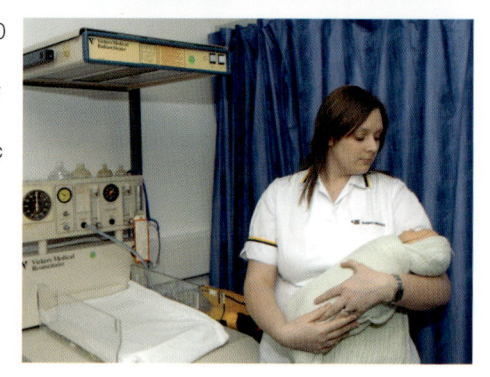

Towards the Modern University

On the Walsall Campus a similarly large development was undertaken to create new teaching blocks, a Student Village, improved sports facilities and a Performance Hub for the performing arts with a new library within it.

University status required some internal reorganisation and renaming, not least of the Director who now became a Vice-Chancellor. But the bigger story of the years after 1992 is of how the role of the university sector as a whole has been determined more and more from the centre. In the previous era the polytechnics had been part of a national system of education that was administered locally. Now there was a national system administered centrally with the added element that power was devolved to what in British terms are called quangos. (quasi autonomous government institutions) responsible to the government. In the case of higher education the new quango masters became the Higher Education Funding Council, and the Quality Assurance Agency.

*Far left:
The new library in the Walsall Campus Performance Hub*

Administration Building interior

Teaching block at Walsall

Nursing Education

War prompted developments in nurse education. Women nurses were recruited to work in army hospitals in 1854 during the Crimean war. Their experience led to the founding of the first nursing school in England in 1860, the Nightingale School in St Thomas' Hospital, London.

Nursing was unregulated, mainly women's work. The higher status voluntary hospitals trained their own nurses, recruiting from middle class women. Lower status hospitals such as poor law infirmaries and fever hospitals recruited working class women who, at best, had only a basic education and very little training. Nursing was seen as an extension of women's 'natural' capacity for housekeeping and care. As handmaidens to the male doctors they would need to be 'self denying, hard working and amenable to discipline'. They could learn what they needed to know on the job, which would probably be short-term, ending on marriage. Harsh training, social control and low wages made nursing an unattractive occupation. Recruitment and retention was a persistent problem.

Training and education were seen as the mechanism to move towards professional status, which would make the work more attractive. Nurses organised to press for improvements, but class divisions were perpetuated. Women of higher social status established professional associations excluding nurses outside of major hospitals who then turned to the growing trade union movement.

The 1914-18 war caused thousands of women with nursing experience to volunteer for war service. In processing these volunteers the fragmented and unregulated forms of nursing training was highlighted. This led to the Nurses Registration Acts in 1919 which introduced minimum levels of training, examinations and a register of qualified nurses. Training was now delivered by approved hospitals in their schools of nursing but the apprenticeship model persisted. Students were paid members of staff. Teaching was by ward staff, instructing the students as opportunity arose in the day to day work. A move towards dividing theory, taught in a classroom and practice, taught on the wards, was introduced in the 1930s to address a practical problem affecting recruitment. Girls left school at 14 but were not accepted for formal hospital training until 18 or older. By splitting theory from practice girls could attend lectures before their formal training began, gaining later exemption from the theoretical part of their first year examinations.

By the outbreak of the 1939-45 war there was a serious shortage of nurses. War made the problem more urgent. Retired nurses volunteered, and were later conscripted, others were recruited from Commonwealth countries. Large numbers of untrained nursing assistants were necessary. This raised fears that professional status for nurses would be threatened after the war by this experienced, cheaper, workforce. This was solved by establishing two levels of nurse registration – the more highly qualified State Registered Nurse and the State Enrolled Nurse.

The introduction of the National Health Service in 1948 re-structured hospital provision and brought the state employment of nurses, national pay scales and standards. More and better trained nurses were needed, yet recruitment was still seriously below demand. Post-war Britain offered alternative work to women. Girls had better education, they could enter different occupations and pursue further or higher education. Of those that did opt for nursing training, less than half became registered nurses, about one third left in their first year, others did not enter for final examinations and of those that did about 20% failed.

One reason for this was thought to be the low level of prior education of trainees, with no agreed entry requirements. Another was that students were treated as cheap labour with their training subordinated to service needs on wards with a constant turnover of qualified staff. The Platt Report of 1964 recommended the entry requirement for nurse training should be five GCE 'O' levels. Students would get a training grant for the first two years of training and wages for a third. It raised the possibility that nursing schools could be separated from hospitals. The recommendations were rejected but the issues of higher entry qualifications, student grants and greater autonomy for training were to gain support.

The move to higher education institutions for nurse education was initiated by the Judge Report in 1985. It identified the need for a broader curriculum encompassing subjects such as sociology and psychology. There was some dissent on the separation of training from the control of hospitals and a practical problem to be solved if student nurses were no longer to be employees and part of the ward staff. It was calculated that student nurses provided three quarters of the care on hospital wards. This workforce would no longer be available if they were to spend the majority of their training away from the hospital. Divisions in status between nurses were abolished and healthcare assistants were recruited to the hospital workforce.

As nursing training moved into polytechnics and universities from 1989, hospitals no longer recruited student nurses, now developing training with their local universities with joint assessment and practical placements. Some argued that a more academic approach to theory would leave nurses ill-equipped with the necessary practical skills when they moved to the wards. Nevertheless it was decided that by 2013 nursing would become an all-graduate profession. Older nurses would be helped to work towards a degree, further training and professional development would also move to universities.

[23] General Certificate of Education - ordinary level
[24] RCN Commission on Nursing Education chaired by Dr. Harry Judge 1984

Government policy and state funding steered universities in a more entrepreneurial direction. Both Conservative and Labour governments prioritised the economic role of higher education. This element had always been present but, at least at the level of rhetoric, it was never as dominant as it has been since the 1990s – a reflection of the power of 'neo-liberal' thinking. Individual institutions like Wolverhampton were encouraged to develop closer links with local companies to reflect this thrust. They were also urged to think of themselves much more as businesses, competing with one another and becoming risk takers.

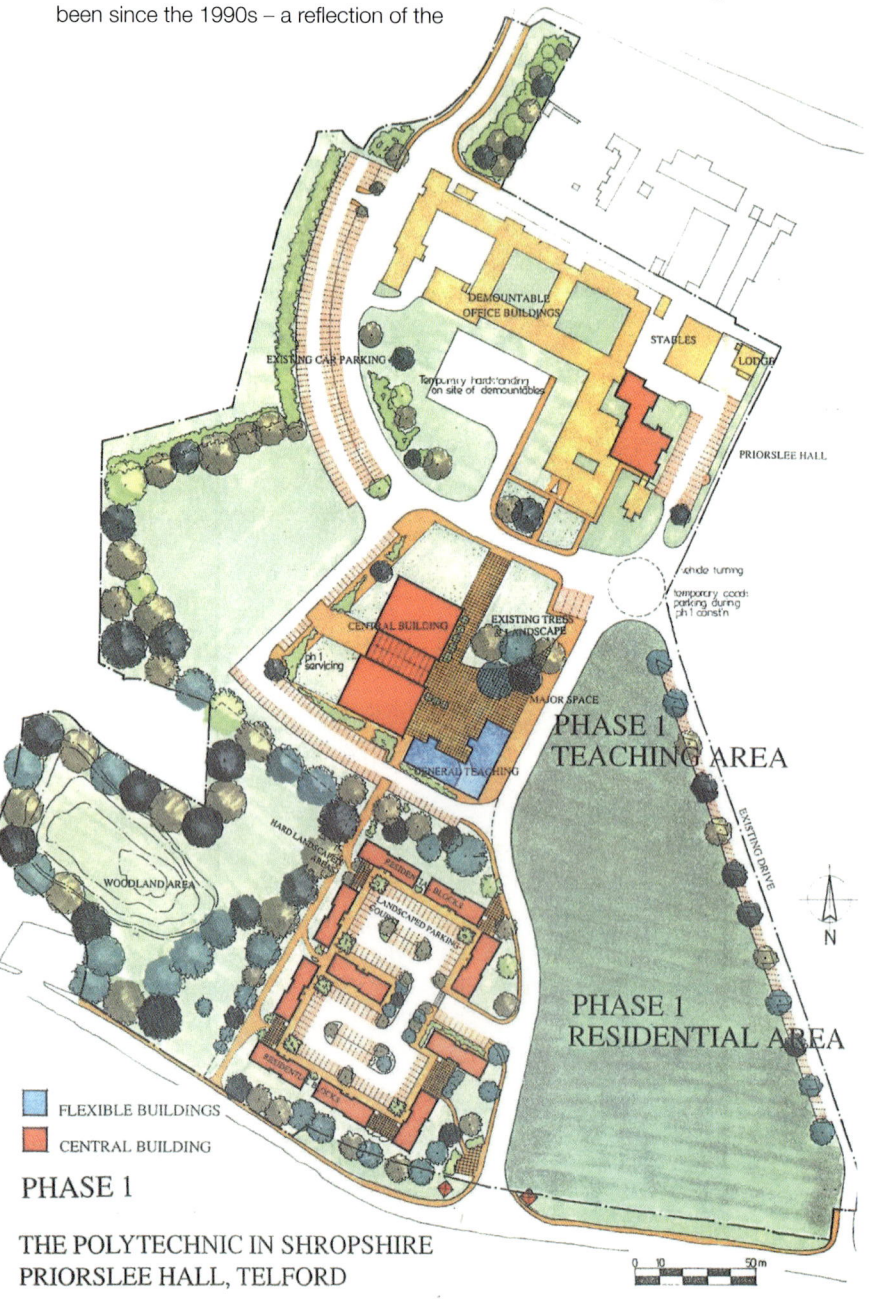

PHASE 1

THE POLYTECHNIC IN SHROPSHIRE
PRIORSLEE HALL, TELFORD

Towards the Modern University

The forms of expansion at Wolverhampton were in part determined by these ideas. One aspect of this was the development of a small campus in Telford in Shropshire as part of a defensive move to prevent other local universities moving into the area. This led to the development of a major site in Telford in two stages, the first completed in 1993. It centred on an eighteenth century listed building, Priorslee Hall, with other accommodation used by the former Telford Development Corporation, soon supplemented by the University's own buildings.

MASTERPLAN

THE POLYTECHNIC IN SHROPSHIRE
PRIORSLEE HALL, TELFORD

A History of the University of Wolverhampton

The Wolverhampton Science Park was a shared endeavour between the City Council and the University. Opened in 1995, the site offered workshops, laboratories, offices and catering facilities. Another thrust, in part motivated by the attraction of student fees in an era of constrained finances, was the more aggressive development of an international profile.

In educational terms there was less change as the patterns in the new University built on the successes of the previous era. The problems lay more in managing the tensions between increasing the quality of education and research, managing student numbers, limited finances and the temptation to take too many risks.

A difficult issue was dealing with the changing demand for student places and year-on-year fluctuations in numbers, budgets and government targets. Universities, like the economy as a whole, are subject to structural changes in demand. For a period, subjects can soar in demand and this happened in the 1990s and early 2000s to areas like computing. But equally demand can slide. This problem was evident in science and technology where, the changing pattern of manufacturing production in the wider economy fed back into changing student demand. In engineering oily rags gave way to computer aided design while in science metallurgy, physics and chemistry declined. Biological sciences and its related subjects grew. No less spectacular was the decline of language teaching where the Polytechnic had established a national reputation in the 1970s and 1980s and one of the biggest, if not the biggest school of Languages and European Studies. Falling demand posed sharp questions as to whether areas should be abandoned or to some extent protected.

Different universities adopted different policies but at Wolverhampton at key points, senior managers pushed to follow demand, leading to various voluntary redundancy schemes and subject closures or downgrades.

Lathe operator at Lee Howl
© Nick Hedges

Below: The new Science Park

Some universities, new and old, failed to negotiate the bigger tensions but Wolverhampton managed to avoid the worst pitfalls until 2009. Then, on July 31 2009, as staff were going on annual leave, the senior management announced that there was a financial crisis with a £12 million operating deficit for the year to which the only solution was a programme of up to 250 potential compulsory redundancies.

This sudden eruption of crisis came as a shock and hit the headlines beyond the region. A modern university needs to ensure that it maximises student recruitment, its main source of income, and meets its targets. Failure to do so can bring penalties from central government. In turn it needs to record its student numbers correctly. Wolverhampton, amongst a number of universities, was hit by failures here but at the same time costs had been rising, because, said the management, of increasing pay. The net result was the hole in the budget.

The crisis provoked bitter conflict as staff unions asked whether the crisis was as great as made out; how it had been allowed to come about and disputed that compulsory redundancies were the only solution. A campaign of opposition was widespread and the University management moved to a voluntary redundancy programme. This led to 150 staff leaving in an atmosphere where the priority seemed to be to save money. They included academics, administrators and manual staff and they stretched from the 'top to the bottom' – 11 professors and deans choosing to go. There was also a squeeze on costs and a restructuring of the curriculum to try to find other efficiencies.

In the next years the fortunes of the University began to turn for the better. The immediate cause in 2009-10 was not so much the initial savings as an increase in income.

Since then costs have been pushed down, leaving a healthier surplus. In January 2011 a new Vice-Chancellor, Geoff Layer (himself a former polytechnic graduate) was appointed, taking office that summer in a more positive climate, saying that, 'the higher education sector faces many challenges in the next few years, but I am confident that by working together we will ensure this is a university we are all proud of.'

Pressures and new opportunities also led to campus changes. The first campus to be closed was at Dudley at much the same time as the new Millennium Building was opened on the South Campus at Wolverhampton. Nearly a century of higher education in Dudley ended but there was a limited opposition, in part because the closure opened up new opportunities for the local further education college. The financial crisis of 2008-9 lead to the closure of the Compton Park Campus where the Business School had been partly located for many years. As with Dudley, part of the campus was sold off for housing development. At the same time the role of Telford Campus was also reconfigured, reducing the amount of undergraduate and postgraduate teaching taking place there and focusing it much more on engineering and short courses, conferences and business development.

The issue of university financing overlapped with that of student financing. In the 1980s the Government began to explore ways of making students pay for higher education. Primary and secondary education was seen as a right to be paid for out of general taxation and grants had been introduced for higher education in the 1950s. It now began to be argued that students should pay a proportion or all of their fees and maintenance costs. This could be by some form of 'up front' payment (which would require a national loan scheme) or a graduate tax after the award of the degree. Early attempts to move in these directions

Triad Gangs, Ancient Bones and German Girlfriends

If *Coming From Behind* immortalised Wolverhampton as Wrottesley Polytechnic in the 1970s, then in 2002 a second satirical novel brought the comic story forward into the world of the new universities. Mil Millington's *Things My Girlfriend and I Have Argued About* is the story of Pel Dalton, a computer specialist working in the library of the University of North Eastern England, – 'a modern forward looking university, a regional university of outstanding quality'. But if the fictional university in the north east sounds a lot like Wolverhampton in the Midlands this is not surprising. Its author was for a time, like the fictional Pel, a computer specialist working in the library at the University of Wolverhampton. Here Millington had begun to write a successful comic blog detailing his everyday arguments with his German partner who had come to England to study and then decided to stay. From the blog came this first novel and then, like Jacobson, a career as a novelist, newspaper and, in a new age, an internet columnist.

Millington's novel weaves the story of Pel Dalton and his girlfriend Ursula and their children with that of a modern university seen from the perspective of the library. One aspect, familiar from Jacobson, is the satirising of the educational management fads which rename the library 'the learning centre' and insist on 'staff improvement' days, made less attractive still by holding them as 'away days' in another part of the university. Here too are the status and aspirational conflicts that Jacobson poked fun at but this time they are between 'the professional librarians' whose status is falling, 'the library assistants' and the IT specialists in the library as well as between them all and the world outside. There is even a passing appearance for the honorary university 'café', across the road, where for decades the stream of early morning manual workers has given way to university staff, high and low, looking for coffee and a fried egg sandwich.

But the bigger story is that of the perils of the entrepreneurial university. A series of chance events result in Pel being catapulted into running the 'learning centre'. But he soon finds that he has risen fast because the university's Vice-Chancellor and Head of Marketing need a patsy. They are fiddling the accounts to pay Chinese triad gangs to recruit overseas students while paying off builders to hide the bones being dug up in an ancient cemetery as they expand the 'Learning Centre' and to bury something far more sinister.

Millington's initial foray into comic blogging seems to have provoked a degree of consternation in an image conscious institution. It was taken off the university servers to avoid embarrassment. But, as with *Coming From Behind*, Millington's subsequent novel captures elements of a time and place and it has become a literary badge of honour. Few would have anticipated that within a twenty year period a fictionalised Wolverhampton would have twice been captured for the comic tradition of English writing that goes back over three centuries.

A History of the University of Wolverhampton

New built for the Polytechnic, now demolished and replaced with the Millennium City Building

Top right: Programme for the opening of the Millennium City Building in 2003.

Right: The Millennium City Building from the Central Square

were defeated as a result of opposition in Parliament and from students themselves, including those at Wolverhampton. The late 1990s, despite vocal opposition, saw the start of a succession of reforms in financing designed to shift a greater proportion of the costs to students. These eventually led to the Coalition Government of 2010 withdrawing the major part of the teaching block funding. This was to be recouped by large increases to the fees paid by students, for which government loans would be provided where needed. With the real cost of higher education rising some argued that this would work to the advantage of élite institutions. It is too soon to say if this will be the case.

Arguments about fees became bound up with arguments about 'reputation' and 'quality'. These are not the same thing. The proliferating league tables claimed to measure 'quality' but were really measuring 'reputation' and 'status'. In 2010 Wolverhampton took the controversial decision to suspend the provision of data to the commercial organisations marketing league tables, arguing that 'these tables disadvantage universities such as Wolverhampton and do not represent a fair picture of our strengths'. The issue was now how far universities, which were equal in name, could become or should aim to become equal in practice. If the development of mass higher education involved a step into the future, the system in England continued to keep one foot in the past where status distinctions continued to play a disproportionate role.

Formally all the UK's universities could now become members of the Committee of Vice Chancellors and Principals which in 2000 became the lobby group 'Universities UK'. But behind the appearance of collective unity and equality, divisions quickly emerged as different universities created lobby or mission groups. These argued for more resources for higher education as a whole, but also to contest the distribution of resources within it. The 'Russell Group' claimed élite status not so much on the basis of its undergraduate teaching but its research work. It concentrated two thirds of all research funding and produced over 50% of all PhDs as well as recruiting élite students from outside of the European Union. A second 'top' group known as the '1994 group' was formed to reflect the interests of what were described as the smaller research intensive universities. The new universities split into a 1997 'Coalition for Modern Universities' which in 2007 became the 'Million+ group' and a 'University Alliance' formed in 2006 which pitched itself as slightly higher in status. Some 20-30, mostly, but not all, new universities remained non aligned.[25] From 1997 the University of Wolverhampton has been one of what became known as the 'Million+ group' seeking to fight the cause of the larger new universities.

An Evolving Research Base

By the time that the polytechnic was created some academic staff were already publishing regularly. Helping staff improve their qualifications was seen as important but going beyond this often seemed to be a matter of personal choice. Support for research came from the general 'surplus' of resources available and various external grants won which supported the acquisition of equipment, 'bought' staff time, and paid for other research costs and bursaries. In this sense, although the value of research was recognised, it also seemed ancillary to the teaching function.

The research commitment at Wolverhampton grew over time. In the 1980s one expression of this was the recognition of professorial status which came in 1985 with the appointment of Roger Epton as the polytechnic's first professor. By the end of the Polytechnic era in 1991

[25] Melanie Newman, 'Do you want to be in my gang?' Times Higher Education Supplement, 19 November 2009.

there were 49 people studying for PhDs, 621 for Master's degrees and 594 for other postgraduate qualifications which put the Polytechnic in the upper half of those offering postgraduate courses.[26] University status therefore built on a long, if uneven, tradition of advanced work. It more or less coincided too with a new national funding regime which gave research a more central role in the University's external profile and its internal organisation.

In 1985-86 the Government began what was then called a 'research selection framework'. The idea was to allocate funding by institution according to the peer reviewed published research outputs. Few appreciated the significance of this approach at the time. When full university status was achieved in 1992 Wolverhampton became eligible for the competitive resource allocation. The resulting funding that came to Wolverhampton, although small in relation to that of élite institutions, began to transform the approach to research. A research profile fed into the emerging university league tables while internally it led to more support and debates about how to organise and encourage research. Over time the succession of research assessment exercises became more onerous and more competitive but also more central to the life of all higher education institutions including Wolverhampton.

It is not easy to agree on a measure of 'good' research and rather in the manner of football clubs the better financed universities can 'buy in' players from lower leagues. The strong focus on selectivity arose from the argument that resources were limited but it too easily flowed into the quite different argument that the available resources should be focused on the very few. The few then became effective lobbyists in their own cause. This has served not only to increase inequalities within higher education but also accentuate regional inequalities as resources have flowed south to the 'golden triangle' made up of Oxford and Cambridge and, in London, Imperial College, the London School of Economics and University College.

The successive exercises have also tended to show that newer universities, in relation to their resources, have punched above their weight and Wolverhampton has sustained a good record over time and in comparison with its immediate peers. But like all of the post polytechnic universities and many of the older ones outside of the élite, it has suffered from the gaming of the system to deliberately increase 'selectivity' despite its positive performance. How far this can be sustained in the future is an open question. The answer does not depend so much on the debate about the immediate funding regime as it does on the capacity to build long-term developments in a university culture that has the commitment and enthusiasm to push out our understanding of the world. As we have seen the roots of this are as deep in Wolverhampton as anywhere else in the university system.

International Trajectories

At the end of the twentieth century people began to talk of an age of globalisation but this neglected the extent to which international elements had always existed. In the case of Wolverhampton, overseas links had been built up early on in periods of working overseas for staff and students. International students had been welcomed in Wolverhampton from at least the 1950s. What is true is that from the 1990s onwards this became a necessity in terms of financing and an opportunity in terms of global education trends.

Non European Union international students bring in large fees. From the 1990s increasing efforts were made by UK universities to attract them. Some provincial universities even set up overseas campuses, seeking to benefit from the 'capital city'

[26] Hansard, 30 April 1993.

effect in terms of recruitment. Wolverhampton did not take this path looking to encourage students to come to the Black Country. Such recruitment became increasingly organised with the university opening its own recruitment offices in Poland and Cyprus, Nigeria, India, Malaysia and China. It also drew on networks of agents, 'educational advisers', in over two dozen countries.

An ever more diverse student body brings traditions and knowledge of a wider world stretching their fellow students and their lecturers. The benefits - social, educational and economic – move in both directions. People come together as human beings to try to know one another better and find out about the world they share. There is even an exchange of recreational pleasures by playing together. In recent years the university has held an international festival for all students on the home campuses with food tasting, displays from around the world and talks. Organised more recently by students themselves, to celebrate diversity, Bollywood dance competes with Zumba and mini Olympics and there is the obligatory Morris dancing - a British 'tradition' whose origins are much more in the twentieth century than its local enthusiasts like to admit.

Educationally too there is benefit. New possibilities (and difficulties) emerge in the classroom and beyond. British students can find insular views challenged in a way that forces them to rethink their position in a society whose power once dominated the world. International students want British based qualifications. This is partly a matter of language, partly status but it also reflects the possibilities of developing a more positive educational experience that can draw on and feed back into the global shifts that are taking place.

There is economic self interest too. British students and staff gain access to insight into regions and economies that they may want to access in an era of globalised employment. Governments encourage the movement of students in the hope that they later become informal ambassadors for wider interests, both national and cosmopolitan, in an era when the world is being tied more closely together.

Internationalisation could also involve going to the students. One way was to set up satellites campuses aboard which a number of western universities did but the capital costs of this could be huge. The more common approach, evident at Wolverhampton, was the development of franchise arrangements with courses designed, validated, sometimes taught by 'flying faculty' and examined by Wolverhampton staff. At the start of the third decade of university life Wolverhampton courses were offered in over a dozen countries being taught in conditions as varied as the extreme cold of the Siberian winter and the warmth of an island of the Indian ocean.

In 2012 the University and its new Vice-Chancellor, Professor Geoff Layer, set out its strategic plan for the next years. It talked of Wolverhampton being 'a major player in the UK higher education sector, contributing to knowledge transfer, economic development, wealth creation and social justice' and it being 'a beacon for widening participation'. The aim, said the Vice-Chancellor was to 'provide a broad range of educational opportunities focused on making a real difference to the lives of individuals, communities and businesses.' If the language had a modern ring, the sentiments could be found throughout the history of colleges that fed first into the Polytechnic and then the University – the history we have traced in these two chapters. But to see what these things have meant in practice we need to explore the Wolverhampton experience in more detail, starting with the students who have come into it in such large numbers over the past generations.

A History of the University of Wolverhampton

Developments continue – impression of the planned new Science Building next to the Engineering Block

Towards the Modern University

Chapter three

The Workforce – Students

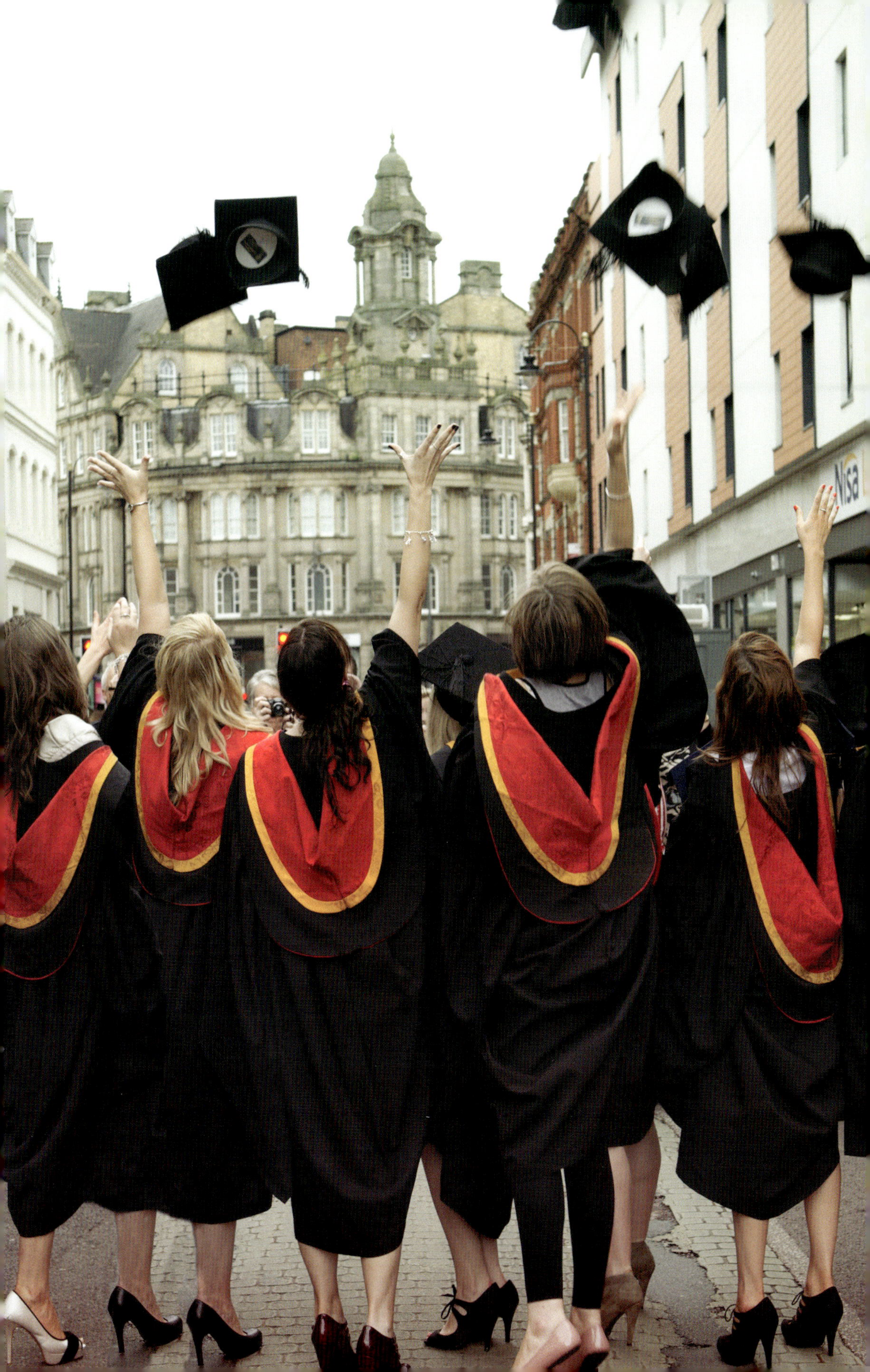
Nisa

Students form the vast majority of the population of educational institutions. They bring life, energy and purpose. Generations of students move on through their courses towards graduation and life beyond, revitalising and challenging as they go. When we look back today it is lost opportunities of the previous generations that stand out. Writing in 1920 H.G Wells said:

> *England in the last three centuries must have produced scores of Newtons who never learned to read, hundreds of Daltons, Darwins, Bacons and Huxleys who died in stunted hovels, or never got the chance of proving their quality. All the world over there must have been myriads of potential first class investigators, splendid artists, creative minds, for every one of the kind who has left his mark upon the world …*[1]

He then went on to argue that 'there is an infinite room for betterment in every human concern'. At that time less than two percent of the population in Britain went to university and over 90% had no more education than what would today be called primary. Wells must have seemed like a deluded visionary to most of those of his day. But less than a century on an ever growing share of the UK population was getting the experience of higher education. Wells it seems saw farther than those who dismissed him.

The first two chapters showed that one part of the history of education is this story of division – of availability and segregation. They also showed that another part of the story is that of overcoming these divisions. Those who supported restricted access and separation have often seemed to be the most influential but in the longer run they have been the losers. The last two centuries have seen the development, first of mass primary education, then mass secondary education and finally, today, we are seeing the creation of mass higher or tertiary education. This shift still has a long way to go and completing it will require a degree of rethinking about the future forms of the tertiary sector. But just as obstacles to mass education were overcome so the obstacles to mass higher education will give way in the future.

In this chapter we look at how the students have changed over time. This is a story of the struggle to realise the sort of potential that Wells talked of and to widen the chance of 'betterment'. It is also the story of a struggle against the pressures of those who argued that more inevitably meant worse.

Study after study has shown that selectivity is as much a measure of social position and background as ability. This is why, for so long, women were deemed less able than men, why ethnic minorities were thought less able than the dominant majority and why the 'lower classes' were seen as less able than the 'upper classes'. Today we more widely recognise the extent to which opportunities to develop and the perception of ability are bound up with life chances. Some still argue for 'better' and 'more objective' tests to enable a more refined selection between those who go to university and those who do not and to decide which university they go to. The enthusiasts for selection do not recognise the peculiarity of the idea of selectivity itself. In fact some global universities already exist where it is possible to gain everything from a basic certificate in literacy to a PhD. If this seems radical we should recall that in Britain the Open University has always admitted students without formal qualifications and the polytechnics led the way with wider access

[1] Quoted R.Pedley, Towards the Comprehensive University, London, 1977

courses. We should also recall the words of a Vice-Chancellor of the City of New York University on the principles of what is called 'open admission':

> *The notion that universities and colleges should be rated principally on the selectivity of their admissions process is a curiously modern one. Like the more stringent of the Catholic positions on birth control, it dates from the beginning of the [twentieth] century. It has no application to 750 years of the English speaking university's existence, and as such can well be regarded as a passing disease. That it may have passed is good news* [2]

But what is a student? The question is more difficult to answer than it might appear. We could think of a school but even if we accept that the definition of a school is uncontroversial (it is not) this does not help us a great deal. A higher education institution is not a school – this was insisted on in the Technical College from the start. There are teachers and students but both are adults, in law this only became so at the end of the 1960s – before then colleges and universities had a formal paternalistic role to their young students. Students come to learn, teachers to teach but students also pay. Students are often talked of as customers but no customer of a normal business is in the position of a student – a university is not a normal business. Students must work and their work is judged. Their work determines the success of the enterprise and consequently the jobs and income of the staff, who are paid to be there and required to manage it. This creates an interdependent relationship which also has the potential for tensions. One way out of this dilemma is to think in terms of co-production. A university is a place to which different people come to work together to engage in co-production, giving, creating and taking as they do so. At one level this is obvious – all work, all labour, all teaching, all learning involves co-production. But the notion is also subversive of the idea of roles and that students are simply there to have their minds filled. They are in the middle of this exchange, this process of co-creation. In the different institutions that fed into the modern University of Wolverhampton this process of co-creation has taken place with successive generations of students. Let us look at some of them.

Students in the Nineteenth Century Black Country

In the late nineteenth century, mass education was about elementary education. It was about schools with classes of sixty children, sitting in straight rows being taught how to read and write but also to know their place. The worlds of the comfortably off who understood the niceties of life – regular food, clean clothes, good manners were lived at one remove from the mass of the workers and their families. Both inhabited a world where there was no radio; no television, no internet and where books and newspapers seemed expensive. This was why the Free Library in Wolverhampton and the 39,000 volumes it stocked by 1900 were so important.

Justifying inequality has always been difficult. Religion was once an important support for the established order. Elementary school children in the late nineteenth century learned to sing, 'The rich man in his castle, the poor man at his gate, God made them high and lowly and ordered their estate'. But religion was weakening and

[2] Quoted Pedley, op cit., p. 72

Christianity had also given rise to a more democratic tradition. In the late nineteenth century a new and ostensibly scientific doctrine of 'intelligence' provided a different justification for educational division. A few were born with ability, the majority were not. The majority needed education but it had to be appropriate to their situation and limited by it. In 1918 D.H.Lawrence, put this bluntly, writing of a dustbin man, 'we can't make a highly intelligent human out of a Jimmy Shepherd' if he had only been born 'moderately intelligent.' 'Every teacher knows that it is worse than useless trying to educate at least fifty per cent of his scholars'.

But was it? There was aspiration, some school teachers tried to do more than the narrowly proscribed curriculum of elementary education, encouraging their pupils to learn more widely. After school had ended at too young an age, there was 'night school' and the Saturday afternoon or evening lectures which promised a little more. But it was still a minority who could access this. In 1877, the Wolverhampton Chronicle announced that in the new Free Library there would be, 'education for the people … evening classes 5 s[hillings] to 1 s[hillings] per quarter'.[3] In a world of insecurity, finding this money, the time and commitment to come regularly was no mean feat. By the 1900s the number doing so had grown but they were still a small part of the population as they would be for decades to come.

For most, leaving school meant work, 'juvenile' labour which all too often was seen as cheap labour. 'Boys and girls up to 18 needed rest, recreation and fresh air', said a prominent speaker at the Technical College prize day in the 1930s, 'but it too often happened that children left school and went into shops and offices, where they worked exceptionally long hours, which made it impossible for them to continue their education'. Even this ignored those who had the physical exhaustion of manual jobs to contend with.

[3] Quoted Express and Star, 15 February 1924

To continue education required commitment. George Chell, when he retired in 1937, after 52 years with the Free Library, Technical School and then Technical College, recalled some of the effort people were prepared to put in.

> *A former student who lived at Wednesfield, worked at Bushbury, attended classes at Wolverhampton three nights a week, a fourth at Walsall, and a fifth at Birmingham, eventually becoming a Whitworth Exhibitioner [i.e. gaining an engineering scholarship], another who when sixty years of age began to study French; a third who at 50 cycled seven or eight miles to Garrick Street and in one winter missed one night only; a workman who entered a course in the free summer classes and graduated foreman, manager and director, a youth who lived at Shrewsbury, 30 miles away and attended school three nights every week.*

Many people had to make significant sacrifices to continue their education. Those who did so were predominately male because the opportunities for women were few. There is a certain irony in the fact that elementary education was co-educational. But once schooling ended the divisions were clear. The local part-time student world was overwhelmingly male and became more so as the nineteenth century progressed. The share of women in the formal labour force fell in the early twentieth century. Women were said to have a special character and capacity that fitted them for home and family rather than education and work.

Early universities were barred to women. It was London University, with its tradition of dissent, that first allowed women to take degrees in 1878. Victoria University in Manchester was the first to theoretically offer degrees to men and women from its inception, although at first no women were admitted. The pressure for equality gradually grew, with the last to give way, Cambridge allowing women to graduate in 1948. Legal rights were denied for a long period and women only gained formal political equality in 1928. Middle class women did not go out to work before or after marriage. Lower middle class and 'respectable' working class women left their jobs on marriage. The 1911 census showed that whereas 66% of single women were employed only 10% of married ones were. Employment for middle class and lower middle class women meant 'respectable women's work' like teaching or office work. The Art School world was a little more welcoming than the Technical College where it was a brave and unusual woman who might think of entering the male dominated world of workshop training. In fact, until 1931, the biggest employment group for working class women would be domestic service.

For a part-time student the financial and time cost of travel to study was an important restriction. Either they had a sympathetic and supportive employer or they had to be able to pay themselves. Until the 1960s travel largely meant walking, cycling or public transport. Willingness to travel was also a function of whether competing courses were available closer to home. Given its position on the edge of the conurbation, Wolverhampton has always been able to draw on recruitment from south Staffordshire, northern Worcestershire and, as Chell suggests from Shropshire.

Students also tended to come from the middle classes, lower middle classes and better off working classes. This was partly a product of the financial barriers though valiant efforts were made to fund scholarships. In the Technical College once the first courses had been passed, advanced classes might be more or less free. The fact that some assistance was available meant that there were opportunities for boys from poorer families to become 'scholarship boys'. This allowed for a small amount of educational mobility and helped to create the myth that a scholarship system did well for the 'talented' sons of workers. But very few could make it this way. Even the middle class and lower middle classes had to scrape resources together in ways that is still common in many poorer countries today.[4] Part-time students on day release from work were in a better position but still had to find resources and time which might delay marriages and affect job choices. For the majority of local young people it is easy to see with hindsight how their hopes and expectations were limited by poverty, hard labour, low wages and the class relations of the Black Country.

Mid Century Students

The years from the 1920s to the early 1960s saw some breaks in earlier patterns of determining who would be a student and what they could study. More students came into the Technical College and its related institutions, the number of full-time students grew but they remained a minority of a minority. For the majority until the 1960s, education ended when the school leaving age was reached, set at 14 in 1918 and raised to 15 in 1944.

Part-time higher education continued to be the dominant form locally – only the most privileged minority went on to university. In the Wolverhampton colleges part-time students continued to live locally though, with increasing car usage, the catchment area widened a little. Full-time students too tended to be from the region

[4] C. Dyhouse, Students: A Gendered History, London, 2006.

though some did come from abroad, even if only for short periods, as with Indian students being trained at the National Foundry College.

The maleness of the majority was beginning to loosen too, although men continued to predominate. Despite the boost to women's employment in the First World War the share of women in the labour force in 1921 was actually lower than 1911 and the share of married women employed fell back to 9%. Thereafter it rose slowly. The Second World War gave it a further push so that by 1961 40% of adult women were going out to work including 34% of all married women. But if opportunities were widening the majority of new women students were expected to conform to traditional female roles.

Despite this, going on to college in whatever form was an important step for a woman even if she went to study 'women's tasks'. For 300-400 women a year in the 1930s this involved studying to become better wives, mothers and companions at the Technical College. The Principal, Fisher said 'he knew of no case of a man attending for cookery, dressmaking or housewifery, though women did invade the bakery classes'. Some too took examinations in 'domestic economy' but in general 'women

Early science students studying in the evenings

Women in dressmaking and cookery classes

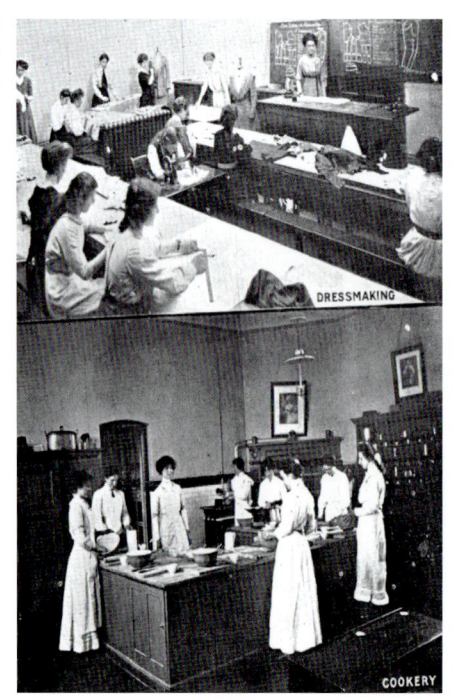

studying homecraft tended to fight shy of set tasks, of homework and examinations'.

Alongside those studying domestic economy, women also dominated in 'secretarial courses' but some were beginning to move into 'professional commerce courses' though status made these predominately male. On the technical side some more women were challenging the rigidities of male-female segregation. 'All classes were open to men and women on equal terms,' said Fisher, 'there was an occasional [female] student of engineering or building, and there was a group of women welders. In the chemical laboratories compatible groups of men and women students worked side by side.'

In 1937 Lady Simon, a leading liberal educational reformer of her day, was invited to be the first woman to distribute prizes to reflect the growing role of women in the college and by this point two women had already been honoured with the annual title of chief student. This did not prevent, however, an on-going problem of a shortage of women's toilets and the difficulty of establishing a separate Common Room for women. In 1948 technical and day release courses were 6% female but another 160 women attended the Technical College 'but few if any … were released from employment to do so'. An exception seemed to be women pharmacists, although the suspicion is that they were allowed to attend because local pharmacies were closed on Thursday afternoons, the time of the classes.

In the Art School the picture was rather different. There in 1948 one third of the students were women and they made up 47 of the 90 on full time courses, but this reflects the higher social status of a full-time art education at this time. Only 14% of the industrial classes were female. Most women studying at the Art College, like those in the Technical College, had only a limited hold in the world of work which they expected to end on their marriage. 'The women's department in the technical college, aims first of all at giving the knowledge of efficient and enjoyable homemaking' it was said in 1948.[5] Even so women were regularly turned away in large numbers because of a lack of places.

Most students were white despite the migration that began to change the Black Country in the 1950s. Contrary to the mythologies of the political right, migrants are often some of the most dynamic people in the societies from which they come. But when they arrive they usually experience suspicion, prejudice and the worst conditions. In the 1950s and 1960s this meant the dirty and dangerous heavy work in local foundries and metal bashing. Later it would mean hard work doing the more menial jobs in the service industry.

Blast furnace crew, British Steel, Bilston © Nick Hedges

[5] *1948 Annual Report, p. 10.*

Publicity photo for the display case at the Hippodrome Theatre

Sheila Holgate-Wright

In the summer of 1944 a fifteen year old girl arrived in Wolverhampton from Liverpool. Sheila had wanted to do science subjects at school but war had intervened. First her school had been evacuated, she stayed at home getting one hour a day tuition from local nuns. Her school returned but most teachers had left for the armed forces or munitions factories. Then the science laboratories were bombed.

In Wolverhampton she started looking for a job, preferably in a laboratory. 'I had to find another way of taking up the things I was interested in'. To equip herself for entering scientific work she enrolled at the Wolverhampton and Staffordshire Technical College to study Physics and Chemistry and improve her Mathematics. At the end of the year she won a scholarship to pay her fees for the next level so considered what to study.

Sheila had found work in the laboratories of the local metals industries and was looking for various classes to help with the job she was doing. It was the Head of the Science Department who gave her the 'best piece of advice anyone could have had', to do a properly constructed metallurgy course leading to a qualification at the end of five years. Sheila was doubtful, only men did metallurgy, could a woman do it? The Head saw no reason why not, so she did, becoming the first woman to graduate from the course. She studied part-time, 'day release' from work plus two evenings a week.

Part-time attendance brought little contact with people on other courses or even reason to leave the basement laboratories. Apart from the tea-break when they would 'nip across Queen's Square to Lyons and have a 1d (penny) bun and a cup of tea'. She had some contact with women pharmacy students and one or two women science students. Most of the time Sheila's fellow students were men, some her own age, half of them older ex-service men. They 'teased me unmercifully, the lads' she 'had to fight for survival', at times thinking of giving up but always deciding she was 'going to battle on however hard it was'. She published in her professions' journals and won an essay prize of the Birmingham Metallurgical Society – "this being the first time a lady had taken one of the Society's prizes the President gave a few words of congratulation and trusted other ladies would emulate the example."

Study and employment went side by side. Local 'industry was still virtually producing as it did in the war'. There were opportunities for trained scientists. Many firms had small research laboratories. She moved from her first job as a young laboratory assistant, becoming a research assistant and then heading a research department. Women were unusual in the industry, the reaction of a Canadian visiting her works "that's the first metallurgist I've ever seen wearing lipstick" became the opening line in Sheila's published survey of women in the industry.

Along with study and a job was fun. Students were encouraged to participate in a College activity that contrasted to their main area of study. Sheila 'joined Dr Percy Young's choir'. In 1946 she joined the Wolverhampton Musical Comedy Company performing at the Hippodrome and the Grand Theatre. Theatre and singing became life-long pleasures. She joined the local photography club in 1948, film was still hard to obtain after the war but her laboratory dark room could be used after work.

With young children and a move southwards, her laboratory work came to an end. As the children got older Sheila became a mature student at a College of Education, embarking on a second career as a teacher. Health considerations made a projected MSc at 80 unwise. Now in her 80s Sheila regularly attends lectures with an interest in emerging technologies –

"I have a pretty well developed sense of curiosity which I'm glad about because life would be pretty dull if you didn't want to know more about what was going on."

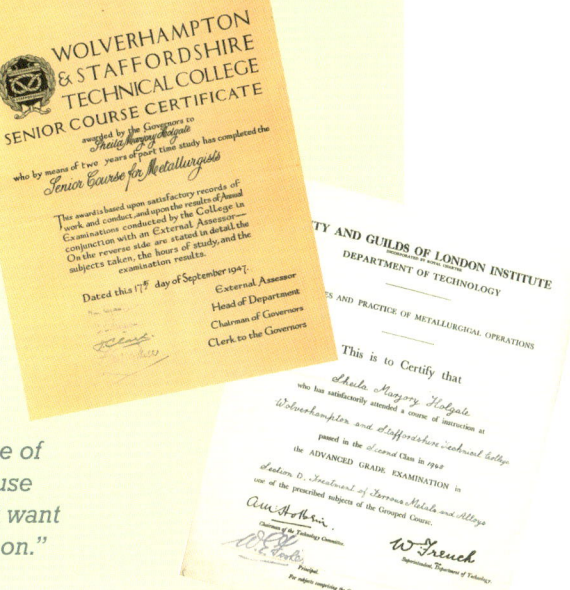

In 1949

Such first generation migrants had fewer opportunities than the native born population. If the doors of the universities were closed to them then so too were places in the various colleges. Stuck in the less skilled jobs, victims of formal and informal colour bars, they found little support from local employers for part-time education. Their efforts and hopes tended to be focused on their families and the possibilities for their children and grandchildren. Realising them would not be simply about opening doors but also confronting the ways in which ideas of difference, superiority and inferiority are perpetuated, often without thinking, on a daily basis.

This applied too with the question of class and education. After 1914 the myth that social divisions were explained by 'intelligence' if anything strengthened. The mass needed a better basic education but little more. All that was necessary was a safety valve to cream off the talented few that chance had allowed to be born amongst this mass. In 1944, this was systemised by the Education Act which divided school children on the basis of the 11 plus into the successful grammar school minority of some 20% and the unsuccessful secondary modern majority who were expected to go on to mass labour. In 1950 Cyril Burt, a psychologist who had inspired the educational segregation that flowed from these ideas told a mass radio audience that:

Metal shearer at Josiah Parkes © Nick Hedges

" *in an ideal community, our aim should be to discover what ration of intelligence nature had given to each individual child at birth, then to provide him (sic) with the appropriate education and finally to guide him to the career for which he seems to have been marked out.*[6] "

Burt would later be shown to have falsified data to support these views but they depended as much on social prejudice as evidence.

At this point students in any form of higher education were still a small minority. The majority in their secondary moderns 'learned to labour'. The phrase has become famous the world over as a title of a pioneering sociological investigation of Black Country schools by Paul Willis which showed how children in the 1970s were still learning intuitively to accept what they could and could not do. (Willis would be, for a time, a professor at Wolverhampton). There was also a process of learning about what type of higher education was possible between and within institutions.

We are fortunate to have a detailed published analysis of the social composition of students at Wolverhampton College of Technology on the eve of the Polytechnic era that reveals some of this.[7] By this point still only 13% of the students in the Technical College were female and 87% male. The data shows how students were funnelled to different courses by a class based school system so that college too was also marked by social divisions in the type of courses that the students were doing. Indeed the data understates this because we are not able to show the proportions in relation to the size of the occupational groups but the pattern is still clear in table 3.1.

---

[6] Quoted C.Chitty, 'Differing views of human intelligence', Forum, 2011, vol. 53 no 2, p. 235-246.
[7] G.Evans, 'Social and educational backgrounds of students at a College of Technology', The Vocational Aspect of Education, vol. 21, no 50. pp. 135-141; see also F.Johne & M.Shamma, 'A survey of Wolverhampton Technical Teachers' College students 1966-67', The Vocational Aspect of Education, vol. 20 no., 45, pp,. 48-64.

	Males			Females		
	Upper White Collar	Lower White Collar	Manual	Upper White Collar	Lower White Collar	Manual
All	35.8%	14.2%	50.0%	71.9%	15.6%	12.5%
Full-time	53.3%	10.0%	36.7%	78.9%	15.8%	5.3%
Sandwich	32.6%	13.9%	53.5%	85.7%	-	14.3%
Block release	40.0%	4.0%	56.0%	-	-	-
Part-time day and evening	26.1%	19.6%	54.3%	-	-	-
Part-time evening	32.6%	23.3%	44.1%	20.0%	40.0%	40.0%

Table 3.1 Gender and Socio-Economic Status of Wolverhampton Technical College Students in 1966

The Poly Generation (1970-1992)

Students, in the two decades of the polytechnic, reflected new aspirations towards higher education. Numbers grew rapidly, 12,484 students were enrolled in 1990-91, an annual intake by this point of around 3,000. A growing number were full-time – the full-time part-time ratio was approximately 2:1. Students came to study a widening array of subjects in the changing faculties and schools. Most wanted to study at degree level, 72% were studying for first degrees and 12% for postgraduate ones. The remaining 15% were studying for HNCs and Diplomas in Higher Education, many of these would go on to transfer to a final degree year.

In a financial sense the first decade of this period was something of a golden age for students. In 1960 the Anderson Committee had proposed that student grants be available to all and under the 1962 Education Act local education authorities were required to pay tuition fees and a means tested grant to all students. Most full-time students had more or less adequate support and vacation work in a labour market with a strong demand for workers. For those without vacation work there was some access to social security benefits. Some even suggested that students were young adults who should be paid a wage rather than a grant in the same way that other trainees were.[8]

The grant system allowed students to experience study away from home so that the numbers of local students initially fell. This added to the sense of post school transition as well as creating more demand for student accommodation and college hostels. From the late 1970s, however, student finances took a turn for the worse. Although tuition fees continued to be paid, the value of student grants was allowed to fall to such an extent that by 1990-1991 students had to be given access to top-up loans through a state backed Student Loans Company. These financial constraints encouraged the beginnings of a return to local study but even so by 1990 at the Polytechnic Wolverhampton, a slight majority 51% were from outside the region.

Home based students had been joined in the late polytechnic years by an increasing number of international students. In the 1980s and early 1990s students came from the European Union, often supported by various short term mobility schemes like

[8] H. & P. Silver, *Students: Changing Roles, Changing Lives*, Buckingham, 1997.pp. 34-35.

the Erasmus programme. Élites in some poorer countries were also sending their children abroad to finish their education, to gain skills, qualifications, status and wider experience through undergraduate or postgraduate study.

In one of the final annual reports of this time it was said that:

> *The polytechnic has since the early 1970s progressively increased its investment and commitment to making higher education accessible to more and more people. We are happy that there is no such thing as a typical student at Wolverhampton Polytechnic.*[9]

The University's Higher Education Shop on the corner of Lichfield Street

We lack some of the fine detail needed to trace the changes because it was not until the 1990s that better statistics were collected. But the thrust of the claim is true and the bigger picture is clear. The idea that education was about fitting particular people for particular jobs and social positions was coming under attack. 'Intellectual talent is not a fixed quantity with which we have to work,' said a major report in 1963, it is a 'variable that can be modified by social policy and educational approaches.' This idea led to comprehensive schooling. Polytechnics like Wolverhampton were better placed to recruit a broader range of students than the universities, many of which remained committed to a narrow social recruitment pattern for too long.[10]

The first to benefit were women who poured into the polytechnic to such an extent that by 1990 they made up 53% of the students. They could be found on an increasing variety of courses building on the steps made by earlier women like Sheila Holgate-Wright. The same applied to ethnic minority students. At the end of the polytechnic era Black and Asian students had come to make up 14% of the student body. In both cases much remained to be done but the polytechnic generations pushed the door open wider. Parents and grandparents could look on to see their children doing things that in most instances they had found impossible for themselves.

There were also the beginnings of a break in the patterns of access across social class. This came partly as a result of the attempt to attract mature students. 'Lack of 'O' levels does not mean lack of brainpower, talent and imagination', they were told. The creation of the DipHE in 1975 was another form of door opening. For people without a family history of higher education, information is vital to access. The opening of the Higher Education Shop, a shop front drop-in information service in the town enabled people to find out about higher education anywhere in the country, including their local polytechnic.[11]

Moves such as these helped to reduce the barriers to those who had 'failed' at school. Individuals could recognise that there might be possibilities they had not dreamed of. But this recruitment pattern also changed because, across a

---

[9] *The Newsom Report, Half Our Future, A report of the Central Advisory Council for Education (England),* London, 1963, p.6.
[10] R.Anderson, *Universities and Elites in Britain since 1800,* Houndsmills, 1992
[11] Opened in 1988 by Ron Dearing.

A Family Affair

As the polytechnic era came to an end, at Wolverhampton one family seemed to capture the spirit of its students and their changing social backgrounds. In the summer of 1992 Michael Kelly had graduated with a BEd degree and was looking forward to a new career as a teacher that October. A decade before he had been one of Britain's 230,000 miners.

Mining had been at the centre of the UK economy for generations. Output had reached 264 million tons in 1910 with over a million miners. But the industry was contracting. Even so it was still a major employer and if pits were long gone in the Black Country itself they could still be found in the surrounding areas. Then in March 1984 the government proposed a massive programme of pit closures. Michael joined the most bitter and, longest industrial dispute of the last half century before the miners were defeated and the industry all but closed. After 2000 fewer than 10,000 miners were left. The strike lasted almost a year. During it the family had survived on his small strike pay and the earnings of his wife, Joyce. But the experience helped change his views. Like most miners Michael lacked formal educational qualifications – he had been employed as much for his muscles as his brains. But this didn't mean he lacked ability.

At the age of 35, he decided to test this out and to do something different. He started an Access course for mature students at nearby Sandwell College. From there he went to the Polytechnic's Walsall campus to begin the training that would lead to a degree and a qualification to teach.

A year later Joyce, his wife, took redundancy from her job and started on the same course. For Joyce 'It hasn't been easy, certainly not financially …I thought I'd feel awkward with a lot of younger students but its been marvellous. And in teaching it helps to have experience on the world and with your family.

Higher education could put strain on personal relationships but Joyce said that 'there's been no competition; we have wanted each other to do well'. And as they graduated, one in the last year of the Polytechnic and the other in the first year of the University, so their oldest daughter Amanda, aged 18, also began a degree course at Wolverhampton.

If this family story was the marketing department's delight it still captured an important part of the transformation that could occur as mature students found a way back into education, challenging earlier ideas about who had talent, ability and intelligence. No less it also shows how this opening up also began to widen horizons for the next generations to come.

wider range of social groups, people were beginning to move towards the possibility of higher education. The data suggests that higher education entrants were still very restricted.

Nationally the middle classes took the greatest advantage of the openings but the balance between the different social groups was changing. The pattern of middle class dominance varied by institution – polytechnics were more open to other groups than universities and some polytechnics like Wolverhampton more open than others – hence its claim to be 'the people's polytechnic' and even before 1992 the unofficial 'university of the Black Country.' At the end of the 1980s even the Conservative government was beginning to talk of a 30% higher education participation rate. This would still leave a 70% non-participation rate but polytechnics like Wolverhampton had already moved significantly in this direction. When Mick Harrison, as the last Director of the polytechnic and first Vice-Chancellor of the University of Wolverhampton looked forward to it becoming 'the foremost mass higher education institution in the next decade and beyond' this would not entirely be windy rhetoric. It might not be the foremost but it would be one of the foremost.

Wolverhampton Students in the New Century

At the start of the twenty-first century Wolverhampton students were even more diverse than at the end of the polytechnic era. The numbers of international students had grown with shifts in nationality, often depending on the situation in the countries from which students came. Alongside this was a broadening social base of home recruitment, although one still marked by the social divisions in society at large. Increases in tuition fees had a disputed impact but one impact was clear, it encouraged more students to study locally again. The student halls and bedsits of Wolverhampton still bustle but by 2010 the share of local full-time students living at home within commuting distance had increased. The growing local diversity of the region meant that local recruitment did not reduce ethnic and nationality diversity – it helped to increase it. Although mature students continued to come, the increasing fees did put those in the oldest age groups at a disadvantage as they had less hope of starting a second career.

The biggest shift was the deepening and broadening of the higher education participation of school leavers. This could not have taken place had schools not changed. More students now get the minimum two A-levels required for university entrance while others succeed by taking A-level equivalent courses. Access was also helped by colleges offering foundation degrees from which people could then transfer to complete their study.

The numbers of women in universities like Wolverhampton has continued to grow. Now they significantly outnumber men across the whole system. The discussion today is more about the under-performance of boys in schools where only 49% get the minimum requirement for higher education compared to 60% of girls. Ethnic recruitment has also continued to diversify. In 2010 the groups with the lowest participation rates were the White and African-Caribbean populations at around 50%. Other ethnic groups had much higher rates so that, although the 2001 census showed them to be around 9% of the population of England, they came to make up over 16% in the numbers in higher education and a third of those in the University of Wolverhampton.

The biggest gaps remain rooted in social inequality 'Wolverhampton is lighting a path of opportunities for students from working class and low-income backgrounds, and that example should be followed right across the university sector', said a government minister in 2004.[12] The statistics measure this in different ways. Some use conventional measures of socio-economic class. Using these, some 50% of Wolverhampton students come from the bottom four classes compared to 30% nationally. Another measure is what is called 'neighbourhood deprivation'. Nationally more than 60% of school children get the minimum qualifications to continue in the 25% least deprived neighbourhoods compared to only 35% in the most deprived. Wolverhampton takes 20% of its students from the most deprived neighbourhoods compared to 10% nationally. A third indicator is free school meals. Whereas Oxford and Cambridge together have only a few dozen students who had free meals at school, Wolverhampton (not the highest) had nearer 300 by the end of the 2000s. The opening up of opportunities can also be seen in other areas such as encouraging students with disabilities to come into higher education.

The ambiguities of educational advance in England mean that this is not a simple good news story. Changes in schools and universities remain controversial and, given the centralism that now exists, in higher education they continue to be at the forefront of sharp political debate – wars even.[13] Big socio-economic gaps remain to be bridged in terms of access. Worse still, these gaps are being reproduced in terms of where people go to study and the sense of fine differentiation of the élite. *'By what right does Oxford and Cambridge lay claim to the 'best' students? Who is to say that Wolverhampton or Kingston, ex-polytechnics with a stronger vocational bent, should not have them?'* asked the editor of the New Statesman in 2004.[14] And with such differences come differences in funding. To correct the imbalances the government in the 2000s did give some corrective funding to institutions like Wolverhampton but the contrast remained huge. In 2004 a local MP raised it in Parliament asking if the government was:

> *...aware that the University of Cambridge gets four times as much money per student as the University of Wolverhampton, ... conversely the University of Cambridge is one of the least accessible to working class students ... while the University of Wolverhampton is the most accessible mainstream university in the country. ... [W]hereas the University of Wolverhampton allows students to work, the University of Cambridge tells prospective students that they will be "sent down", to use its archaic language, if they get a job. That is hardly doing much to encourage accessibility for working class students.[15]*

---

[12] Hansard, 20 May 2004
[13] Melissa Benn, School Wars: The Battle for Britain's Education, London, 2012.
[14] 'A levels are just rationing devices', New Statesmen, 23 August 2004.
[15] Rob Marris, Hansard (House of Commons Debates), 20 May 2004 : Column 1107.

Student Academic Experiences

Students coming into higher education have always done so with a mixture of expectation and trepidation. The scale is enormous; the buildings are large, their design can be deliberately intimidating. When the original main College building was planned in the 1930s the aim was clearly to use the architecture to convey a degree of status, authority, even awe, with the attention drawn to the ascending staircase and the sky through a stained glass window. The large iconic buildings built since then are designed as statements rather than as inviting, comforting environments. The opportunities created by higher education have to therefore be taken in an environment that might seem quite alien. Newcomers come with a nervous mixture of hope tinged with anxiety, suspicion, fear and even, for some, dread. This is compounded by the fact that most continue to come from families where the earlier elitism of higher education denied similar chances to their parents and grandparents.

Students come to learn but also

Examining Inequality, Education and Policy

The economist Steve Machin continues to play an important role in UK debates on education. He is a professor at University College, research director of the Centre for Economic Performance at the LSE, a past visiting professor at Harvard and the Massachusetts Institute of Technology. Machin's work ranges from the most abstruse exercises in econometrics to careful dissections of educational policy, schooling and achievement in modern Britain. He tracks how inequality and social mobility function and how they are affected by educational change. He looks especially at issues like education, gender, ethnicity and the impact of wealth and poverty. Nor has he been afraid to take on the government of the day when he feels his research has been misused.

Machin argues that his data shows how 'Educational inequalities emerge even before children start school... Educational disadvantages acquired during schooling (and pre-school) strongly impact on whether an individual participates in post-compulsory education... Furthermore, educational inequalities do not stop growing when people have completed their full-time education... we should not regard large socio-economic gaps as inevitable. This partly has to do with the choices that are made in educational policy'.

But why should he be interested in this? Perhaps part of the answer lies in his own background. Machin comes from the Black Country. Born in 1962, between 1982-1985 he studied at Wolverhampton Polytechnic where he got a first class degree in economics. From there he went on to do a PhD at Warwick and eventually to become an editor of the Economic Journal, a position once occupied by Marshall and Keynes, the two greatest economists born in Britain.

Thanks to the changes in higher education and the creation of the polytechnics like Wolverhampton, Machin did get, in H.G Well's terms, 'the chance of proving [his] quality'. But his research is also inspired by the desire to look for evidence about how we can do still more in the future. In 2010 he was awarded an Honorary PhD in Social Science by the University of Wolverhampton watched by his parents and family who still live locally.

But for students what matters is not only how they get to university but how they get on once there.

to be challenged. What that might mean is suggested in a story told several times by a past Wolverhampton Vice-Chancellor who overheard a rowdy group of students talking. One, a young women, was telling the others 'I have just been to the most fantastic lecture – it was on the Enlightenment. It was mind blowing.'[16] The idea that students at Wolverhampton could and should study and be excited by philosophy would be no surprise to the early college educators. The idea that they could do so to degree level, would have been astonishing.

Not all teaching has this effect. Studying in a university involves sweat and effort too and this does not come easily. It requires a degree of self discipline, skills that must be learned. Whether this can be done is not entirely in the hands of students themselves. Looking back at the era either side of the polytechnic years we see something interesting. Until the 1960s, apart from in teacher training, people came into the colleges as full-time workers and part-time students. Now in an era of high fees and loans they come as full-time students and part-time workers. A study of one Wolverhampton first year cohort in the 2000s found, for example, that 70% were doing paid work and less than 30% had spent more than 15 hours a week on a campus. A significant number anticipated that their biggest challenge would be to find time for their study.[17]

One way of dealing with this has been through technology. Wolverhampton, like all universities, has made huge investments in computers and social leaning spaces. These enable students to have 24 hour access to global learning, albeit subject to hidden institutional tensions about copyright, intellectual property rights, payment of access fees for databases and journals etc. They also enable students to be offered an element of distance leaning – even whole degrees were proposed this way. But ambition here also runs ahead of achievement. One problem is the overestimation of student IT skills. Being adept at computer games and applications did not mean being able to access, evaluate and use good quality information on the internet. In any case there is a limit to the extent to which 'techno fix' can overcome the lack of social and cultural capital that hinder many students in mass higher education.

Just as no school can overcome the deficiencies of society at large so can no university. But they can compound or lessen them. The academic experience in a university has to have, therefore, a degree of self awareness which is not easy to achieve. Students must learn the formal curriculum and a mass of documentation survives to show how this has changed over the past century. But they must also engage with a hidden curriculum of assumptions and class room practices that it is harder to recover. Very often it is this hidden element that makes the difference – encouraging the student to move in a new direction as happened to students like Sheila Holgate-Wright or the Kellys or, conversely, discouraging them.

There is also an informal curriculum outside of the classroom. One aspect of this, emphasised from the early days of the College, is that students are and should be treated as adults. Insisting that students be aware that college and university is more than a school is not always easy to achieve in practice, not least when there are performance pressures. Even the technologies of today play an ambiguous role here – allowing students access at all times but also allowing that access to be tracked.

One nationally funded study, for example, run from Wolverhampton, found that students appreciated being reminded by text that their library books were due or being told that classes were cancelled due to unforeseen circumstances. They were less enthusiastic about 'educational

---

[16] C.Gipps, *Who Goes to University? And why it matters*, Wolverhampton, June 2011
[17] M.Leese, 'Bridging the gap: supporting student transition into higher education', *Journal of Further and Higher Education*, vol. 34 no.2, 2010, pp. 239-251.

uses' of messaging. 'Students use their mobiles for their social life and contacting family and perceive their education to be separate… Some students felt that the texts were a breach of privacy, particularly if they arrived at inopportune moments, when they would just delete them. Many students also begrudged the cost of replying to a text.'[18] Staff misunderstanding students is just as common as students misunderstanding staff.

Is it worth it? The sceptics continue to say that too many go into higher education. Institutions, and their graduates, have always faced condescension as they have been brought into the university system. Subjects too face the same reaction. 'He gets degrees in making jam/ At Liverpool and Birmingham' was once a 'jingle' sung by those at the 'ancient' universities. Such views need to be challenged with evidence – the evidence of real achievement. Let us take an example. Nursing education in new universities, for example, still has to fight to establish its credibility as a university subject. 'Much of Florence Nightingale's life was spent trying to break free of the social and intellectual suppression of women. She did not want her nurses to be servants or medical handmaidens, she wanted them to be educated and think for themselves.'[19]

Today nurses have a better chance of doing this in part because of their higher status and university based training. The single biggest problem in any hospital, for example, is infection control and the need for something as basic as hand washing. Once, hospitals killed as many patients as they cured, perhaps more, because doctors and nurses did not understand its importance. Today they still battle to ensure that the highest standards are maintained. A part of being an effective nurse is in understanding why this is so important and how hand washing is not just a simple task of hygiene but a social behaviour within part of a larger organisational system controlled by organisational power. Sometimes the simplest things turn out to be the most complex and a failure to confront this has resulted in literally millions of unnecessary hospital deaths in the last two centuries. Confronting the problem requires an understanding of all its dimensions, it needs knowledge and the confidence to challenge bad practice that comes with not training but effective education, a sense that was captured by a Wolverhampton student nurse, 'during my placement on the neonatal unit I found that infection control was extremely good. The nurses on the unit are extremely strict and ensure that when anyone comes into the unit, they must wash their hands and remove their coats. I also observed nurses doing an audit on how often the doctors washed their hands.'[20] In this way not just nursing students like these but students more widely are learning to research and understand recalcitrant problems in both nature and human organisation – an education which at its best allows them to confront authority with genuine knowledge.

There is no more powerful day on which to see the meaning of achievement than when studies are over. Essays have been done, exams passed, degrees announced and the students come to collect their parchments on graduation day.

Graduating

Graduation itself is a rite of passage, a public passing out. It involves a formal ceremony in which individual achievements can be recognised and the institution can show itself off – at least to the local world if not nationally. There is therefore an element of planned theatricality in its ceremonies. The problem in an earlier period was that the big awards tended to be nationally awarded. Those awarded a London University external degree through study at Wolverhampton, for example,

---

[18] http://www.guardian.co.uk/digital student/texting. M.North, 'Push the button Texting sends out mixed messages'.
[19] M.Williams, 'Nurse education has had a bad press', British Journal of Theatre Nursing, vol. 9 no. 6, 1999; M.Williams,. 'Reflections on a perioperative career, 1970-2008', The Journal of Perioperative Practice, vol. 19 no.3 , 2009.
[20] D David Holyoake, 'The awkward feeling campaign: confronting poor hygiene to improve hand washing', Nursing Times, vol. 106, no. 35, 2010.

Wolverhampton & Staffordshire Technical College

21st ANNUAL PRESENTATION OF PRIZES AND CERTIFICATES
Session 1952-53

Organ Recital   7.15—7.45 p.m.
Academic Procession   7.45 p.m.

Order of Procession

Full-time Lecturers
Heads of Departments
Officers of the Students' and Teachers' Union
Principal
Clerk to the Governors
Wolverhampton and Staffordshire Technical College Governors
National Foundry College Governors and others interested in the National College
F. Bray, Esq., C.B., and H.M. Inspectors
P. H. Wilson, Esq., O.B.E., and Sir Gilbert Flemming, K.C.B.
The Mayoress, The Chairman of the Governors, The Mayor

WOLVERHAMPTON COLLEGE OF ART, LICHFIELD STREET

DIPLOMA DAY

The Chairman requests the pleasure of the company of

....

at the Diploma Day, of the College of Art, Wolverhampton
7 p.m., Monday, 2nd October, 1950

Mrs. BEATRICE L. WARDE

of the Monotype Corporation will give the Address, distribute the Prizes, and open the Exhibition of Students' Work

The Workforce – Students

The First Degree Ceremony held at Wolverhampton

WOLVERHAMPTON COLLEGE OF TECHNOLOGY

PROCEEDINGS AT A DEGREE CERE[MONY]

30th JUNE, 1967

PROCEEDINGS AT A DEGREE CEREMONY
30th June, 1967

The procession will enter the Hall at 2.40 p.m.
(*The audience is asked to stand during the procession.*)

THE CHAIRMAN OF THE GOVERNORS, Councillor W. L. Hughes, J.P., will declare the ceremony open.

HIS WORSHIP THE MAYOR OF WOLVERHAMPTON, Councillor E. Y. Fullwood, J.P., will welcome Lord Kings Norton.

THE PRINCIPAL OF THE COLLEGE, Mr. Robert Scott, will give an address.

THE HEAD OF DEPARTMENT OF MECHANICAL ENGINEERING, Mr. C. J. M. Lee, will present to Lord Kings Norton, Chairman of the Council for National Academic Awards, graduates who obtained degrees of the Council in the years 1965 and 1966.

1965
Bachelor of Science in Mechanical Engineering

First Class Honours
  Roy Dungar
  Richard Andrew Grant
  William Arthur Rowley
  Michael Edward Patrick Wykes

, Division I
  Malcolm Ronald Hill
  Keith Thomas Symonds

Division II
  Kenneth Allan Causer
  Keith Benjamin Holyoake

  Amiva Kumar Sarkar

1966
Bachelor of Science in Mechanical Engineering

First Class Honours
  Raymond Leslie Hough   George Rodgers

Second Class Honours, Division I
  Robert Clive Brown   Anthony Douglas Roche
  Keith Daniel Guest   Derek William Stanton
  John Roger Purshouse

Second Class Honours, Division II
  Peter Chantrill   Malcolm David Pattinson
  Graham Leslie Irving

Third Class Honours
  Sujit Kumar Bhattacharya   John Seal
  Jonathan Edward Pope   David John Woodman

LORD KINGS NORTON will give an address.

THE VICE-PRINCIPAL, Mr. J. H. Williams, will thank the Mayor and Lord Kings Norton.

THE CHAIRMAN OF THE GOVERNORS will declare the ceremony closed.

The procession, including the Graduates, will leave the Hall.
(*The audience is asked to stand.*)

Music will be played by the WOLVERHAMPTON SINFONIA ORCHESTRA
(Conductor: Mr. James Eastham. Leader: Mr. John Hilton.)

Guests are invited to have refreshments in the Refectory
(Ground Floor) after the ceremony.

Graduation Ceremonies take place in Spring and early September, at the Grand Theatre, Wolverhampton.

could graduate at a major ceremony in London presided over by the London University Chancellor – usually a high member of royalty. Colleges were therefore anxious to develop their own ceremonies which also had status. Prizes could be distributed and local qualifications recognised with an invited speaker, a stage party made up of staff, local dignitaries and employers – before the graduates and their families. These prize days acted as de facto graduation ceremonies and were usually held in the main halls of the colleges which themselves had been designed with such events in mind. As the different colleges came together in Wolverhampton, the focus switched to the main hall of the 'Marble' building. But this was soon too small and the Civic Hall began to be used with multiple ceremonies performed, eventually twice a year. Then the ceremonies were moved to the Grand Theatre with its capacity for 1,200 people. Each ceremony now begins with an academic procession from the University to the town, a short but symbolic distance through the streets of Wolverhampton.

Graduation Day Rituals

The idea of academic dress goes back to the Middle Ages when students were in clerical orders. Gowns were worn by staff and students in older universities to indicate membership. They might be worn by some staff in schools, technical and teacher training colleges on a daily basis during the 1960s to indicate academic status. Academic regalia is now only seen as part of a public ritual. Today each university has its own colours and version of the cap, hood and gown which also vary by the level of degree. In Britain there is a modern classification system for academic dress and even a Burgon Society – devoted to its study and the real and imagined traditions that it involves. In the polytechnic years degrees were validated and awarded by the Council for National Academic Awards. The first CNAA based award ceremony was held in 1967 with the chairman of the CNAA present. In this devolved ceremony the academic dress was determined by the CNAA. With University status, Wolverhampton was able to award its own degrees up to PhD level as well as honorary degrees to mark local and national achievements.

There are two major national academic gown suppliers – Wippell and Ede and Ravenscroft. The University of Wolverhampton works with Wippell. In 1992 and 1993, with thirty new universities, staff from the garment suppliers worked 'manically' to create new academic wardrobes. They use a special language of dress. There are gowns for undergraduates ('Oxford Bachelor' style) and mortar board hats. Master's and PhD awards have different gowns with different decorations. There are specific 'bonnets' for senior awards and specific types of 'Aberdeen hoods'. There are materials of damask and taffeta, velvet and imitation silk. There is Russell cord, gold cord and tassels. And there are the colours – in the case of Wolverhampton, those of red and gold. For the modern autumn graduations at Wolverhampton, Wippell bring 2,500 hoods to adorn those who wish to walk across the stage 'properly dressed' to the applause of their friends and family.

But, as anthropologists tell us, the informal practices and dress codes of graduation day are also rich in symbolism. There is public ritual here too with pride to be displayed and friends to be impressed. There are new clothes and suits, whether to wear a tie or not, new shoes, hair styles, make up and jewellery. There are cars to arrive in, family to bring. There is the walk across the stage, the applause, the occasional trip, cheers and whoops from friends and family. There are professional photographs to be taken and a mass of unofficial ones, individual and group – sometimes with lecturers. There are graduation booklets to be clutched and memorabilia to be bought. There is a remembering of good and bad times, a leaving and a saying goodbye but also a looking forward to a new and perhaps still uncertain next stage.

Chapter four

The Workforce – Staff

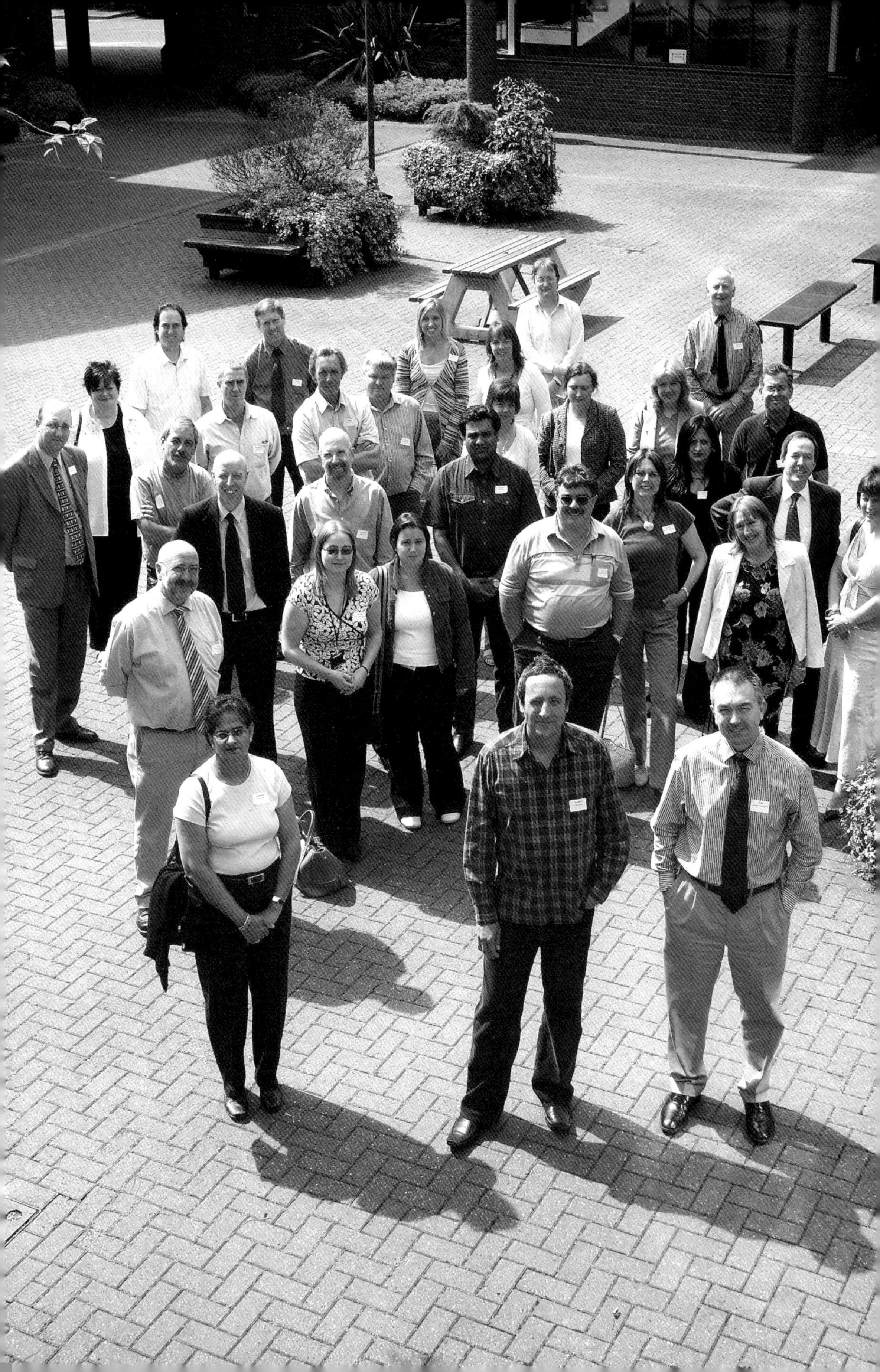

A History of the University of Wolverhampton

People who staff universities in the United Kingdom work in a substantial sector. In 2009-2010 higher education institutions employed over half a million people. They are labour intensive organisations, which spent £14.6 billion on staff costs, 56.8% of their total expenditure of £25.9 billion. The University of Wolverhampton today employs nearly 3,000 people in one form or another. Alongside those with permanent contracts are visiting lecturers and casual staff. Permanent staff are nearer to 2,500 people and rather less on a full-time equivalent basis. The precise figure varies from year to year in relation to the overall health of the institution. Alongside the teachers and researchers, are librarians, technicians, people working in finance, IT, human resources, marketing, print services, catering and accommodation services.

There are administrative staff operating the procedures of a huge, busy organisation which must work safely and within the law. Buildings are maintained and cleaned, new equipment is installed, old equipment is serviced and fixed. Caretakers and security staff work from early to late, often unnoticed until things go wrong. Like any organisation a university is a world in miniature in which people often pass by without recognising the extent to which they depend on one another.

Transport and Security staff

This chapter tries to unravel part of this story. It is not easy. Organisations, and not least universities, are built around a degree of status and hierarchy. Bertold Brecht once wrote a poem called 'Questions from A Worker Who Reads' in which he asked,

> *Who built Thebes of the seven gates?*
> *In the books you will find the name of kings.*
> *Did the kings haul up the lumps of rock?*

Such questions helped to inspire a generation of historians who wished to tell a more rounded story – history written not from the top of the hierarchy but from below. This can be hard, the records we are left tend to be top down. We know about the past Principals, the Directors, the Vice-Chancellors and their executives, we know about many of the academics. We know the architects of the University buildings, the firms that 'did the work'. But as to those who hauled the 'lumps of rock' – even the marble of the University's centre piece building we know little or nothing. We know little too of those who worked in offices or across the estate keeping the University functioning in other ways.

It can be assumed that organisations are run from the top down, that what matters is what is decided at the highest levels. Professors leave a record in the books and papers that they write. Teachers hope to be remembered by their students. Sometimes long-serving individuals at the top of the organisation are able to seize key moments to shape the future as Chell, Fisher and Scott did, but

The Portraits in the Board Room

The story of those at the top of any organisation can often be found in the portraits in the boardroom. In Wolverhampton some of the past Chairmen of the governors (they have been men) stare down alongside the past Directors and Vice-Chancellors (one woman).

There are stories in titles – the official ones and the unofficial ones. The 'in between' status of different colleges and schools that fed into the University was reflected in the titles of those at the top. The Art School for a time had Headmasters; the Free Library had Secretaries and Chief Librarians; the Colleges had Principals, the Polytechnic had Directors and the University has Vice-Chancellors.

In the early decades the various heads often had long periods at the top. Fisher was followed, after a gap of a few years, by Robert Scott who saw the College turn into a Polytechnic over two decades. Today tenure has become rather shorter. Since 1969 there have been six 'Vice-Chancellors' also with professorial titles, although the first two never had these names or titles.

Robert Scott 1957-1978
George Seabrooke 1978-1985
Michael Harrison 1985-1998 
John Brooks 1998-2005 
Caroline Gipps 2005-2011 
Geoff Layer 2011-

For most of these, heading the institution was the culmination of their careers but with younger appointments the possibility of moving on also exists. The sense of what the job at the top should be has changed away from that of a senior academic to that of a manager – encouraged in this direction by both legislative changes and fashions for leadership speak. But has what the job actually involves changed as much?

The scale is very different. The only time today that most students will recognise a Vice-Chancellor is at their graduation ceremony. There is a senior supporting management team whose own titles and status have changed too. But beneath the grandeur of office there is perhaps a greater level of continuity in what it means to be a student or a member of staff or a Vice-Chancellor of a mass higher education institution than we might think.

they can only do so because of the capacity of the people they lead. Mostly people at the top come and go, down below things are more stable than is often appreciated and that stability, invested in individuals who can stay sometimes for decades, is often vital to an organisation's survival and development.

This is illustrated in the story of Keith White. He came to the Wolverhampton and Staffordshire Technical College as an apprentice in 1958 and spent his whole working life helping the institution to change to a College of Technology, Polytechnic and then University. Retaining a strong local accent and known for his blunt speaking, he retired a few months short of fifty years' work in January 2008 – acerbically rejecting the idea that he might stay a little longer to make it a complete fifty. First as a technician, then in maintenance, and finally as 'clerk to the works', for half a century little of the university expansion or its day-to-day activity could have gone on without him and the people around him. But although the University marked his retirement with the presentation of an antique watch he characteristically asked for no leaving collection saying that he wanted to leave 'quietly, without any fuss or ceremony' and no picture publicised the presentation. 'Without fuss or ceremony'. The phrase illustrates the problem of trying to capture the wider story of those who work in an organisation.

Numbers, Structures and Processes

The process by which the University was formed out of mergers was complex. It would be hard in the best of circumstances to tell the story of all the staff employed by its constituent parts over the last century and a half. But it has been made harder because many of the records disappeared as colleges were merged into a greater whole. The narrowest lineage that runs from the Wolverhampton and Staffordshire Technical College to the University today offers the best opportunity.

The most obvious part of this story is the huge rise in staff numbers from a mere handful in the early days to nearly three thousand today. A part of this growth is the development of organisational functions beyond teaching. In 1921 the Technical College guide listed 70 members of the administrative and teaching staff in addition to the Principal, Fisher. Forty-one of these supported engineering and technology, 29 of them were in commerce, languages (including Russian) and domestic economy. Only two, Fisher and the head of the department of metallurgy and chemistry had a PhD and a slight majority (38) listed no qualification at all. The remainder had first degrees, professional or workshop based qualifications. Seven were women, all in languages and domestic economy and only the Italian teacher (Mrs Taylor) was married. But the most important thing about teachers at this point was the predominance of part-time lecturers in those listed.

By 1950 the managerial and teaching staff had risen to the Principal, 7 Heads of Department, 25 Senior Lecturers, 25 full-time Assistant Lecturers and 180 part-time teachers. The General Office, headed by the Secretary of the college was now staffed by 10 clerical workers, 3 of whom worked in two roles as office and library assistants. There were now 12 technicians maintaining the laboratories. General maintenance was covered by a Head Caretaker with six assistants and 10 part-time cleaners.

As the Art College merged with the College of Technology to form the Polytechnic in 1969-70 titles changed and new categories of jobs were named. Now the Director was joined by 2 Associate Directors, 5 Deans and 12 Heads of Department with 334 Lecturers. Alongside 5 research staff and 67 Technicians there were 2 Industrial Liaison Officers and 15 Computer Centre Staff. The Secretary's Department now comprised a Registrar, an Accountant, 60 administrative staff and 13 library staff. The physical requirements of people and buildings were serviced by 9 maintenance and 8 security and caretaking staff with 4 catering, nursing and domestic colleagues.

Although staff numbers increased through college mergers, these only partly explain the growth. By 1986-87, with the Polytechnic soon to leave Local Authority control, the Directorate comprised the Director, 1 Assistant Director (doubling as Polytechnic Secretary) and 2 Deputy Directors. There were 461 academic staff with 27 researchers. Computer Centre staff had doubled to 31, technicians increased to 118. Administrative staff had more than trebled to 214 and Library staff risen to 57. At this time figures were only given for 19 salaried caretakers and 7 salaried catering staff which implies there were other workers paid differently.

The current staff numbers today of 2-3,000, depending on the type of count, can be broadly split into three categories. Around 35% of staff are academics. 48% are recorded as technical and administrative staff, 17% as manual staff. These figures show the extent to which the University has developed as a bureaucratic organisation, reflecting the wider patterns in society at large. Attempts to explain bureaucratisation nationally have created a small industry, not least amongst academics teaching and researching modern society. Growth in scale is an obvious factor – the bigger the organisation the more effort is needed to run it and growth has been the dominant characteristic of this University. There has also been a broadening of tasks, alongside work in the classrooms and its direct support, other functions have been taken on – enterprise development, marketing, a chaplaincy, a theatre, transport and much more. With growth and multi-site operations there has also been an increase in complexity. To deal with this, systems are needed that tend to be taken for granted until they fail. In a multi-site library, for example, books need to be returned to any site but still end up on the shelves at the right one with most library users not asking how this is done. Staff expect access to their computer accounts twenty four hours a day, wherever they are in the world, but with little appreciation of the effort that lies behind this 'magic' of the twenty-first century.

Administration Building exterior

There is also specialisation and professionalisation of function. In a huge organisation what people tend to notice is the front facing offices that deal with students, staff and the community. But without the 'backroom functions' little of this could occur. Growth has led to an expansion of this hidden area. By the turn of the new century the numbers involved were so large that many of these staff were grouped together in a new building. Here their work is carried out on huge open plan floors that can be observed through plate glass doors – a design, depending on who you ask, that is either a testament to the genius of modern architecture or that turns the 'back office' into a white collar factory.

These explanations focus on the rationality of organisational development and bureaucratisation. But organisational theory also points to a more self-interested side. Some stress the extent to which those running large bureaucratic organisations have an interest in increasing their pay and status by expanding their role in the system. Others stress the extent to which similarities in structures and processes between organisations arise because of pressures towards copycat behaviour. These pressures are partly coercive, from the outside, laws and regulations have to be followed. There is policing by regimes of inspection, accreditation and external performance measurement. But copycat pressures also arise from the need to be seen to be doing what others are doing. This can give rise to various organisational and procedural fashions. The story of polytechnics and universities is therefore the story of changing organisational forms and processes that come and go or are continually reborn with new labels – students as clients then customers; management as efficiency, quality, total quality, quality assurance and so on. The archives of any university, including Wolverhampton, are a testament to these changing approaches but the focus of this chapter is the people whose working lives are shaped by them. These are the people who keep education in a lively population and sprawling estate functioning day-by-day, whatever the current organisational approach.

The Teaching Staff

As the work of the predecessor colleges, the Polytechnic and then the University, has grown so has the number of academics teaching and researching. Today there are some 800 full-time equivalent academics in post. They are overwhelmingly full-time (despite casualisation in some parts of the wider British university system). This is very different to the early days. Looking back Fisher described the early teachers,

> *Meeting in a school after working hours instead of in a factory or on a building job, the teacher, himself a craftsman strives to initiate his pupils into all the mysteries of that craft. He was prepared to make good, so far as lay in his power, all the deficiencies of general education and to pass onto his class all that modern science lay within his reach and seemed to be applicable to their work.*[1]

We know too little about these earlier generations of part-time teachers who came into the various colleges after their day jobs. It is hard too to get an exact trajectory of when the balance tipped towards full-time permanent staff. This is compounded by the way figures are compiled. There is a difference between 'headcount' and 'full-time equivalent' numbers. Many people have part-time contracts which

[1] Express and Star, 13 February 1924.

are conflated to give a picture of 'full-time equivalent' staff. By headcount, part-timers were still predominant into the 1950s. In 1950 the Technical College had 57 full-time academic staff (and five vacancies). There were seven academic departments, each with a head, 13 responsible lecturers and 25 full-time assistants. Alongside these 180 part-time teachers were also employed. In full-time equivalent terms the part-timers had probably just been over-taken. The status of part-time staff has also diminished. Early on they are named in college guides in a way that makes it impossible to distinguish from permanent staff. From the 1950s they became more of emergency cover, to help deal with growing numbers and staff absences. Later generations of part-timers have tended to come from future academics looking to earn some money and gain the experience necessary for them to get future permanent positions. By the 1970s we can roughly estimate that the full-time equivalent number of part-time staff was only around a dozen across the whole of the Polytechnic. By headcount there were many more, as there are today. A few hours work teaching could be enough to keep a person's head above water after life on a grant (or later loan).

As the number of permanent staff grew (including those with fractional contracts) so their diversity also increased. In the early years, like the students, part-time staff had come from the local community. Full-time permanent positions could be filled by people applying from anywhere in the country and increasingly internationally (though subject to the vagaries of immigration rules). The predominance of men also gave way to more women, and married women at that, as the prejudice against their employment was overcome. But this took a long time. The Governors' Report of 1937-38 records them accepting 'with great regret the resignation (in view of her approaching marriage) of Miss K.E Ferguson, MSc, Head of the Women's Department.'[2] Her successor would be Miss Challen. Ethnic diversity has also increased too as second and third generation children of migrants have overcome some of the prejudices in society that had held their parents back.

Some stories weave together the breaking down of barriers. Laura Serrant-Green was born into an immigrant family where her mother worked in the kitchens of the local hospital. With her mother, at work, she 'saw the best and worst of how professionals treat support staff. She taught me that no matter who you are in healthcare, we all have important roles'. It made her want to become a medical doctor but at the last minute she changed her mind. Laura decided to take one of the first nursing degree courses. 'You could have been a doctor', she was told, with the sense that nursing was second class even though she could 'support … the whole person at the point of need'. But her career did not stop – her 'proudest achievement' was 'getting my PhD in nursing. I became a real doctor – and a nursing one at that'.[3] She went on to become a professor and Director of Research in the University's School of Health and Wellbeing.

Staff qualifications have also increased. In fact the importance of improving the quality of academic staff is a permanent theme in the history of the University and its predecessor colleges. Over time the average qualification level has risen so that first degrees have become essential alongside any professional qualifications, then Master's degrees and today PhDs are increasingly demanded of staff when they are appointed. Longer serving staff are encouraged to complete a doctorate while in post.

Education is about human interaction even if the humans are separated in location, communicating electronically. This means the ratio of students to staff is important. Here there is a puzzle. The numbers of academic staff has increased in

---

[2] *Wolverhampton and Staffordshire Technical College, Twelfth Annual Report of the Governors 1937-1938, 1938, p.8.*
[3] *Laura Serrant-Green, 'You could have been a doctor', Nursing Researcher, vol. 16 no. 3, 2007; 'Nursing Life: Sixty seconds with Laura Serrant-Green', Nursing Times May 17-May 30, 2011.*

A History of the University of Wolverhampton

Workshops and informal lectures

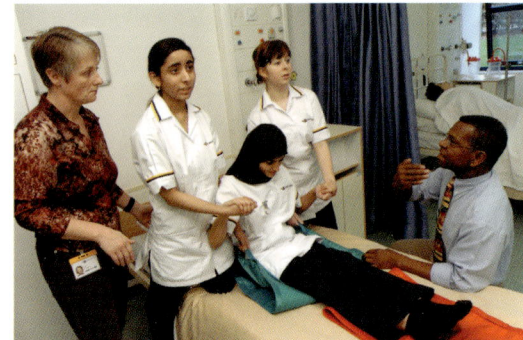

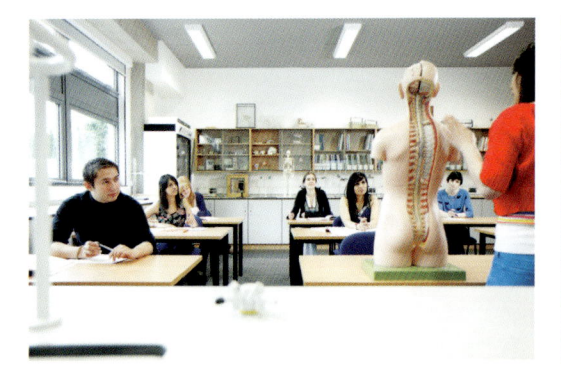

a broadly stable relationship to the numbers of students – the bigger relative increase has been in other staff. This is partly because some of these have taken on roles previously done by academics; it is also because contact has been reduced. In the early years in the technical college, for example, a part-time evening course could involve the commitment of three evenings a week in sessions of up to three hours each, or a day and two evenings a week – not very different from the class contact on an undergraduate degree today.

There was considerable unevenness in staff: student ratios within and between the various colleges that fed into the university. At the lowest were the tiny numbers in the newly formed Technical Teachers Training College in the early 1960s where the new principal said 'temporarily, the staffing ratio is rather better than 5:1 (neglecting In-Service and short courses) but every lecturer is fully extended.'[4] With the creation of the polytechnic these contrasts began to be evened out. In the first years there were even suggestions that the student: staff ratios were more favourable than in the traditional university sector though it is not clear that these calculations reflected all the work that was done. Even if true at the start, the trend was towards rapidly increasing SSRs as they came to be called.

There was to be little respite from this. As the new universities emerged, staff and student ratios became less popular as a measure of resourcing but they still have an underlying value and point to continuing significant contrasts. A lecture is, to an extent, a lecture whether it is given to fifty, 500 or recorded for a limitless audience. But a seminar becomes something different as numbers rise from around a dozen participants (1970s) to two dozen and then 30 or more. In the laboratory-based subjects, limits to class size for 'lab' work are set by the size of the labs or computer suites. Here the pressure is reflected in the number of classes that need to be timetabled as larger numbers of students try to get the experience they need, assisted by demonstrators and technicians.

The demands of teaching in accessible higher education are considerable and Wolverhampton staff, together with other staff in the sector, have pioneered new approaches and refined old ones. Elements of this were evident in an earlier era but there were also complaints. In 1963 it was noted that 'As far as teaching is concerned it will be noted that in most departments there is a need for a greater amount of student involvement and less note dictation. In the technologies and sciences for instance more attention needs to be given to demonstrations and unnecessary distinctions between theory and practice should be avoided.'[5] Teaching became more innovative in the 1970s. In earlier years teachers and students could assume they had been trained to process information in the same ways through similar educational experiences. That is no longer the case. People gather from the education systems of many different countries, from varied vocational courses, from experience of school decades ago and from work. Their levels of formal attainment and modes of learning can be accommodated in a class of 20 - a lecture audience, sometimes of several hundred, poses rather more challenges.

Fantastic and innovative teaching can be done in large classes but it would be foolish not to recognise that they also bring practical problems. In education, as in health, there is something of a national 'inverse care law' at work where resources flow to those least in need rather than most in need, not least staff resources. On a day-to-day basis even the most innovative of teachers can be worn down by the grind of dealing with this. But they keep going and the best systems are those which encourage

[4] C.L Heywood, 'Wolverhampton Technical Teachers College', The Vocational Aspect of Education, vol. 14, 1962, pp. 11.
[5] Ministry of Education, Report by HM Inspectors on Wolverhampton and Staffordshire College of Technology, London 1963, p. 6.

and support them to do so, as part of a common journey on which the students too need to play a role, conscious of how their experience is moulded by society at large.

Yet the importance of student/teacher interaction remains, the inequities of the education system continue to condition what goes on in the classroom. A key element is disparities in resourcing which continue to affect the student: staff ratio. One of the ways that increasing numbers have been dealt with has been through the use of educational technology, in part to economise on staff, in part to extend the frontiers of teaching. Today the forms may be more 'high tech' but from the days of the Free Library in Wolverhampton and the first lantern slides and film shows, it has been the mass sector that has been more innovative, perhaps of necessity, in using new forms of technology. Indeed sometime the criticism might be that some have been too enthusiastic in seeing 'techno-fix' as a solution to bigger educational problems.

Administrators

This is another group of staff who have left a documentary record. They have some presence in the formal records but they can also be seen in the notations in course guides, scribbled notes, reports and records of meetings. These give us glimpses of the people whose work has kept the procedures of the institutions moving, year after year. But the record is less full than for the academics. In 1963, a team of government inspectors reported that 'in a college of this size it is easy to overlook the administrative staff, especially when, as here, it is efficiently unobtrusive'.[6] In the first decades of higher education, support for running the various colleges was limited even if, as with the Wolverhampton and Staffordshire Technical College, it already was a significant size. In the first days of the Technical College the College Secretary's office not only served the Principal but acted as a shop where students could buy the notebooks in which their progress was recorded and the paper and materials that they needed for their courses. Here too they could also come to get the tram and bus passes that allowed them cheaper travel to and from college. The Art School and other colleges also ran in similar make-shift ways.

Facilities still had to be created and maintained, students recruited, fees and deposits collected, classes arranged, timetabled and taught, progress recorded, examinations arranged. Bills too had to be paid, not least staff wages and expenses. Some of these tasks were done outside the College, by local authority staff. Other tasks fell to the teaching staff including recruitment, 'The Principal and Staff will be in attendance between 7 and 8.30 for five consecutive evenings each September' prospective students were told in the 1920s. Still other tasks might be devolved to the students themselves through the Students' and Teachers' Union. By 1950 the clerical staff had expanded to ten, still under the control of the Secretary of the College. Heads of departments also had clerical assistance.

A more formal central management structure developed over time, and especially from the late 1950s. By the early polytechnic era it had begun to look recognisably like that of today though it was still very much about individuals rather than large teams. Alongside the Polytechnic Secretary, who was now also Clerk to the governors, was the academic registry, the finance office and the establishment officer. This, largely male group, was supported by various assistants and a team of largely female 'clerical officers, secretaries and shorthand typists'. They still are – their vital role captured in Laurie Taylor's story of Maureen who holds things together at his imaginary Poppleton University,

---

[6] Ministry of Education, Report by HM Inspectors on Wolverhampton and Staffordshire College of Technology, London 1963, p. 6.

The Workforce – Staff

> *Maureen is always at work, when at work she is always in her office, and when in her office she is always fully aware of what is going on. As the academics stagger through their days in a haze of confusion …. Maureen is always on hand to deal with student questions, the intricacies of assessment documents and the running of the department. A few academics take the managerial shilling and become authors of complex business plans but in the main it is Maureen, for a salary which is probably half that of most academics, who literally services the academic world.* [7]

Qualifications were also growing on the non teaching side. 'It is pleasing … to add a note of praise for the graduate college Secretary and his department' said the inspectors in 1963.[8] The post of College Secretary had always been a high status male one but here we also see a new word 'graduate' reflecting the start of a process by which the qualifications of the non teaching staff would also rise as the nature of their jobs changed.

And if academics worried about their work loads so too have the administrative staff. In the first Polytechnic years, for example, their numbers were held down, resulting in what the Academic Development Plan of the time described with candour as 'serious deficiencies in the services provided… with the final effect of the incorporation of the Faculty of Education not yet clear, it appears unlikely to result in a significant overall improvement'.[9] In the 1980s too, pressure continued to rise as expenditure was held down. But numbers did rise as they have done since, though so too has the load of inspection and recording.

These two groups, academics and administrators worked with their colleagues from a range of occupations vital to the functioning of the series of organisations which created the University. Some of this can be seen in the records of the development of services, such as libraries in which people worked. The ease of access to effective computer facilities must evidence the work of generations of specialist staff

---

[7] Quoted M.Evans, *Killing Thinking, The Death of the Universities*, London, 2004, p. 79.
[8] Ministry of Education, *Report by HM Inspectors on Wolverhampton and Staffordshire College of Technology*, London 1963, p. 6.
[9] *Academic Development Plan*, 1979, p. 27.

developing knowledge as technology changed. However, the jobs of other colleagues have left no documentary records. Their work and its value to the organisation can be inferred in the story of the physical construction of the estates. People on the ground, knowledgeable about the physical environment, must have enabled construction workers to access and work safely. New buildings must have been cleaned, serviced and guarded. Supplies must have been distributed. Their work can also be traced through records of the activity of students on this built estate, because they enabled it to happen. Here we trace workers through the structures that impacted on them and the organisations they created.

Unequal Worlds, Unequal Rewards

The work we do is still the central determinant of who we are, no less in a university than elsewhere. Despite its ostensibly more democratic ethos, higher education is full of hierarchies bound up with class, status and power. These hierarchies overlap but also conflict. Amongst academics the creation, in the mid 1980s, of a professoriate based on research produced tensions with those who believed that teaching should have equal status. The competing hierarchies of the academics clash with those amongst the non-academics where the existence of a single pay scale also does not prevent a perception of difference. In each case the opportunity to rise up the local hierarchies is structured by who you are and your background in the same way that these factors impact on student access and performance. This story of differentiation of the workforce in terms of status, pay and conditions reflects the wider social divisions in English society.

What determines, asked one reformer in the 1970s, that writing a research paper is more difficult or more rewarding than, say, teaching English as a foreign language? Or, on the non-academic side, running the university on a day-to-day basis. Why should one require a vastly greater level of pay and status than the other? The paradox of higher education is that while we break down and analyse the irrationalities of hierarchies and how they are constructed we also inhabit and live them. While the new universities challenge and contest differentiation they also work within it, reproducing its assumptions externally and in their own hierarchies. Part of the humour of Howard Jacobson's fictional account of Wolverhampton in its polytechnic years is its playing with these distinctions. Mil Millington's fiction does the same thing for the new university. Perhaps in a more democratic future students will struggle to understand these distinctions in the same way that we struggle to make sense of the divisions of medieval Europe.

Meanwhile the hierarchies from the college to the university years have always been dominated by older white males. This domination is reducing. The University has had one female Vice-Chancellor, there are female Deans, Professors and Heads of various service departments. Progress for minority ethnic groups has also been possible. But in both cases the pattern is still one of inequality. In 2009 60% of all the University's employees were female but their numbers diminish as one advances up the hierarchies. 15% of staff had minority backgrounds but the same pattern existed there with the figure for Deans, Professors and Department Heads falling to 6-8%. The biggest share of minority ethnic groups collectively was to be found amongst the University's manual staff.

It would be naïve to think that prejudice and discrimination has not existed in the history of the colleges and this university or any other. Today it is less obvious, banned by law, deterred and monitored by processes and data. But still inequality persists. Some of the reasons have been well analysed including in research commissioned by the University of Wolverhampton. One major study of women in research, for example, which used Wolverhampton as a case study pointed, amongst other things, to the extent to which women were encouraged even pressured, to take on teaching and administrative roles that involved caring for students.[10] On the administrative side too this is evident. Women predominate in student facing roles as they do in the human resource department 'caring' for staff. Ethnicity and gender discrimination can come together as they do amongst the staff who arrive early in the morning to clean and maintain the organisation.

Before the Polytechnic became independent from local authority control in 1988, it and its predecessor colleges, had a clear 'public sector' and 'local government' base. This meant that from the aftermath of the First World War, pay and conditions were set by agreements negotiated nationally. Academics were on what came to be called the Burnham scale. This was established by a committee in 1919 under Lord Burnham, first for elementary school teachers, then extended to secondary and further education in the local authority sector. Negotiations set the scale, conditions and level of jobs, posts would be advertised with phrases like 'in accordance with Burnham'.

Centralised pay scales had many advantages but it meant the governments of the day could use the system to seek to hold down pay. This was less of a problem when inflation was low – more when it speeded up. Disputes over levels and comparability broke out periodically. In the early 1970s, for example, pay in schools, further and non university higher education had fallen behind. In the new polytechnics this was said to be discouraging recruitment and encouraging some academics to switch to administrative positions for better pay. In 1974, the Houghton award allowed some catch up before inflation again had an impact. But even today the salary scales for the mass of academics build on these earlier scales.

Colleagues are further segregated by their type of contract and conditions of employment. There is a distinction between a service relationship in which a salary is exchanged for services, and a labour contract in which quantified work is exchanged for a wage. These are perceived to indicate the status of the work. In universities this distinction is reflected in divisions between academic staff with 'permanent' jobs and the majority of staff. The looser service relationships do not specify hours of work, allow for working away from the institution and offer more generous holiday entitlement. The more constricting specific labour contract is explicit about hours of attendance in the workplace and description of duties. Neither may reflect the actual hours people work, it is a minimum that is indicated, many staff work much longer.

The University has remained committed to nationally negotiated pay scales with various annual increments to reflect experience. Nor has the University's senior management looked with favour on suggestions that pay should be regionalised, seeing this as negative for the institution and the region. There is a national bargaining structure for negotiations on sector pay for the majority of higher education staff. The Joint Negotiating Committee for Higher Education Staff (JNCHES) comprised the Universities and Colleges Employers Association and staff Trade Unions. This negotiating committee replaced ten separate structures, with the specific intent of establishing parity across the sector. The workforce was considered in two sections, academic and non-academic, with separate sub-councils and separate pay scales. A linked pay spine was introduced in 2004

[10] V. Fisher, 'Women in research in British universities – an institutional case study', International Journal of Management Concepts and Philosophy, vol. 5 no. 4, 2011.

and a pay settlement was agreed in 2006. National pay agreements are not mandatory, although the majority of universities do apply them. There has been some division over whether academic and professional staff should continue to collaborate with other groups in the negotiating bodies.

Organisational inequalities are reflected in pay levels. In the UK in 2008-9 the median income was around £25,000. In UK universities as a whole, in that year 14% earned more than £50,000 and 18% less than £20,000. But the differences were also reflected by type of work. For academics the median salary was £43,000 at that time while for administrative and support staff it was £28,000. The salaries of the 'other staff' were much less as those who worked in catering and support facilities clustered in the 18% earning below £20,000. Even so work at the University compared well for all staff working at the University compared with the general pattern in the Black Country.

The pattern for senior staff is more complex. So long as colleges and the polytechnics remained linked to the local authorities, senior pay was also limited by the local government situation and comparability issues. Why, for example, should the head of a polytechnic not be paid in line with a senior local government official? Would it really make sense to pay someone running a central services unit in a higher education organisation more than his or her equivalent running a possibly larger equivalent local government unit? This produced conflicts in Wolverhampton as elsewhere. Polytechnic Directors positioned arguments for independence in many guises, but one key factor was a desire to have more freedom for setting pay at the very top, including perhaps their own. In 1987, for example, it was noted at Wolverhampton that:

> *The grading of posts has been a somewhat contentious issue... [T]he local authority... wished to see a close comparability with the posts in the Civic Centre... [and upgradings of senior staff]... were not as substantial as had been requested by the Governing Council, but were all the Authority was willing to accede to. A number of other posts have been upgraded, largely because of the difficulty in filling some posts when advertised. At these middle levels, the Authority has not been quite so unwilling to see upgrading made.[11]*

Freedom from local authority control had some significant consequences for internal pay in a new university like Wolverhampton. For most staff their conditions of employment were simply transferred, but for senior staff it allowed the reconstituted new Governing Council and senior management greater freedom over top pay and appointments. Basic pay could now be increased and more fringe benefits and performance elements added (they varied over time). Below the top level some other staff were also excluded from nationally agreed rates in favour of those set at the discretion of the senior management. This applied, for example, to Deans and the University professoriate as well as some service Heads. Here pay is also subject to individualised annual appraisal.

The overall result of these changes for the university sector as a whole, and Wolverhampton in particular has been to widen differentials and increase inequality within the institution. Current pay ranges from just over the national minimum wage to some £230,000 a year. This mirrors British society as a whole. At the start of the twenty-first century what some saw as

---

[11] *The Polytechnic Wolverhampton, Institutional Review*, 1987, p. 61

Rock of Ages

When the front building of the University, the 'Marble', was being built in the early 1930s George Chell and William Fisher must have walked its dust strewn corridors with feelings of satisfaction about what was being created. Chell had already had over forty years helping to develop a night school into a college. Fisher could reflect on a decade as Director, helping to plan how a ramshackle set of buildings would give way to the beginnings of a modern campus. He would preside over it for another two decades. Together they gave eighty years of their working lives to the development of a predecessor college of the modern University of Wolverhampton.

Today we are told that this is no longer possible. We live in a precarious and flexible world where no one stays long in the same place. But we need to be careful. The statistics do not necessarily support this view. It is easy to reproduce the fashionable story of the day and not look hard at the evidence or even notice the world around you. Many other staff invest their working lives in the same place. Keith White is one example but there are others. Each year the University gives long service awards for 25 and 40 years.

They make interesting reading. The story is told of a peasant living in central Europe who lived his life in several countries without ever leaving his village. This can happen to people in organisations too. Sometimes you have to go out to the world to get change but sometimes the world comes to you. Perhaps Barbara Hodson, a senior Laboratory Technician, felt like that in 2010 having begun at the Dudley College of Education as a trainee technician in 1969 and seen it change to a Polytechnic, then become part of a University, only for it to disappear while she remained. So too might Stuart Mason who joined the School of Art a year before. In 2011 another technician, Robert Hooton, and a member of the Institute of Learning, Steve Jeffs also recorded forty years. Alongside them are significant numbers who have recorded twenty-five years or more. Pauline Lim, for example, trained as a local nurse, became a midwife and then finished her career with nursing a university subject and she a university lecturer in the area she served.

The structure of a work force is a bit like looking at the structure of a rock formation. There are thicker bands from times when expansion was fast, thinner ones from times when it was slow or there was even contraction. But all the time new layers are being laid down as new people come in and the rock formation on which an institution is built changes over time.

the Anglo-Saxon model of capitalism was producing large differentials between those at the bottom and the top. Although the gaps were not as great as in the private sector, universities soon developed some of the largest in the public sector.

Organised Voices

In the new century university staff make up an important part of public sector trade unionism. Trade unions exist to represent the collective and individual interests of employees and to look forward to a vision of a different and better society. They were illegal in Britain until 1824-25 as a result of what were called the 'Combination Acts'. Early trade unionists, therefore, who came into the various working men's colleges in mid nineteenth century Wolverhampton needed both commitment and a degree of courage. At this point it would have seemed strange to think that there might be a time when white collar workers, women as well as men – might support trade unions.

In fact teachers in schools began to organise early but they did not see themselves as traditional trade unionists. Neither did the first college staff. A desire for respectability, paternalism in the running of institutions and professional aspiration overcame any sense of worker solidarity. The staff could come together socially with the students and for a long period small staff associations functioned – sometimes with their own bars.

But today University staff tend to be members of either UCU, the University and College Union, which represents the academics, or UNISON, which represents the administrative and manual staff. Together they form the two unions recognised by the

University's management for the purposes of collective bargaining. They act as the collective voice of the staff in the institution as well as defending individuals in terms of grievances and disciplinary actions.

Both organisations have a long history but their significance at Wolverhampton really dates from the 1950s and 1960s. UNISON was formed by a merger of three unions in 1993, two of which had branches in the University and the Polytechnic before it. NALGO, the National and Local Government Officers Association, was the union for the white collar staff and NUPE, the National Union of Public Employees, for the smaller number of manual staff. The third COHSE was for those in the heath services so some of the staff who joined from nursing had involvement with it. NUPE was seen as a more traditional trade union and had been formed in 1908 but it was actually NALGO which had been created first, in 1904. The smaller numbers of non academic staff in the constituent colleges of Wolverhampton limited the possibilities of union growth. From the 1950s, however, the numbers of staff who could join grew and the organisation threw off its image as a professional association, joining the Trades Union Congress in 1964. Nationally NALGO's membership expanded from 100,000 in 1940 to 300,000 in 1960 and 700,000 in the 1970s including a significant number in the new Polytechnic at Wolverhampton. In the early period these members were part of the larger Wolverhampton branch reflecting its, and the Polytechnic's, local government links.

The lecturers' trade union made the same shift away from a primarily professional orientation. Academic trade unionism began at the start of the twentieth century in the new technical colleges. In the traditional universities it took much longer. In 1904 the Association of Teachers in Technical Institutions was formed, appointing its first full-time secretary in 1923. Membership was stronger outside of the West Midlands but pioneers did join in the Wolverhampton Technical College. Membership really took off from the 1950s and the ATTI became the first teachers' trade union to join the TUC in 1967, shortly after NALGO. By 1972 the ATTI had 40,000 members and a strong base on Wolverhampton Polytechnic. It was strengthened further by the merger of the training colleges which led to it becoming NATFHE, the National Association of Teachers in Further and Higher Education in 1976.

union that incorporated further education staff, as well as the radicalism of some of the policies of the day. In opposition, a small Association of Polytechnic Teachers was formed but at Wolverhampton this only got the support of a few individuals. Nevertheless some of the same issues arose again after 1992, especially in the old universities where some looked askance at a link with former polytechnic staff and those in further education. But over time opposition diminished – in part because of the increasingly similar problems faced by staff in old and new universities alike. The result was that in 2006 a merger took

Staff in court-yard at Telford campus

After 1992 the rationale for two separate unions in higher education – one representing academics in older universities and the other those in the newer universities – weakened. Issues of status prevented an early merger. This problem had also been apparent in the 1970s when some in the polytechnics resisted the idea of a

place between the Association of University Teachers and NATFHE to form a new union, the University and College Union, with two branches at the University of Wolverhampton, one at Wolverhampton campus and one at Walsall.

Today UNISON and UCU represent staff interests through a joint committee. But as the Polytechnic developed there were some tensions between their forerunners. In the 1970s NALGO and NATFHE disagreed over which staff should be represented by them. The hybrid nature of some posts created the basis for what the Times Higher Education Supplement called 'bitter demarcation disputes' and Wolverhampton was one of the centres of these.[12] Research assistants were one such group, but their position was relatively easy to resolve in favour of 'higher education [i.e. academic] conditions of service' and therefore possible membership of the academic union. Much more contentious were other groups who were appointed on Burnham pay scales but with local authority conditions of service – hence the formally hybrid nature of their posts. These included senior librarians, senior computer staff and registrars. Only in 1980 was agreement formed to find a way to resolve these elements of formal hybridity though many informal elements survive.

Over the longer term, however, unity between the unions has been more evident. The need for trade unions arises not from ill will but from the structural tension between the interests of those running any organisation and those employed by it. The argument that universities do not need unions as they consist of professionals doing jobs together focuses only on the common purpose. This exists, as we have emphasised, and is reflected in the day-to-day co-operation between senior managers and the trade unions to resolve particular issues. This does not eliminate the structural tension – indeed many of the day-to-day problems arise because of it.

That serious potential conflicts of interest exist is most obvious at times of threatened redundancy. These, as we have seen, occurred for the Polytechnic as a whole in the early 1980s and for the University in 2008-2009, but they have existed at different times for particular sections. Redundancy is often presented from the top as a 'necessary evil' sometimes even 'a brave choice' but those threatened with it are hardly likely to see it this way. It raises questions about the nature of the stewardship of any organisation and why the 'evil' should be inflicted on some at the expense of others and the organisation as a whole. For the individual too the pain of redundancy has been increased by the reduction of redundancy terms in the UK. In Wolverhampton these have been significantly more generous than what statutory pays allows in law but they too have fallen over time.

In a crisis then the day-to-day co-operation becomes harder to achieve and structural conflicts become more evident. This structural tension exists between those running organisations and their employees. It has been argued that part of the logic of recent higher education reform (and what is called the new public management) is the attempt to heighten this tension. This is done by increasing the ambiguity of the position of university executives themselves. Whereas once they might see themselves as representatives of their organisations, lobbying for resources from central government, now governments want them to be conduits of government policy within their organisations.

As the University moves forward, therefore, the necessity of having a strong staff union voice will also continue to be important. Both at the level of national policy and within the institution, staff trade unions make an important contribution. They do so by protecting the interests of staff as 'workers' but also helping to defend the wider interests of staff and students in terms of an education based on the ability to think and challenge freely – an idea that goes back to the very first days of those who thought about creating the mechanics' institutes in places like Wolverhampton in the 1820s.

[12] *Times Higher Education Supplement*, 1 May 1980

Chapter five

A Small Town in a Big Conurbation

GO eat

"Feeding your expectations"

Over one hundred and eighty years ago the technical institutes and libraries in Wolverhampton established meeting places. People came together to find fellow thinkers, talk, research and read shared publications. This still happens today. The importance of that original role – providing a meeting place – is a vital part of any discussion of universities.

Providing a physical place for people to come together has long been suggested as the justification for universities. In 1854 Cardinal Newman, in his classic discussion of the purpose of universities, hoped that if scholars from different disciplines were exposed to each other in one physical place, they would, '...learn to respect, to consult, to aid each other. Thus is created a pure and clear atmosphere of thought, which the student also breathes.[1]

Physical attendance assists the academic process, enabling students to be socialised into disciplinary cultures. It allows for face-to-face discussion and cross-disciplinary contact that cannot happen elsewhere in a society lacking public space.

The formal purpose of universities is study. The curriculum, research, academic concerns and outcomes for students inevitably dominate discussion. Much intellectual activity can be accommodated in cyberspace. But our intellects are embodied. People gather in large numbers on English university estates, arriving from across the world, different parts of the UK and the immediate locality. They eat and excrete. They meet, talk and sometimes sleep. They make friends and enemies, find sexual partners and fall in and out of love. Some live on site, others attend regularly and frequently, some visit intermittently. People gathering together require shelter, facilities, food and drink.

At the University of Wolverhampton people gather on sites spread across a major industrial conurbation. Collectively these offer the facilities of a small town. Cafes, shops, restaurants, sports centres, libraries, theatres, a faith centre, advice services, public transport, security and refuse collection. It is a small town community, more cosmopolitan and outward looking than most, with unity, divisions and degrees of engagement, like all populations. This chapter is about the myriad activities that active, interesting and varied individuals and groups create and the places they use.

Their focus can be surprising. A group of students were asked to suggest an image that summed up the University for them. They offered three – an iconic building, themselves sitting together socialising and various snacks. Why snacks? Because, they

[1] J.H. Newman, The Idea of a University, (1854), New York, 1996, p. 77.

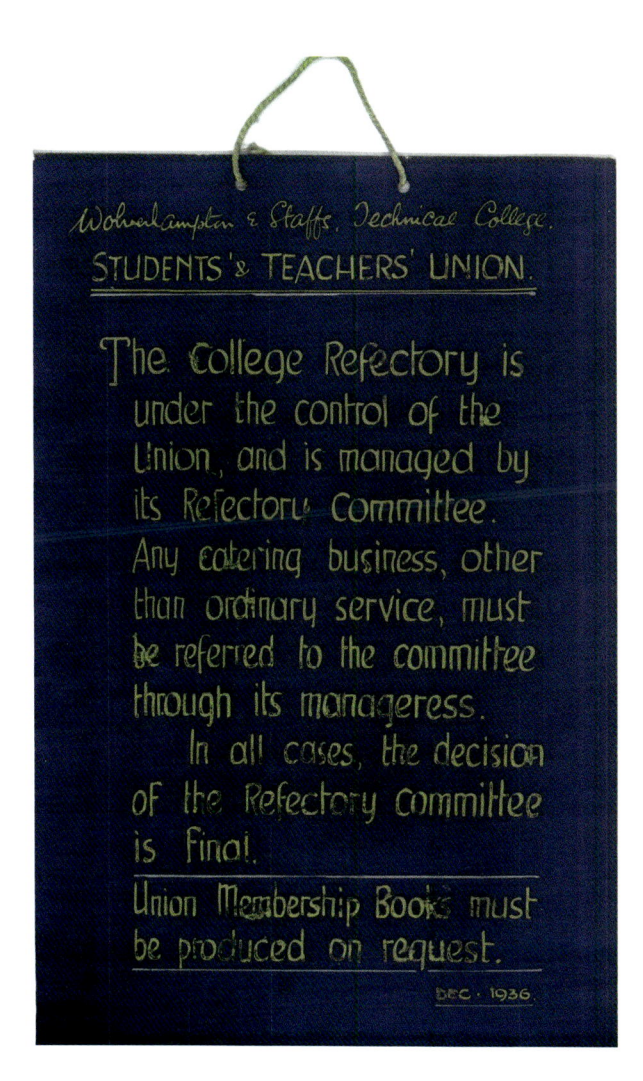

Wolverhampton & Staffs. Technical College.
STUDENTS' & TEACHERS' UNION.

The College Refectory is under the control of the Union, and is managed by its Refectory Committee.
Any catering business, other than ordinary service, must be referred to the committee through its manageress.
In all cases, the decision of the Refectory Committee is final.
Union Membership Books must be produced on request.

DEC. 1936.

between staff members and students in the College Union. They worked together to provide facilities, create a variety of social clubs and hold management to account. From 1904 the purpose of this Students' and Teachers' Union was to promote 'professional' interests, 'social and sports activities' and 'to represent the general body of students'. They helped to run the first College library and they continued to run a refectory until the 1960s. But by this point even the Government Inspectors thought that students ought to have their own organisation.[2]

The Students' and Teachers' Union had the Chairman of Governors as President and the College Principal as Vice-President. The new 'Students' Union' explained, as they came onto campus each day their first thought was what they were going to eat. This idea of people talking, laughing and eating in a variety of buildings is the backdrop to the small town of university life. Areas for socialising, living, playing, and performing have been provided as part of the general estate and within Students' Union facilities. The Union has had a constant presence, although with different forms and fluctuating vitality.

The Students' Union

In the early Free Library and Technical College there was no division gradually developed a form of democracy with the membership electing officers, some of whom were paid for a year's sabbatical from their academic studies. The move from the old to the new Union was a contentious process, positioned on the cusp of a shift in status of the College. There was a gap between the energy of a few and the inertia and indifference of the many, a recurring theme in university activism.

'Until January, 1966, a Students' and Teachers' Union had existed for over thirty years. Its failings were obvious to those of us who arrived at College in October, 1965. It catered for a type of night-school establishment, with much of the organisation

[2] Ministry of Education, Report by HM Inspectors on Wolverhampton and Staffordshire College of Technology, London 1963, p. 10.

of the Union being left to former members well past their student age. It was apparent then that the College had soon to adapt itself to its new function as a regional College and, possibly, a Polytechnic. At the Annual General Meeting in December, 1965, and at an Extraordinary General Meeting in January, 1966, changes were made in the Constitution, transforming the Union into its present state. With few exceptions the Union was formed to be run entirely by students… Through the year and a half since its reformation the Students' Union has developed, though perhaps not quite as much as many of us would have preferred. It has grown stronger in asserting its rights in several scuffles with outsiders who seem to be unable to realise that the College and Union have grown into something more than a "Tech" '.[3]

This local change mirrored a national time of change for young people and a rise in student activism in the 1960s. The National Union of Students (NUS) had been created in 1922 but student associations in technical colleges and teacher training colleges were not allowed to join until 1938. The NUS began with a belief in promoting international co-operation between students who would mature into the leaders of nations. By the mid 1960s it offered insurance, travel, and welfare service for students, negotiated concessions and provided a vacation work bureau. Another NUS role, growing from the 1950s, was as a significant research and campaigning force in areas of direct educational impact such as grants, teaching and accommodation. A wider political engagement became increasingly visible in the 1960s. This partly reflected the growing numbers of students, partly the changing level of radicalism and involvement in a wider range of issues. The first constitution of the NUS explicitly rejected political engagement, this was changed in 1969, student protest and campaigning could now be co-ordinated nationally and internationally.

Locally the big issue was the eruption of race into mainstream politics through the role of Enoch Powell, a senior Tory who led opposition to immigration and represented Wolverhampton for nearly twenty-five years. Students tried to get him barred from speaking at the College and when that failed, tried to shout him down, raising debate about freedom of speech in the process. But the campaigns of Powell, and those like him, produced a new unity, one report of the time describing students, mainly from Wolverhampton College of Technology and the College of Art, marching with the Indian Workers Association to petition Powell in his Wolverhampton Conservative Association office.[4] It also led to the formation of the College Civil Rights Group. Other collaboration followed, an inter-faith group in the town reacted by determining to present a more cohesive vision. They worked with the Art Gallery, Nick Hedges, then a photographer hosted by the Polytechnic, and art students. Visiting places of worship they took intimate pictures of local people and held an exhibition showing the diversity of ethnicity and faith in the town. This exhibition drew the largest number of visitors ever recorded by the Gallery at that time. Local students could also be found opposing the Vietnam War, even supported by the Head of the Art College. But behind the headlines union members were also organising their College life. Students in 1967 were greeted with this message:

"

You come at a time when the College has just been designated as a Polytechnic… and the Union is developing to meet the extra demand put on it by a much larger number of full-time students, whilst

[3] *Wolverhampton College of Technology Students' Union Handbook 1967/68, p.9*
[4] *The Star, Sheffield, 4th May 1968*

A Students' and Teachers' Union

As a new Students' Union was formed in the 1960s, the 1967/68 Union handbook told the story of the 'Origins of the Union':

'Our Union owes its origin to a volunteer Committee of Students and Teachers from the old Wolverhampton Free Library Evening Classes….. This volunteer Committee organised the first Annual Soirée and Re-union as far back as 1884, and it was from this social venture that the foundations of the present Union were laid. Membership at that time was purely optional and a number of students and staff paid a subscription. With the opening of the present building in 1933 came automatic membership to the Union of all registered students, their nominal registration fee becoming their Union membership subscription by virtue of a College Governors' resolution of 1933. This was the only permanent income of the Union. Other income came from various financially successful functions organised by the Union. With this new situation, the Students' and Teachers' Union as it was then known, since some 40/50 teachers regularly joined on a purely voluntary basis, was re-organised and became responsible for the corporate life of the College. A Chairman, Officers and a representative Students' Council were elected annually, administering through various Committees the College Refectory, Sports and Athletic Clubs, various social activities, Dramatic Society, Common Room, and various other affiliated societies which functioned from time to time when the necessary support was forthcoming. The first Union Magazine was published in March, 1948, and the first Annual Rag Day was organised in 1949 resulting over the years in approximately £15,000 for national and local charities….'

With the growing numbers of full-time students a further change in the Union came about in January, 1966, and the Union became the "Students' Union", teaching staff ceasing to be eligible to join. The old Dramatic Society (Studio 61) was disaffiliated, and later on the refectory administration was taken over from the Union by the College authorities. Naturally with many more full-time students came fresh enthusiasm for various student activities, and some old societies were revived.'

at the same time being mindful of the still much larger number of part-time students. The Union is expanding in a number of ways, during the past year a large number of new societies and clubs have been formed, a new Union bar opened and dances have become a regular feature... Looking to the future, work on the provision of a new Union building has already commenced and plans have been made for the Union to have its own sports grounds.[5]

By this time there were several committees, a Social Secretary, Sports Secretary, Education & Welfare Secretary, Bar Chairman and Editor of the Union newspaper, Marble. Three years later the list of Officers shows the difference between intention and the reality of getting people to put their energy into organisation. Of 16 officer posts six were vacant.[6] The Polytechnic entrants brought an increase in full-time mature students who in 1978 created their own union to articulate their concerns separately.[7] This only lasted a couple of years before they amalgamated into the general Union, which has continued to represent all students.

By 1983 the tone had changed, partly reflecting changes to the student body, with advice on how to avoid the pitfalls of privately rented accommodation and advice for overseas students. There was a broader agenda reflecting changes in society with advice on contraception, sexually transmitted disease, rape and sexual assault, drugs, arrest, legal aid, benefits and grants.

Engagement continued in the 1980s with involvement in some of the political parties of the time with Communist, Labour, Socialist, Socialist Workers and SDP Liberal Allliance groups. These ran alongside single issue campaign groups like CND, Amnesty International, H Block Armagh, Friends of Palestine. The rise in identity politics was apparent in the Women's Group, Women's Self Defence, Afro-Caribbean group and Gay Society. Ideas could be discussed in the Mooting and Debating Society, perhaps to the accompaniment of the preoccupation of the Real Ale Society. Some took up arms in the wider political debates of these years, not least the conflicts in industrial relations and the prolonged miners' strike (1984-1985). A few activists later became local councillors, even MPs and the occasional Vice-Chancellor could later be found whose CV included their time as a more radical student activist. The political groups of the present day Union reflect a narrower spectrum of organised political parties – Conservative Future, Green Party, Labour Students. Mature students and students with disabilities have formed new groups. There is a greater emphasis on fundraising, enterprise and employment.

The Union provided a hub around which activity could form. It offered physical facilities, advice, some financial help to its members and negotiated discounts. Its own financial health, however, has fluctuated. Early accounts of the Students' and Teachers' Social Union show profits on social events and a surplus in the Library fund. By the late 1940s there is some concern at repeated losses in the Union's money, made up by the College. This seems to have improved, with the 1962 Refectory Account showing a continuing surplus not accounting for the tea supplied to cleaning staff. With the new Students' Union the finances took another dip leading to management of the refectory being taken over by the College authorities. The situation was improved with some substantial funding from the local authority in the 1980s for running costs. However, in more recent

---

[5] *Wolverhampton College of Technology Students' Union Handbook 1967/68, Chairman's Message, p.3*
[6] *Wolverhampton Polytechnic Students Union Handbook ,1971/72*
[7] *H.Smith, The Origins and History of the Polytechnic Wolverhampton, Wolverhampton, 1983, p.112.*

Political, Grubby and Beery?

There was 1980s nostalgia for the perceived political identity of past students with an appeal for constant challenge in the present, shown in this extract from a Students' Union publication.

'Long-haired, beer-swilling, scruffy, dirty, aggressive yobboes! The student image generated by the activists of the 60s still exists in the minds of the populace, despite the fact that students nowadays bear, unfortunately, no resemblance to those bastions of freedom of speech who did us so proud two decades ago.

It was in the age of campaigns, demonstrations, etc. that this image was generated. Students realised that the greatest gift given to them by the education system was time, and a chance to analyse the systems from the 'outside' – a chance not given to many in the rat race of the twentieth century. Given this chance, they started to exercise their rights of freedom of speech, seeing the inequalities and injustices that the 'powers that be' perpetuated or swept under the carpet. After all, the government, police, courts etc. can't always be right. Thus, they fought against racism, sexism and injustice, with courage, determination and, above all, enthusiasm.

This fight must continue despite the attitude of a large proportion of students that the Union should not get involved in politics. If you close your eyes and hide under the bed, problems do not disappear. The argument that you should only study at college and not become an activist because you are funded by the rate payer is a fallacy. It is because you are supported by society that you have a fundamental obligation to fight on behalf of society against inequalities... Finally, to reinforce the argument, here are a few examples of campaigns being fought by the Union: racist fees and quotas for overseas students, grants and cuts, CND, anti-apartheid, People's March for Jobs, women and gay rights'.

A History of the University of Wolverhampton

*The Students'
Union today*

A Small Town in a Big Conurbation

years the Union came close to bankruptcy – all the Student Union bars closed, shops were taken over by the University and staff transferred to the University establishment. But the Students' Union still offers a focus for political and social activity for each new generation, 'run by students, for students. We are here so you can get the most out of your time at University. We represent you, help you take part in sport, societies and student-led events, provide opportunities for paid and voluntary work and offer independent advice on anything related to being a student.'

The willingness of successive institutional managements to help the Union is some indication of the importance of its role. The social aspect of student life is given prominence in student satisfaction surveys. But socialising is not just about entertainment and finding ways of getting on with each other. The surveys show that fellow students are an important source of advice, providing motivation to work, learning through discussion and help in understanding the material provided by academic staff. This happens outside of organised course time, in social spaces. In many of these places is food.

Cafes, Restaurants and Bars

From the earliest colleges to today, canteens, cafes and bars appear in descriptions of the sites. Just off the various campuses private cafes and bars share in the informal culture of a university town – some compete in the evenings for the claim of the 'hottest student nightspot'. Food was an attraction in the basic Common Rooms that preceded the current range of facilities. In the early colleges attempts were made to create some limited social spaces. It was the new buildings that allowed these to be incorporated into the design. The 1933 'Marble' building provided a students' common room and refectory where societies and social functions were hosted by the Students' and Teachers' Union. By the 1960s the student handbook talks of a snooker room and Student Common Room with a rack of magazines and newspapers. Soft drinks, milk and chocolate were available and cigarettes in a vending machine. There was also a plea, 'last year… the cleaners refused to clean the room because of the state to which it had deteriorated.'[8] The plea was unsuccessful, two years later the cleaners again refused – it had become too dirty to clean.

These facilities, even cleared up, were very limited. The College authorities refused to open the site on Sundays despite protest. Students organised premises in the town. In 1967 the Union opened a bar in the upstairs room of a pub, open from 12.30 to 13.45 Monday to Friday, and 19.30 to 22.30 every night. It offered beer, snacks, a juke box and a hand football machine. Advice was given on cafes in the town as there was no 'coffee lounge' in the college.

Expansion in the late 1960s led to a new Student Union building on the Wolverhampton Campus with its own bar. This was enlarged in 1976. As the various College mergers occurred, student facilities were integrated across the different sites, though not equally. By 1983 the 'St Peters Site' Student Union building had two bars, a coffee bar, two television rooms, a common room, bank, shop, and sports facilities.

[8] Wolverhampton College of Technology Students' Union Handbook 1967/68, p.17

At Dudley there was also a bar and TV room and a dance floor where discos were held regularly. Compton Park too had a bar. Bars on three sites were now open daily seven days a week and until 23.00 on Fridays and Saturdays. They sold beer, lager, cider, spirits and soft drinks. Food had also improved with crisps, nuts and hot and cold snacks on sale. The Union also ran a shop on each site, and Polytravel at Wolverhampton, all profits going to keep prices low and develop services.

Alongside the Union facilities there was growing provision by the Colleges, then Polytechnic and, finally, the University. Some services had always been necessary to provide for residential students, staff needing to eat and for more formal dining and entertaining. From the 1960s, at Wolverhampton and then on the other campuses, refectories, canteens and coffee bars were opened for the use of all students and staff. This was party in response to the physical needs of thousands of people on a daily basis. It also reflected an acknowledgement of the way that education and learning is bound up with meeting and talking. By 1989 catering outlets across three sites of the Polytechnic included a refectory, a buttery, a restaurant, a snack bar, a wine bar, two coffee bars and two other bars, between them offering service from 6.00 to 21.00. The scale of this activity has continued to grow, by 2010 catering staff offered hot and cold food and drinks through seventeen restaurants, cafes and snack bars. Food is always available, in refectories from morning to late evening and from vending machines at all times.

A description of the food consumed in the Students' and Teachers' Union refectory gives an idea of the scale of catering. Out of the 4,000 students about 160 ate in the refectory each day – consuming over one hundred weight (over 50kg) of potatoes, 30 pounds of bread and £6 worth of meat, accompanied by 32 gallons of tea and coffee.[9] This contrasts with the quantities today with the catering facilities used by over two thousand people every day. Countless cups of tea and coffee are available all over campus. The refectories now serve tens of thousands of breakfasts from sausage baps to full English and provide 2,000 main meals each month. Potatoes provide the bulk – tons of chips and 16,000 jacket potatoes a year. A decision to promote fair-trade products has resulted in 300,000 items being sold from coffees to chocolate and flapjacks. During the nine day period of graduation ceremonies, 12,000 glass of sparkling wine were served in celebration.

Such provision costs money and there has been a constant tension over whether it should be subsidised, done on a full cost basis or for profit. At times this has produced conflicts as in the 1980s when students gave the following back-handed compliment:

[9] The Wolf, Wolverhampton & Staffordshire Technical College Students' and Teachers' Union, February 1955

> *Any mention of our luxurious hostel accommodation would be incomplete without a mention of the wonderful refectory service. There is a refectory on each of the three sites. The menus are sometimes varied and the food never lacks character. Incidentally, the prices only ever come down when the Students' Union wins a hostel rent strike. Last year our glorious President negotiated a 12% reduction in food and snack prices as a result of our rent strike. Funny thing, the chips still shrink in length as they miraculously do each year!* [10]

GOeat

"Feeding your expectations"

GO café

café hot drinks
Freshly prepared for you

	Small	Regular	Large
Espresso Short strong black coffee		£1.20	£1.85
Americano Espresso with hot water to make a smoother coffee	£1.60	£1.95	£2.30
Cappuccino Espresso coffee with steamed milk topped with chocolate	£1.75	£2.20	£2.50
Café Latte Steamed milk added to an Espresso	£1.75	£2.20	£2.50
Mochaccino Indulgent coffee, chocolate and steamed milk	£1.95	£2.40	£2.75
Hot Chocolate Steamed milk and chocolate	£1.85	£2.30	£2.65
Flavoured Latte Served with steamed or ice cold milk Caramel, Vanilla, Hazelnut, Almond, Seasonal	£2.20	£2.65	£3.20
Tea PG to go		£1.60	
Tea Herbal, Fruit & Fairtrade	£1.40	£1.60	£1.95

café cold drinks
Still Mineral Water (500ml bottle) Natural refreshment	£0.75
Soft Drinks (500ml bottle) Assorted carbonated drinks	£1.20
Fairtrade Juices Part of your 5 a day	£1.40

café snack
Flapjacks	£0.99
Muffins	£0.99 to £1.80
Pastries	from £1.25
Crisps	from £0.50
Confectionery	from £0.55
Speciality Cakes	from £1.90

café selection
Sandwiches	from £1.45
Panini	from £3.20

"Feeding your expectations"

COSTA SERVED HERE

Products offered subject to availability

Although chips are still a favourite, the food has changed from a menu of pies, stews and roasts with traditional English puddings.

Now there is a wide range of international dishes, vegetarian options and salad bars reflecting peoples' different backgrounds

[10] *Poly Passport Students' Union Handbook 1983/84*

A History of the University of Wolverhampton

Changing forms of Information Technology

Working Anywhere

The earliest computers were huge, specially housed and available only through specialist intermediaries. The WITCH (Wolverhampton Instrument for Teaching Computation from Harwell) computer of the 1950s, although advanced for its time, had less power than the modern devices we can carry in our pockets. It's arrival was so exciting that groups of people came to see it. When a mainframe IBM 1620 was bought in 1964 it got local press coverage. Kit was expensive and shared, WITCH came from Harwell, the Polytechnic bought second-hand equipment from Lanchester Polytechnic and donated their old IBM to Oswestry College. Despite various equipment upgrades these were centralised resources, with specialist data preparation staff working shifts. Its use in teaching was limited to instruction in computer applications and the developing Computer Science courses. Staff could use it for their research and consultancy but students had little access.

By the late 1980s the Computer Centre had multiple smaller units that could be more easily used. 'The service is provided using both microcomputers and central minicomputers. Over 600 microcomputers (Apricots, IBMs, BBCs and CP/M micros) are in use, and over 250 terminals are connected to a network of five Prime minicomputers. These are distributed in clusters of various sizes throughout the Polytechnic. Some are reserved for regular sessions devoted to specific courses, others are available for individual bookings so that students can carry out further work in their own time.' Eleven rooms equipped with microcomputers were available for booking. There was still a central data preparation service 'the results can only be as accurate as your own handwriting.'

By 1991 access to terminals had grown dramatically, the Polytechnic had over '1,500 IBM-compatible microcomputers, several hundred of which are linked into 22 local area networks' as well as 'large Prime computers with more than 5 Gbytes of disc storage', in its time it was as advanced as anything found elsewhere. From 1994 websites were developed. Students were allocated personal storage space on the University server from 2000. Wolverhampton developed its own in-house system – WOLF – the Wolverhampton On Line Framework to allow students to access materials on and off the campus at any time. Now the use of information technology in higher education is big business, dominated by global companies. There are now 5,000 PCs distributed around the sites. The smaller, cheaper and more portable computers have become, the more freedom we have in where to work. At first laptops could be plugged into the network. With the advent of wireless connections from 2000, access to resources is from anywhere on any site with ever smaller devices. Typically around 3,000 user-owned devices log-in each day.

and tastes. There is pride in this breadth of service and in all meals being cooked from fresh ingredients delivered daily. Students get to try dishes that are new to them. Catering staff enjoy discussing different culinary traditions with students. There can also be surprise as students, short of money and unfamiliar with local traditions, create new favourite fusions. A fried egg provides a topping for a bowl of rice or for a daily order of strawberry jam on toast as kitchen staff try not to refuse a request.

People working in the catering outlets recognise the value of these places as informal areas where students can relax, away from the pressures of the formal teaching areas. They also see them as places where people from different backgrounds can mix in ways that would not be possible outside the University. The only down-side to spending time in cafes and bars is that it usually involves spending money which many do not have. So people find other ways to come together, sometimes capturing spaces for different ends as when conversations take off in toilets or the quiet of the library gives way to the hum of socialising. The distinction between social and working space has been gradually eroded by the use of electronic access to resources. There are now computers in cafes and food and drink in libraries.

Some forms of studying require concentration, quiet and a degree of solitude. Prospective landlords were told in an early Polytechnic leaflet that students need 'good conditions of study… the bedroom if it is large enough or a separate sitting time where there would be no interruptions'. Such conditions would have seemed a luxury to past generations of part-time students and possibly still are today for many home based and mature students. Group work, however, requires other people and talking, leading to the creation of informal learning areas and a revolution in the use of libraries. Technology has changed their role from repositories of books and periodicals. As universities have become more 'customer' focused, students expect resources to be available at times convenient to themselves. Libraries have adapted continuously to respond to demand.

Libraries

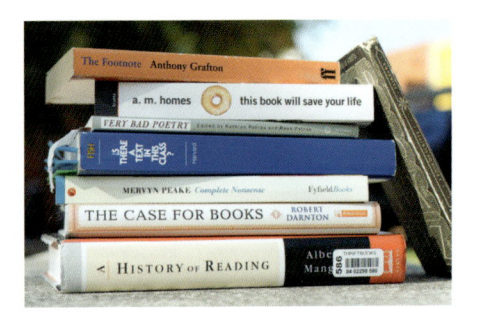

Different forms of 'libraries' were core to the rise of formal technical education in Wolverhampton. They passed their precious stock of books on to each other through the series of early institutions. For decades thereafter though libraries became one of the weakest aspects of the various colleges and especially the technical college. In 1912-13 the library had limited stock 'including many of the standard works dealing with the subjects included in the School Syllabus. It is hoped ultimately to cover every branch of the School curriculum. A writing table with stationery is provided'. Students who subscribed to the Union had free access, other students were expected to pay at least one shilling a year towards new books.

A report in 1950 describes the Technical College provision. 'The Library is housed in a light and gracious room on the first floor of the College, which is also used as a private study room: it can accommodate about 25 students at a time seated at small tables. A small store nearby is used at present as a book store and the library staff work in the Library itself.'[11] Students could not borrow books. By 1963 the stock had increased but the space had not, it was 'accommodated in a small room. The staff comprises a newly appointed qualified librarian and two part-time untrained female assistants. Staffing and accommodation are, at present, inadequate.'[12] Library funding was increased but access was still limited to weekdays. 'the Library is situated immediately over the main entrance of the College and is open at the following times during term – Monday - Thursday 9am to 9pm, Friday 9am to 7pm.' In 1969 the Students' Union pressed for weekend access, it was reluctantly agreed to open on Saturdays mornings for a trial period. Unfortunately only four or five students used it and it was promptly closed again.

Although small, this library proved useful to many people beyond the College staff and students. Part of the tradition of libraries is their accessibility to all which librarians defended. One debate over the status of the library offers information on its users. Defined as a 'public library' it qualified for a 10% discount on the purchase of new books. This status was under threat so the Librarian of the time kept a visitors book, between 1969 and 1975, to document use by people who were not part of the College and then Polytechnic. It shows a range of people from local industries, teachers, school children, scholars, students from other institutions and residents with a deep interest in a variety of subjects. Alongside all levels of study and research they visited to compile booklists for stocking their own libraries. Others came to see what was newly published in their field at a time of fewer publications and before the days of electronic access.

The move to Polytechnic status brought minimum standards for libraries imposed by the CNAA including on holdings, space and the ratio for students and seating. By 1971 the library had developed, although to what extent is dubious. One view is offered in student information 'The Polytechnic Library consists of the main library on Stafford Street, the Faculty of Art and Design library and the management library at Himley Hall... The Library does not exist merely to store books and to lend them. It offers as well a place to work, the daily newspapers, a wide range of periodicals, and a do-it-yourself coin in the slot photo-copying machine.' Another view appeared in a report of the same year which argued for resources, acknowledged developments but made the limitations clear.

'There can be no doubt that the Interim Library accommodation at present in use in the Polytechnic is a great improvement on the old Technical College Library accommodation. This is so evident to all who knew the old Library that there is a danger of our being too easily satisfied. New carpets and bright curtains can all too easily produce a complacency which prevents us from looking beyond to the comparative poverty of the bookstock. The satisfaction of showing visitors pleasant reading areas can blind us to the fact that the Library is understaffed and that consequently few services can be offered beyond processing and issuing and receiving books.'[13]

By 1976 libraries were open during the vacations but the facilities were still very poor.

In January 1977 the situation changed when a new four-floor building opened – the Robert Scott library on the Wolverhampton site. In one jump the Polytechnic moved from poor facilities to having some of the best, some said the best, physical library amongst the new polytechnics with space to develop extensive collections. In the same year the Teacher Training Colleges at Dudley and Compton Park became part of the Polytechnic, their library stock becoming available to all students. The Robert Scott

[11] *Report by H.M. Inspectors on Wolverhampton and Staffordshire College of Technology, November 1950*
[12] *Report by H.M. Inspectors on Wolverhampton and Staffordshire College of Technology, February 1963*
[13] *Library Development Plan, The Library Committee's Recommendations to the Academic Board*

library acted as the 'sun' around which various satellite specialist libraries on different sites revolved – the Art and Design Library, the Law Library, the Business Library, the Education and Humanities Library. Opening times had lengthened to twelve hours a day Monday to Friday and Saturday mornings. By now too machinery had increased with photocopiers, microform reader printers, VHS video machines and cassette players.[14]

Two decades later a major new development was built on the site of the Robert Scott Library, The Harrison Learning Centre was officially opened in 1999. This had computers, some of which could link to the internet allowing the first remote access to catalogues of other libraries, and handle electronic mail for registered users. There were databases held on CD-Roms, more sophisticated copiers, now card rather than coin operated. There were video cameras, video editing suites, satellite TV, overhead projectors, CD players, laser printers and video-conferencing facilities.

The internet and electronic storage has changed what libraries are for. Once they were the only place where people had access to shared books. In 1912-13 the Library contained about 600 volumes and 23 periodicals, by 1950 this had risen to about 4,500 volumes. In 1963 this had more than doubled to 11,000 volumes. In the first year of the Polytechnic the stock had risen to approximately 25,000 books but it was noted that this gave a ratio of 9.6 books per full-time equivalent student at the same time as Wulfrun College of Further Education had a ratio of 16:1 and the Library Association recommendation for Polytechnic Libraries was 75:1. Just before the mergers of 1977 the library had 82,000 books, 2,200 periodicals and growing collections including photographs and slides. Book stock takes space, at one stage the Scott library brought in rolling stacks to accommodate its growing collection. Site closures and mergers have brought additional stock, including the incorporation of nursing and midwifery specialist libraries. In response Dudley library was extended and large new libraries built at Walsall and Telford.

Book stock has nearly quadrupled in twenty years, from 105,000 in 1998 to 405, 417 in 2011 at the City Campus alone. The 23 periodicals of the early library have now become 20,513.

Faced with space problems another solution is stock deletion – a necessary adaptation for some and the destruction of a precious heritage for others. The pressure on space has increased the demand to replace physical books and journals with their electronic versions. Electronic publications allow the provision of a vast array of resources and allow access from anywhere. They are the preferred version for new material and journals but there are unresolved issues about the ways in which they are used by students from the ease of plagiarism to the question of the depth of engagement with 'the text' on the screen.

These changes have affected the work in libraries bringing new forms of specialism. Some old tasks have been mechanised, physical resources can be logged out and in by machine (176,618 issues in 2011). Some interactions have been distanced, a rota of staff can offer help through instant messaging and phone. The scale and complexity of resources has created areas of work. Library staff are the guides helping students to navigate an overwhelming wealth of information. It became necessary to teach students and staff how to use the resources through workshops, tours and Help Zones. They also have to deal with a wider range of issues as thousands of people come through the doors, 1,187,656 in the Harrison Centre alone during 2011-12. Concerns over lack of access have been solved by being open every day, all day until midnight. Twenty-four

[14] Polytechnic Student Guide 1988/89

A Small Town in a Big Conurbation

From Libraries to Learning Centres.

128

A History of the University of Wolverhampton

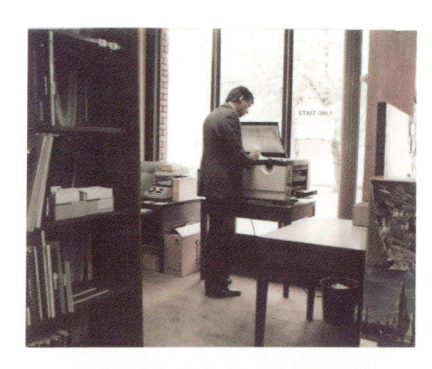

A Small Town in a Big Conurbation

130

hour access is currently being trialed. Today the University's libraries are still open to the public with anyone able to visit and work in them and, for a fee of £35 per year, borrow from them.

Places to Live

The early colleges catered mainly for local or regional students who did not require residential accommodation. The exceptions were those colleges deliberately founded to serve students from further afield. Custom-built, segregated halls had existed at the Dudley College of Education from its outset in 1908. The National Foundry College, after 1945, drew its students from the whole of the country and internationally.

National Foundry College Residential House study and lounge

They were required to stay in the two houses provided for the duration of their course.

As the Technical College developed its regional role and looked towards a national one, the first student and staff hostel was opened in 1965. Brinsford Lodge was a collection of single-storey huts organised around a central block. It had been built during the 1939-45 war to house the workforce of an armament factory. After the war it was used as a men's residential college with courses for demobilising forces personnel. In the 1950s it was used to train Malayan teachers preparing for independence from the UK in 1957. In 1964 the College took it over as accommodation for 250 students in individual bedrooms.[15] Each block held around a dozen students and, in addition to the bedrooms and bathrooms, provided minimal cooking and laundry facilities. Blocks for women and men were segregated with rules prohibiting movement between the two. There was a dining hall, common room, two televisions and a quiet study room in the central block with a gym and tennis courts on site. Parties at weekends could be arranged with bands and a bar, and frequently were. The Lodge closed in 1982, amidst opposition from students, by which time modern hostels had been built closer to the main Polytechnic site.

Part-way through the 1973-4 academic year the Polytechnic opened a newly constructed self-catering hostel, Randall Lines House, named after a local Director of Education. Demand outstripped supply, in 1975 the Students' Union was appealing in the local press for people to take in students at the beginning of the academic year. In October there was a 'sleep-out' demonstration in Wolverhampton to protest at lack of rooms. There was also a 'rent strike' in 1975 to try and force the Polytechnic to reduce rents.

The integration of the Teacher Training Colleges in 1977 brought their

[15] Brinsford Lodge: The Story of a Malayan Teachers' College in England, 1955 – 1964, Brinsford Alumni Association Malaysia, 2009

A Small Town in a Big Conurbation

University Halls of Residence

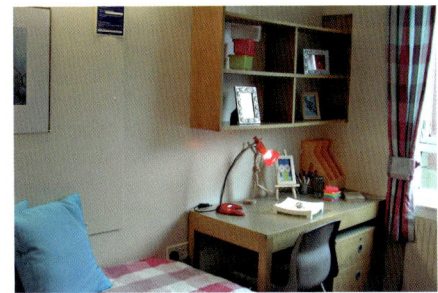

132

residential places into the Polytechnic. The Technical Teachers' College at Compton Park housed 144 students, Dudley College of Education 370. In the same year more accommodation, Lomas Street, opened at the Wolverhampton site offering 310 places. By 1980 therefore, despite being unable to offer accommodation to all students wanting it, the Polytechnic could claim that Wolverhampton had more hall places than any other Polytechnic of the time.[16]

What is considered essential for student accommodation has changed in time – from a basic bedroom with a bathroom and toilet shared by 12 people to en-suite bedsits. What was once high quality is now marketed as 'economy'. Shared television rooms and film shows are replaced by limitless entertainment through wireless networks in all halls. The first purpose – built hostel was a five storey building with 285 rooms clustered in corridors of 12 bedrooms with a communal bathroom and kitchen. The next design was organised in nine smaller buildings with 310 bedrooms in clusters of seven people sharing one bathroom, toilet and kitchen. Later developments show a further reduction in occupancy density. At Walsall Campus 106 rooms were separated into six bedrooms per corridor with communal bathrooms and kitchens. The newest accommodation offers bedrooms incorporating a small bathroom. On the main Campus there are 461 of these rooms in 13 blocks, still organised in corridors of seven sharing a kitchen but now with a communal seating area. This lounge and kitchen space shared by seven people is also offered in the Student Village at Walsall with en-suite rooms for 338 students. The Telford Halls of Residence offer the lowest occupation density with corridors of four to six students sharing the kitchen with en-suite bedrooms for 100. Women and men now routinely share corridors unless requesting a room in a segregated building.

Prices of University accommodation have risen, in part because of inflation but also in real terms, though the quality has also improved. One important change has been the ending of the system which allowed overseas students to be charged higher rent. In 1979 they were paying between 80-150% more, although gaining some additional catering in some instances. Today the prices do not vary by student but according to quality, with an en-suite room costing 40% more than an 'economy' one.

Some of the older hostels were lost with the closure of Dudley and Compton Park sites. The ground floor of the oldest block has been converted to a nursery for 50 children of students and staff. By 2012 there was also competition from privately built accommodation blocks. However it is still the case that a minority of students are residential. Most live in the wider conurbation. Part-time and mature students are more likely to be local people with job and family commitments in the area. In one survey over 80% of the University's students lived in their own or their parents' home, with 71% living within 20 miles of the University outside term time. Others rent in the locality.

This combination of sites in different towns and students living across the conurbation presents difficulties for organised social activities, but they have always been overcome. By 1963 the elements of social life were in place even with restricted facilities.

> *It is not easy in a college with a high proportion of part-time students to establish and maintain a wide variety of social, cultural and intellectual pursuits. Student association is possible in the common room which serves also*

---

[16] H.Smith, The Origins and History of the Polytechnic Wolverhampton, Wolverhampton.

as a games room and this provision is well used. Several sports teams thrive, and there is mixed social activity through regularly arranged dances and local charities benefit from the annual Rag Day.[17]

Town Events

The tradition of 'Rag' encompasses social event, sport, street drama and community action. The term is reputed to go back to the nineteenth century when affluent university students collected rags for the poor. Local 'Rag' events started in the 1940s, an opportunity to both raise money and engage in various stunts. A press report describes the impact:

> Between 400 and 500 students in fancy dress were let loose on Saturday in the streets of Wolverhampton, demanding money for charity. The annual 'rag' of students of the Wolverhampton and Staffordshire Technical College was organised on greater lines than before. A larger number of decorated vehicles, about 30 in all, took part in the afternoon parade through the town. In the evening the customary torchlight procession was held… the torches were thrown on to a pile to become a bonfire. By special arrangement, Wolverhampton fire brigade was on hand to put it out.

In later years the nature of 'rags' produced the occasional suspension and some conflict with surrounding residents and Councils. In 1967 Wolverhampton Council refused to allow street collections during 'Rag', effectively cancelling it. On its return in 1969 it was billed as a last chance. A press report describes a week including a football match between men and women, a sponsored walk to Birmingham several races around the town – on tricycles, on stretchers, a three-legged run, a relay race and a chariot race from Walsall to Wolverhampton. There was a regatta on the park's lake, kissing for cash, 'drink a pub dry' and eat as much as possible contests. If it all got too much things could be thrown at students in stocks. In the evenings there was jazz, a Rag Ball, a concert, a dance at the Art College, a barn-dance at Brinsford and a final dance at the College.

> Rag is a time when steam may be let off, but always bearing in mind the true purpose of the whole thing, that is to collect money for needy local charities, who in many cases, rely on our small contribution each year to keep going. You students, by collecting money on Rag Day, for these charitable organisations of Wolverhampton, can show your appreciation to the town for the hospitality that it has extended to you during your academic year. The previous highest total being just under £1,000.[18]

But enthusiasm was not high 'If you don't bother coming then the party isn't going to be much good… If people just take the trouble to become involved in Rag it will

[17] Report by H.M. Inspectors on Wolverhampton and Staffordshire College of Technology, February 1963
[18] Wolverhampton College of Technology Students' Union Handbook 1967/68, p.16

A History of the University of Wolverhampton

be really great.[19] 'Rag' continued for many more years, Dudley 'Rag' raised £8,200 for charities in 1982, but fizzled out, although other forms of community involvement have gone from strength to strength.

Formal social events were once a part of the academic year. An annual soirée for students and teachers had been started as early as 1889. In 1904 there were three annual socials – a gathering of current students, a reunion for past ones and an excursion. The nature of these occasions is indicated by the organisers' purchases, chessmen in 1906, playing cards in 1910. In 1907 ball room powder, pins and rosettes cost £4.4 shillings, possibly regretted as the event made a loss of £4.4 shillings. The Annual Social Gathering of 1908 provided whist prizes of 12 shillings 3 pence. A formal end of year Ball continued until recent times and the Students' Union had frequent gigs and dances.

[19] Wolverhampton Polytechnic Students Union Handbook 1971-72

135

The mood changed in the 1960s – from the paternalistic:

> *Approval was given for the sale of beer and cider at the Students' Union dance to be held on 5th March, 1966. Sales would be made by a licensed caterer and continuance of the scheme after 5th March would depend upon the Principal's being satisfied as to supervision and conduct at the Dances.*[20]

to a more recognisable and endearing style:

> *ENT '68 – all you new Hippies arriving at College... Tech. Rave-Ins. These take place in the Main Hall at College each and every Saturday night... For the last three Freak-Outs we have had such names as "The Artwoods" "The Eyes of Blue" and the one and only "John Mayall"... Each year, on the last Friday in January, we hold our Annual Ball and last year over 1,400 people came ... to see Zoot, the Zombies, John Mayall and the 'N Betweens, plus three jazz bands, at the Civic Hall, where we raved non-stop for six hours.*[21]

The final days of the College of Technology were seen out with a Ball:

> *With two top pop groups, The Who and the Love Affair, last night's annual Wolverhampton College of Technology students' ball was a 1,500 sell out before the doors opened. It was the last annual ball to be held by the college as such. Soon it is to be merged with the College of Art into the new Wolverhampton Polytechnic.*[22]

All around these staged events there were groups of people gathering. From the first decade of the 1900s there have been college debating and dramatic societies. By the 1960s students had formed an Overseas Students' Association and a United Nations Students Association, and by 1971 a new Flying Club and the Mechanics Society had negotiated concessions from local aviation businesses and garages.[23] The Polytechnic years saw a huge growth in activity. In 1983 the Students' Union could report over 90 societies. Some illustrate colourfully the changing nature of the student body. The rise in postgraduate students is apparent in the inception of a Post-Graduate Society. The national and ethnic diversity of the Polytechnic population shows in the range of international societies. Asian, Chinese, Latin American, Iranian, Malaysian, Nigerian and Zimbabwean. There was still room for the sharing of personal passions in the Railway, Amateur Radio, Ornithological, Motor, Motor Cycle and War Games Societies. By 2013 gaming had several groups, although electronic based. Baking has become a social group rather than a part of the early core

[20] Joint Education Committee February 1966-7
[21] Wolverhampton College of Technology Students' Union Handbook 1967/68
[22] Express and Star 25th Jan 1969.
[23] Wolverhampton Polytechnic Students Union Handbook 1971-72

curriculum. Other nationalities and ethnicities are represented with the Palestine, Saudi, Nigerian and Brit-Asia Societies.

The Theatres

There have also been drama groups since the early 1900s. When the Music Section was created in 1944 it was unique in technical colleges and became a central part of college life. By 1971 the Music and Drama group were recruiting for choral singing; classical guitar, instrumental classes and ensembles; musical documentaries; multi-media concerts; poetry and jazz; play production; improvised and experimental drama; stage management and design, travelling theatre; pocket opera as well as arranging visits to regional and national productions.[24]

Early performances were in rigged up classrooms and halls, then the new lecture theatre. The lack of space did not hamper action. Arts Societies have operated as 'dramatec', Studio 61 and PolyArts. Dance and contemporary dance companies have formed and musicians have come together around folk, jazz/funk, rock and alternative music and the ukulele. Student Union groups put on annual revues, performed classic dramas, political works and their new plays. 'One Hundred Years Ago' a new play about the workers of the Black Country based on a Factories Inspectors Report of the appalling working conditions at a local firm was written to mark the TUC Centenary in 1968.

Staff and students have played in instrumental groups, orchestras, bands and ensembles. Choirs, orchestras and dance groups put on joint performances. Art students created costumes for productions, their final shows were open to all and their fashion shows were covered extensively in the local press.

Literary and poetry magazines have published new work. For decades

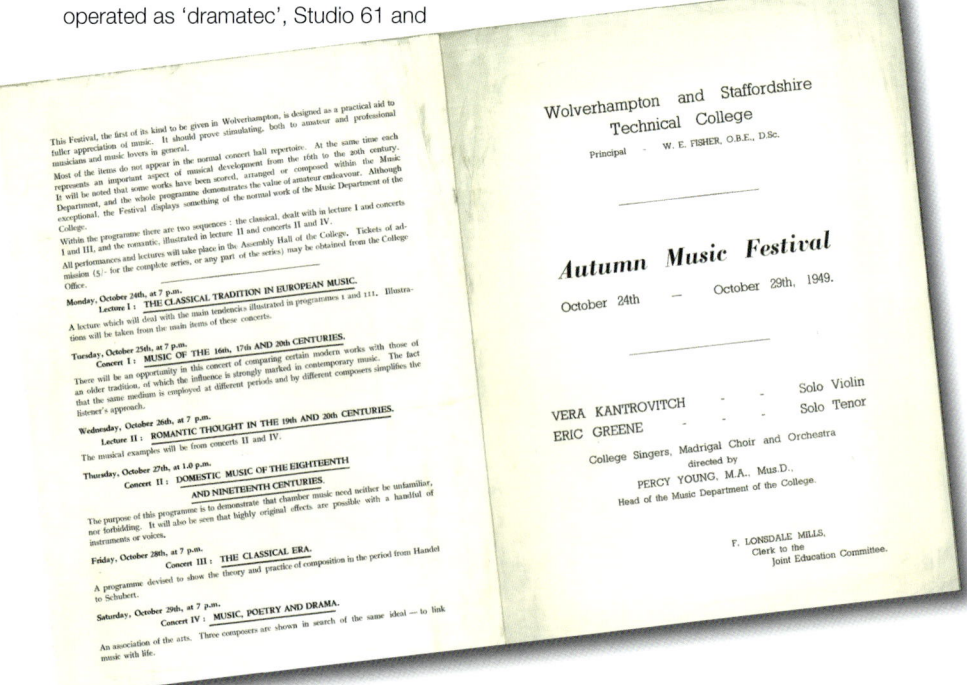

[24] Wolverhampton Polytechnic Students Union Handbook 1971-72

A Small Town in a Big Conurbation

From the frocks of the 50s in the Dress Parade to the cool chic of the 60s Fashion Show.

fashion parade 1960

THE DRESS PARADE

The University's Arena Theatre is used by students and locals

there were seasons of free lunchtime programmes. These one hour sessions offered an eclectic mix of music, poetry and recitals. Staff and students played music, put on shows and sang together. Local orchestras, choirs and drama companies put on their work. Young musicians from local schools received encouragement and an audience.

In the Polytechnic era the Arena Theatre became a venue for student performance and place of entertainment for the town, attracting national and international touring companies and musicians. Students with elements of performance in their curriculum had a stage. Facilities have stepped up another gear with the The Performance Hub opening in 2011 on Walsall Campus. The ethos is the same, to provide a venue for the area not just the University. It offers a programme of events and facilities for musicians, dramatists and dancers, a theatre, studios and two recording studios. This is in stark contrast to the technological limitations that are passing from memory. In 1908 the organisers of the Annual Soiree paid £3 for 'hire of Cinematograph'. The College 'Sound Film Sub-Committee' decided in September 1937 to buy a Bell & Howell Sound Film Projector for £328.16s.9d. Sadly this was found not to be 'in accordance with the required specification' and the December meeting opted instead for 'a Bell & Howell silent film projector for use in the College (cost £51.8.6)'. Film shows were put on in Colleges and hostels, major entertainment events before we could watch a film anywhere, anytime.

A Small Town in a Big Conurbation

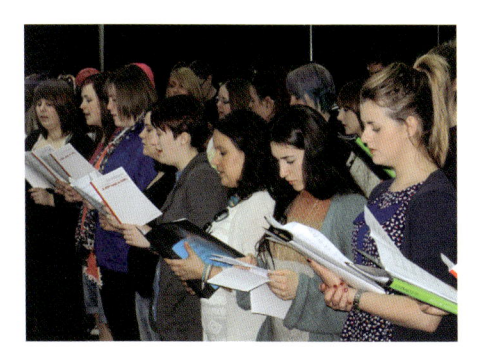

A History of the University of Wolverhampton

A Sporting Life

Sport is done for enjoyment. When it becomes 'organised' other elements are overlaid. In the early days of the Technical College physical training for all students was timetabled for once a week. Now at least it is voluntary! Sports facilities have grown from a time at a borrowed sports field in 1932 to the current Sports Centre with a 12-court multi-activity sports hall, a six-lane floodlit athletics track, all-weather floodlit pitch, throws and jumps area, dance studio and swimming pool. This Centre became an official training base for the 2012 Olympics.

With or without pitches, tracks, gyms and pools, sport has been keenly pursued by students individually and through local leagues. In 1950, sports clubs included Association Football, Athletics, Badminton, Cricket, Fencing, Hockey, Rambling (including camping and climbing), Rugby Football and Swimming. A Staff Sports and Social Society was also active. Even in borrowed facilities the Union staged Inter-College Sports meets, the Soccer Club and Rugby Club became successful although pleas for a greater turnout of supporters had to be made. By the end of the 1960s even more clubs had formed, Mountaineering, Pot-Holing, Cross-country and Road Running, Table Tennis, Tennis, Ten-Pin Bowling and the Wolverhampton Welsh Society which was essentially a Rugby Club. Basket Ball and Judo were added the following year.

The lack of facilities must have been restricting because as soon as they improved there was a flurry of activity. By 1983 there were sports halls on three sites offering squash courts, swimming pools, tennis courts, playing fields and pitches, athletics tracks, gymnasium and weight training rooms.[25] New clubs sprang to life, some, like Frisbee, of the moment. Others were more durable, Aikido, Karate, Gym & Trampoline, Snooker, Netball, Volleyball, Squash, Water Polo and Canoe. The Students' Union now owned three minibuses which clubs could use for away matches. New clubs could go further afield for Wind Surfing, Sailing, Hang Gliding, Skydiving, Horse Riding, Hiking and Sailing, it is not clear where the Ski Club went.

Staff (usually, but not always, the men) joined in with everything from team games to running along the local tow paths. Sport inverted hierarchies – the students played and beat the staff, an academic team lost to the manual staff in five-a-side football. In the early 1980s, some joined a Deputy Director in lunchtime runs only to find he was better than they thought. Now there are new groups playing American Football, the Ski Club has been replaced by Snowsports, Kickboxing and Cheerleading have a presence and an old favourite is back with Ulimate Frisbee. For all these events, activities, outings, fixtures and performances to succeed, people need to know about them.

[25] Poly Passport Students Union Handbook 1983/84

Let the People Sing

Percy M. Young was appointed director of music in 1944. He would quickly establish himself as a prolific author and musicologist, a well known figure in British classical music for nearly six decades. Having a music department run by such a commanding figure was a bold move and one which the Education Department's Inspectors found puzzling, suggesting it be reviewed when Young left. In the event Young stayed until 1966 when he retired to work freelance.

Young energetically expressed the best of the post war social democratic ethos. In one part of his life he was broadcasting regularly on the BBC and meeting with the great British composers, and many of the international ones, of his time. In the other part he was rooted in the West Midlands using his college to reach out into the community. Young once wrote that 'English operas should have their premieres in Wigan, where, we believe, people have a capacity for enjoyment and criticism unimpaired by the decrees of fashion.' To people in Wolverhampton he brought music, musicians and composers. But he was also passionate about football, writing histories of it and eventually the centenary history of Wolverhampton Wanderers. His commitment was not just intellectual. He served for a period as a Labour Councillor, was a Head of the Community Relations Council, sat on various local health boards and was a School Governor. Probably no figure since has had the same capacity to link the College/University with the local, national and international communities of their time.

He not only encouraged the development of music as a subject in its own right but also as part of the general studies programmes. In the late 1950s, reported one of his junior part-time lecturers, 'over a hundred students have chosen music; they listen to it and discuss it in groups of ten and twenty'. If not every student appreciated this, others left with an enriched experience. One reported that his encounter with Bartok had 'improved my social outlook tremendously, and my love of music is much more sincere and deep.' For others music might simply provide a moment of calm and reflection, 'these lessons had a more practical use for me, helping me to relax between the two engineering lessons'.

Music and choirs brought staff together from across different occupations as this note suggests,

'The John Kempson Singers were formed in 1972 from staff of The Polytechnic and invited members of the general public. They now have a high reputation locally for their interpretations of 20th Century Past Songs, Sacred Music and Madrigals. ... John Kempson, Department of Production Engineering, the founder, studied the cello and chamber music at the Birmingham School of Music and has played in festivals and as a member of the City of Birmingham Symphony Orchestra. David Rendell, of the Department of Physical Sciences, was, whilst an undergraduate, assistant organist at The University Church Oxford. … Richard Anderson, also on the staff of the Department of Physical Sciences, took up the oboe whilst still at school and played with the Devon Youth Orchestra. Later he was a member of the Bristol University Orchestra. Philip Bradfield is the warden of Randall Lines House and before coming to Wolverhampton directed singers and instrumental ensembles at Edinburgh University and Leicester Polytechnic. He is particularly interested in Renaissance and Early Baroque music. Martin Hill is on the staff of the Maintenance Unit and has a high reputation locally as a solo tenor and chorister. '

Music and dance remains part of the University's work in the School of Sport, Performing Arts and Leisure. It was fitting that at the end of 2011 the University's new Performance Hub was opened by Gareth Malone who had become famous through his TV programmes showing the potential of ordinary people to come together to make astonishing choral music – something seen and practised by Young in his years at Wolverhampton.

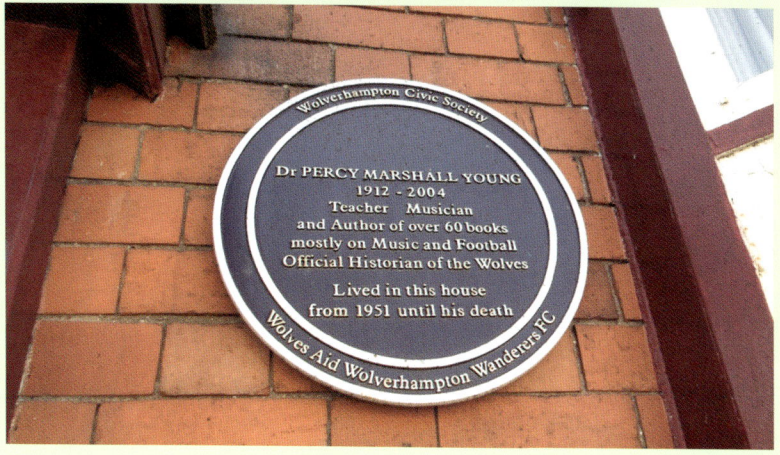

The Town Criers

In any large population keeping people up to date with current and forthcoming news and events can present problems. For a brief period the Students' Union broadcast a radio station. In the University today a range of electronic means make it simpler. Students and staff can post on social networking sites, message, tweet, email and create electronic newsletters. Societies and groups with shared interests create websites and forums. This was not always the case, surviving copies of print newsletters testify to the dedication of small groups of people struggling to keep communication alive.

Staff and student journalists reported on debates, complaints, developments and sports fixtures. They publicised forthcoming social and academic events, offered advice and satirical comment. All this was accompanied by pleas for contributions, irritation at criticism of content (unaccompanied by offers of assistance) and inadequate budgets. Paper still matters – including flyers, advertisements, leaflets and posters competing for attention. A corporate ethos dictates that notices should be on notice boards. The need to be seen dictates they should go where they are noticed. There has been a continuing battle over what is private College/University space controlled by the authorities and what is public space. Today this extends to cyberspace.

This battle has been sharper because of the presence of the School of Art and Design. Its walls are still more chaotically adorned than other parts of the University. How could it be otherwise when a major part of art in the last century has been to challenge elitist views. 'The streets are our brushes, the squares our palettes' Mayakovsky had declared at the start of the twentieth century. The sculptor Gabo said in the Realist Manifesto that, 'Art should attend us everywhere that life flows and acts – at the bench, at the table, at work, at rest, at play; on working days and holidays; at home and on the road'. Today street artists declare the world as their canvass.

A Small Town in a Big Conurbation

The Students' Union and University now produce electronic newssheets

146

The University has its own public art – its architects thought that its very buildings were an expression of this. There are sculptures and monuments. But there is also an official 'street art' on the School of Art Building where a huge light installation flashes out in the darkness as a beacon to the city or, say some cynics – as a calling sign for a passing alien spaceship.

A Mini Welfare System

Whilst such a large, busy, purposeful place can be exciting it can also be intimidating and difficult to navigate successfully. There has been a national trend to develop support services to help students cope with academic and social problems. Wider access to university has meant students grappling with a greater range of difficulty. The mode of study has been altered through various forms of part-time and modular study, meaning people are students for longer. Access is easier for students with external commitments but juggling jobs, study and looking after others piles on the pressure. Money can be a major preoccupation. With large numbers of students living away from home and country, so a greater complexity of academic, financial, work, legal and social problems has grown. The range of potential reasons for non-completion has increased. Assisting students through their studies is important to universities. Today too student retention, satisfaction and completion are necessary to institutional income and survival. In response a range of personal and study support services have developed. Specialist support contrasts with diminishing contact with academic and administrative staff. A combination of a decrease in the staff: student ratio and a rise in administrative workload detracts from the time and energy academic staff have for students. Technological developments have also reduced face-to-face contact with academic and administrative staff.

At the University of Wolverhampton new students can register on-line and thereafter undertake all administrative and financial tasks through the University website. Problems can be dealt with through electronic help desks. Course information and materials are managed through electronic systems, including communication with staff and peers. These are very efficient systems which allow large numbers of people to process large numbers of tasks, but they are also impersonal.

Student 'welfare' in its widest sense is one of the tasks of the Students' Union, which enlarged its own Advice and Support services in the early Polytechnic days. It was kept at arms length from the official services, in order to be a more effective advocate for students in conflict with the Polytechnic.

> *The aim of the Advisory Services is to provide a comprehensive range of information and advice covering the needs and problems arising from and particular to, the students of the Polytechnic... The Advisory Officers each have a specialisation, eg. accommodation, careers but are also available for general counselling and advice, so that students who have come to know one officer can seek their advice on a quite different area.*[26]

Independence from the University is still emphasised in what is now 'The Students' Union Advice & Support Centre' which is described as offering advice and case work in housing, academic, money and debt problems as well as providing support for international students.

The variety of student support services which developed in the University of Wolverhampton indicates the importance ascribed to them. A range of institution wide services offer practical advice, help with studying and with personal difficulties.

A College Chaplaincy was formally established in 1966 with Geoff Wynne the Chaplain being a point of stability for five decades.[27] The Chaplaincy team were drawn from different Christian denominations, Anglican, Methodist and Roman Catholic. One member of the team would be available in a designated room each dinner-time. By the early 1980s a new Chaplaincy Centre had been built at the Wolverhampton site, staffed by male clergy from denominations of the Christian church. These have now been joined by a woman Methodist, a Rabbi and an Imam. It has always been stressed that the Chaplaincy team is available to people of all faith and none. They organise lectures and discussion groups on questions of ethics and spirituality,

[26] Wolverhampton Polytechnic Students Union Handbook 1971-72
[27] Wolverhampton College of Technology, Administrative Board minutes, 22 Sept 1966

encouraging debate. A room has been set aside on the busy main site for reflection and prayer, which can be used by everyone. By 1983 a long running Students' Union Christian Society was joined by a Jewish and an Islamic Society. There are now ten faith groups including Hindu and Sikh groups.

Big sites, lots of people, all sorts of activities – wonderful and yet it can be frightening. The bigger and busier the site, the more intimidating it can be 'To most new people the Poly seems big and confusing and people seem to bustle past knowing exactly what they're doing'. One student explained 'arriving at a college absolutely new to ones-self is a terrifying experience'. going on to describe not knowing what to do or where anything is and possibly wearing the wrong clothes.[28]

The University provides support services but that does not mean that students will use them. They may choose to avoid them, miss information publicising them or not have access at suitable times.

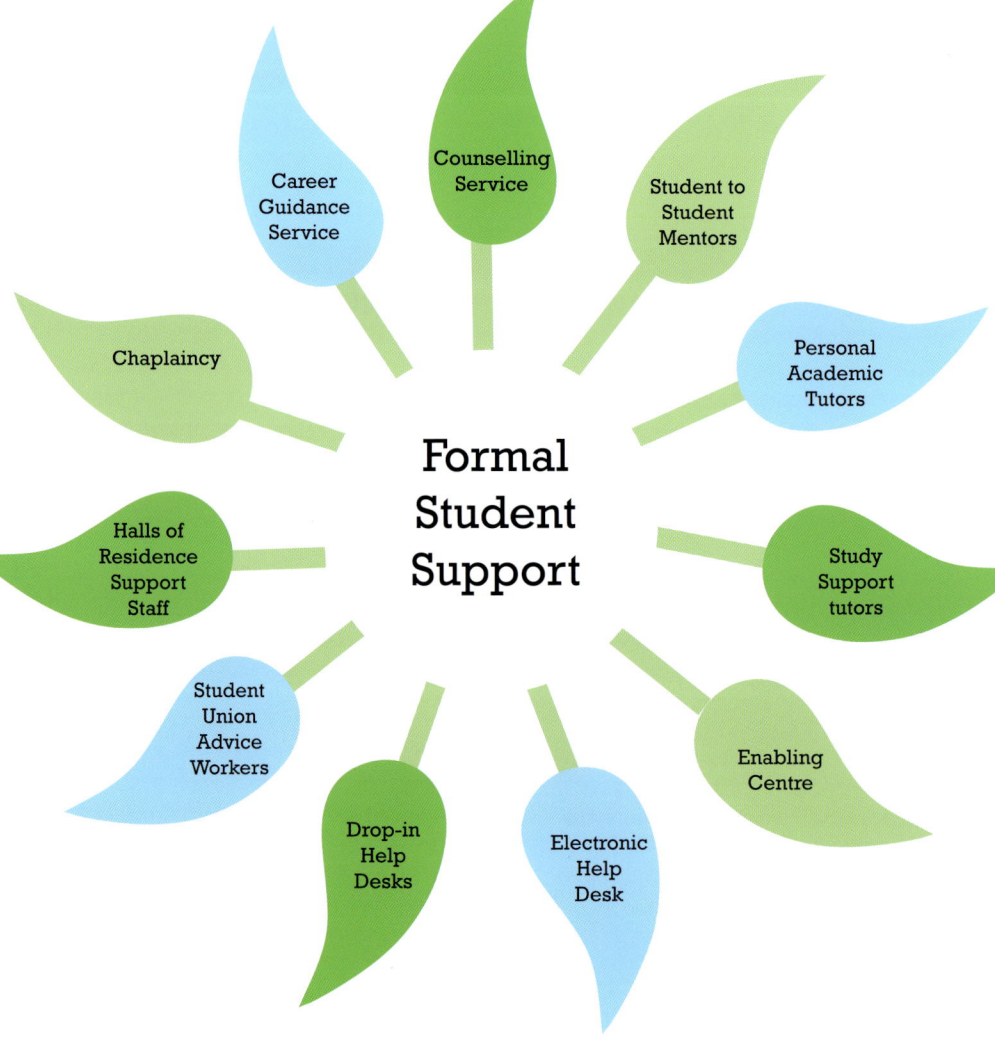

Formal Student Support

- Counselling Service
- Career Guidance Service
- Student to Student Mentors
- Chaplaincy
- Personal Academic Tutors
- Halls of Residence Support Staff
- Study Support tutors
- Student Union Advice Workers
- Enabling Centre
- Drop-in Help Desks
- Electronic Help Desk

[28] 'Marble' Vol 4(2) No.25 'Freshers Point of View' and Poly Passport Students Union Handbook 1983/84

Students most needing help may have most difficulty seeking it. Multi-site universities too have particular difficulties. Fortunately, alongside the formal services, an informal network functions with ever present help from caretaking, catering and security staff. They work in the public areas of the University, across all sites, 24 hours-a-day, 7 days-a-week. They answer questions, lots of questions, any question. Information derived from an intimate 'on-the-ground' knowledge of the institution and from generations of students is joined with availability. They can chat, offer comfort, reassurance and encouragement. They become familiar and they are always there.

The Transport System

One of the first things a student has to work out is how to get around. The Polytechnic developed as a multi-site operation involving, at its peak, five campuses within a 15 mile radius of Wolverhampton, the distance between the two furthest being some 25 miles. Inevitably there had to be a degree of specialisation by campus. But the desire to integrate courses and student life also required a degree of movement between sites and common facilities. Brinsford Lodge hostel five miles from the town centre meant daily coach services were needed to transport students to and from the main campus in the centre of Wolverhampton. This need for people to move around led to the development of an internal transport system which used local coach firms and then University owned coaches. There is now a shuttle bus service operating in a continuous loop round each site, free to staff and students.

Private transport creates the problem of where to leave it. In the early years this centered on the provision of bike racks but as transport changed so did the difficulties. A university has been described as a group of staff fighting over car parking. This problem is not new. There were complaints from a student about lack of car parking in 1966. Parking affected the planning of new Polytechnics buildings. 'Stage VII will not be approved unless we can assure him that we can provide the car spaces to make up for the deficiency of spaces in Stage I. This will probably mean putting the building on stilts.'[29] Not everybody obeyed the rules 'There had been a disturbing rumour that people other than the college staff had been using the college car park. The Chairman said that this would have to be investigated.'[30] By 1988 the Polytechnic management stated that students would not be offered parking places. Few staff have an allocated parking space which continues to be a concern, particularly for lower paid staff for whom car parking charges are a real financial problem. The sites outside of town centres had car parks and this was a factor in decisions about where to work. Today the many thousands who come each day battle for 2,100 car parking spaces, 1,674 for non-residents, cursing those who get there first and looking enviously at the reserved spaces – a victim role not shared by the thousands of others who use public transport.

Opening Up, Clearing Up and Keeping Safe

Someone has to get up early to open the doors, turn off the alarms and check the heating and once, stoke the boilers. They usually do so un-thanked but if they did not do it nothing could happen. This is part of the Cinderella world of the small town – taken for granted. Keeping open 24 hours-a-day, all year means staff working in shifts, as some leave for the night others arrive. This demands commitment too. Cleaners on the hilly Dudley site once put socks over their boots to trudge through the snow to get in to clean the rooms of the rest of the staff. It is an onerous task. Today the multiple sites have 42 residential and non-residential buildings all of which have to be cleaned and maintained. In them people generate 1,500 tons of waste a year. Today only the clinical and construction waste does not yet have a further life. 7.5% of the rest is used for heating and 79% recycled. Large public areas and social venues have to be supplied. Gardens, grounds, pitches and those car parks are kept in good condition. All the activities of this small town happen in spaces that will then be used for something else. That means staff setting up and clearing away – continuously. There are only glimpses in the records, new uniforms when war time rationing was relaxed, extra pay for a caretaker for a Sunday event in the 1950s. Yet the scale of activity shows they were there and what they did was vital to the life of the University.

Alongside the desire to foster a sense of belonging and relaxation, a tension exists as the security of people and property is maintained. Night time security used to be one man and his dog, no longer.[31] In an earlier age too the Students' Union brought in outside security staff to help:

Being slap bang in the middle of a town like Wolverhampton, and all three of our sites offering very cheap entertainment with regular late bars all means that we have to take every precaution to ensure the safety of our members. Having learned from bitter experience and with the Polytechnic reluctant

---

[29] *Administrative Board - Minutes of meeting ,21 Feb 1969 2*
[30] *Administrative Board - Minutes of meeting, 18 Jan 1968, 6(c))*
[31] *H.Smith, The Origins and History of the Polytechnic Wolverhampton, Wolverhampton.*

to help us, we have engaged the services of a local firm, KLM Security. They are always recognisable, they are the policeman-like objects in uniform – but I'm sure you will all find them infinitely more amiable… Remember they are there only for your protection. [32]

Now the University has its own security staff in police style uniforms, linked to City police by radio. These are the people who enable learning centres to stay open until late and who staff twenty-four hour facilities. They control access through the use of electronic gates, ID cards and CCTV cameras, some of the three million said to exist in Britain. They watch over the buildings, the car parks, the grounds and the playing fields. They guard the population. Without this work the University could not open and operate, none of the activities of this small town could happen. Yet these people are the least recorded. They often function as first responders, having to think on their feet as they deal with people in distress combining security, community support and comfort.

The Town Museum

You have to ask the way to it. Only a few people, unofficial volunteers go there. It has no curator. But when you ask 'who do you think are?' you need its precious resources.

Of course before you get there you can ask people. Organisations are said to have memories but they do not. It is people in organisations who have memories. These people carry the past into the present. That can be irritating, memories are fallible, stories gain in the retelling and no one should try to live in the past. But people with experiences and memories matter.

They are the people you first go to if you want to know how to do something or why things are done the way they are. They are points of stability in a crisis because they have been there before and so take things more in their stride. For good measure they may also know where the bodies are buried. (Hopefully not, readers of *Things My Girlfriend and I Have Argued About* will say, under a library extension).

But we also need the written records of an organisation and its place in the world - but which written records? There is a mass of official documentation that we have drawn on here – reports from inside and out, surveys, books of press cuttings. But these tell you only about part of the story. The academics who wrote leave their tiny marks for the future but what of everyone else – where are they? Of course there is the ephemera. Beware that word for this is what goes first into the dustbin - it may be the bigger story. The programmes of dances and socials, the tickets for events, a letter trapped in the leaves of an old volume of minutes, comments hurriedly scribbled in the margins, the group photographs from another time. This too is the story and some of our pictures try to capture it.

But the half hidden museum has a problem. No one gives much to it anymore – 'it is all on the internet' people say. But what is there is only accessible as long as the sites are accessible and with the press of a button they too, and their precious heritage is gone. In the museum, before the volunteers saved them, some of the earlier records were eaten by mice. Now for a time they are safe but fragile. But who is protecting and caring for the internet records of this or any other organisation? These records too are part of our story, they may be your story too.

---

[32] Poly Passport Students Union Handbook 1983/84

Chapter Six

The World Beyond the Open Doors

OUT·OF·DARKNESS·COMETH·LIGHT

How does a university relate to the wider world? At different times, different students and staff have come to the University of Wolverhampton and its forerunner colleges. They have developed themselves, created things, generated new ideas and then moved on, ultimately across the world and sometimes beyond it. William Willis graduated from the Wolverhampton and Staffordshire Technical College in 1951 with an ONC and an HNC, after two years of full-time study financed by an armed forces grant. Having worked locally for a few years he followed his sister, a GI bride, to California where he soon began working for the world's largest observatory telescope maker, drawing 'a lot on the knowledge I had gained in my course'. From there he went to NASA where he 'worked on the Galileo, Mars Observer and Hubble space telescopes'. 'I was a specialist engineer for the shutter and filter mechanisms that were on the wide planetary camera. It was this camera that took many of the famous Hubble pictures you see today'.

But the impact that a university has is also measured in the historical accumulation of smaller stories which together feed into local, regional, national and global developments. Like a stone dropped into a pond the biggest splash is close at hand but the ripples move out in widening circles. These ripples are formed of economic, cultural, social and civic influences. The stone that creates them itself has different sides – the university as a complex organisation and business, the university as a generator of knowledge and ideas, and the university as a transformer of people.

Location, Location, Location

Location matters and location tells a story. Wolverhampton, like many new universities, is self-consciously urban. The traditional universities were not – deliberately created in smaller provincial towns. Some of the new universities of the 1950s tried to continue this tradition with greenfield locations. The physical detachment suggests a story and so does its rejection in favour of the city. When nearby Birmingham University was being created, Joseph Chamberlain said, in 1898, that:

> *To place a university in the middle of a great industrial and manufacturing population is to do something to leaven the whole mass with higher aims and higher intellectual ambitions than would otherwise be possible to people engaged entirely in trading and commercial pursuits.[1]*

To have colleges and then a university located near to where people lived and worked in their hundreds of thousands spoke to a different ethos. This was the message in the creation of the new urban red brick universities in the late nineteenth century. Even so Birmingham University was then located in the leafier suburb of Edgbaston.

With its Technical College and Art School roots in the centre of an industrial city, a university like Wolverhampton did not have this luxury. This was not always appreciated as a positive element. In the early 1960s, the Labour Party argued that industrial towns like Wolverhampton needed a university but supporters on the local council thought that any location should be a new one, on the edge of the conurbation, perhaps in a stately home. 'Wrottesley Hall provided an ideal site' said one report and

---

[1] Quoted A. Briggs, 'Development in higher education in the United Kingdom. Nineteenth and Twentieth centuries', in W.R. Niblett ed., Higher Education. Demand and Response, London, 1969, p. 98

the writer Howard Jacobson would use the name 'Wrottesley Polytechnic' for his fictional account of Wolverhampton in the 1970s. Others proposed nearby Himley Hall and its estate. This had been one of the homes of the Dudley aristocratic dynasty with grounds designed in the eighteenth century by Capability Brown. Sold to the national Coal Board in 1945 it was then bought by Dudley and Wolverhampton Councils and was used by the Polytechnic for a time for its top level management courses. The current Walsall and Telford sites to an extent also reflect this ideal of a green, statelier campus within the urban environment, as did the Dudley and Compton Park sites before. But the major part of the University in Wolverhampton has historically developed at the centre of the town which was designated a city in 2000, some half a century after this status was first requested from the government of the day.

Developing a campus, initially for several thousand and then for many times that number, albeit on several sites, has been a major undertaking and the more so on the Wolverhampton site where growth has involved redevelopment, clearing old housing and old industrial units for new roads, buildings and car parks. Urban redevelopment led to Wolverhampton being encircled by a ring road which now splits the town centre campus. The building of the School of Art & Design in the late 1960s, on the north side, resulted in some local protests but initiated an ongoing movement of the main campus northwards as the area was developed commercially, by the local football club and the Asda supermarket chain.

In Wolverhampton the new Technical College buildings of the inter-war years were next to many of the major bus stops so people might rush in to use 'the best toilets in town'. In the winter the odd tramp might be found warming himself on a radiator. Later hundreds crossed the campus from the local car parks to the civic and town centres. After the war there were suggestions that the informal openness should be built on and incorporated in a new campus design. But the resources, and perhaps the will, were not available to realise this. The actual development has been much more piecemeal and access has become more controlled, partly embodied in building design but also CCTV, identity cards and security staff and gates. In the less densely occupied campus locations local children, dog walkers, bike riders and runners still amiably co-exist.

Similarly when both students and staff were part-time it was easier to carry the local community into higher education and higher education back out into the local community in ways which 'just happened'. But as higher education has become more organised on a full-time basis, with a student body and a purpose that has become more diverse, the potential linkages have grown. So relations with the wider world have become more organised. But the continued presence of a large university in the centre of a big city remains the point of departure of any analysis.

The Local Economic Impact

Colleges, polytechnics and universities have a significant impact on the economy of the areas in which they are located. They generate incomes and jobs. Money that is spent with local suppliers, in local shops and bars, on local transport, feeds round the system creating incomes and jobs for others. This is what economists call the multiplier effect. Of course not all of the money is spent in the immediate region, part of it will 'leak' away. The size of this leakage will determine how big the multiplier effect is. The boost also has a double character. There can be a one-off effect from developing and equipping new buildings and a continued effect from the income spent on a day-to-day basis. In principle we can measure this effect and the net impact of a university compared to what might have happened if it had not existed in the region.

In the case of Wolverhampton and its forerunner colleges the importance of this boost has grown as the relative size of the University has grown and the wider Black Country experienced economic transition. In the 1950s and 1960s, for example, the area seemed to be at the forefront of advance. 'In industry trends tend to be set in the West Midlands and followed up throughout the rest of the country,' said the local newspaper, and spending on the Technical College 'in an expansive area like the West Midlands ... would be thoroughly justified'.[2] A generation on the role of the Polytechnic and later University seemed to be much more about resisting relative decline and assisting in regeneration. Over time too the exact distribution of the impact has varied, partly as the balance of activities has changed between the different colleges and University sites at Wolverhampton, Walsall and Telford (but in the past also Dudley).

Estimating the size of this boost for any higher education institution is difficult. In the mid 1970s, for example, it was suggested that each student 'injected into the local economies' of Wolverhampton and Dudley between £1,300 and £2,600 a year – a significant sum once inflation is taken into account and the Department of Education warned of 'substantial economic and social consequences' in Dudley if a higher education base was lost there.[3] The Department of Education also pointed out that local higher education spending in the Black Country did not necessarily follow the economic cycle. Not to have it, 'would be especially serious at a time of depressed economic activity' – a point whose

[2] *Express and Star 17 September 1963; 19 September 1963.*
[3] *Rudi Herbert, A study of educational policy making local level: a case study of the merger of Dudley College of Education and Wolverhampton Polytechnic, 1974-1976, University of Birmingham, MEd Thesis nd. (WA), p. 75.*

significance has grown with time.[4]

In the late 1980s Jackie Lewis, an economics lecturer at the then Polytechnic, was asked to calculate the impact of the Polytechnic. In doing so she pioneered a more robust calculation and developed an approach to calculating the impact of a higher education institution, elements of which have continued to be used in a number of other studies of the local economic impact of universities in the UK. Her calculations suggested that with 1,300 staff the Polytechnic also generated jobs for up to 2,000 more in the Black Country.[5] It would be a fascinating but demanding task to replicate these calculations for later years using the subsequent refinements to the approach and later data. But we can set out some of the elements that matter.

The University itself is a significant economic factor in its own right. By 2010 its turnover had grown to over £160 million and it employed nearly 3,000 full, part-time and casual staff. This compares well with Black Country private sector companies which have tended to contract in size or shifted the balance of their activities beyond the region. In terms of the public and semi-public sector the University stands behind the local councils and hospital trusts in terms of jobs and turnover but is certainly the third biggest part in Wolverhampton. However jobs and turnover tell only part of the story because these figures do not count the 20,000 plus students and visitors and capture only a part of what they spend.

How we analyse the total multiplier impact depends on the period we are looking at, who is doing the spending and the nature of the local economy. In earlier times spending was more localised. Architects and builders were local or regional. Even goods that arrived by train could be brought to the colleges from the station by local horse and cart. Today spending on new buildings and everyday goods and services involves dealing with bigger national suppliers rather than the local ones of earlier decades. But recent concerns with sustainability have begun to suggest that a more local focus may have merit. The local impact of staff and student expenditures also depends on who is doing it and what they are buying. Staff salaries account for over £90 million of the modern University's expenditure. Academic staff are more likely to travel in from longer distances, therefore their local spending effect will be smaller than the rest of the University staff who are more likely to be drawn from the Black Country and its surrounding areas. Although their individual spending is less, it is the students who have the least leakage using local shops and services perhaps to the greatest degree, although the amount of internet shopping is unknown. Taking Lewis's estimates from the late 1980s and the more recent ones for other Universities we might very crudely estimate that in addition to the jobs and income that the university directly creates, it also supports a further 3-4,000 jobs locally.

The most obvious impact of having a large student body on the local economy is in housing. The thousands of students looking to live away from home create a significant demand in the local area of a university. University halls of residence have been one solution and, as we have seen, for some students 'living in halls' is part of the rite of passage of being 'at uni'. But by 2012 of the 1.3 million full-time students in the UK only just over a fifth were in university halls. The rapid growth of higher education created, therefore, a thriving set of local rental markets as landlords and letting agents supplied rooms and houses of varying quality to students. Sometimes this could create frictions as areas came to be subject to 'studentification'.[6] It was very lucrative and 'buy to let to students' fed into the property booms of the turn of the twenty-first century. The returns on letting to students also began to attract big

[4] Herbert, op cit., p. 83.
[5] J.Lewis, 'Assessing the effect of the Polytechnic, Wolverhampton on the local community', Urban Studies, vol. 25 no. 53, 1988.
[6] See, for example, D. Smith, 'The Politics of Studentification and '(Un)balanced' Urban Populations: Lessons for Gentrification and Sustainable Communities?', Urban Studies, vol. 45 no. 12, 2008 November, pp. 2541-2564.

investors moving student lets from a fringe market to something of interest to global business – especially as the market proved resilient in the face of economic difficulties with returns over 10% a year. 'Student property has performed exceptionally well as an asset class compared to traditional investments over the last year', noted one report on 2012. 'In fact, it has outperformed every other commercial property class and delivered consistent returns throughout the economic downturn.'[7] In Wolverhampton this led to three major private developments to challenge both University accommodation and the small scale landlords. Fiveways Hall was developed by the Opal Property Group Limited, the UK's second largest student provider. Fresh Student Living redeveloped a large former office block opposite the Grand Theatre, and Victoria Hall Ltd (a company with halls in four countries) opened its huge Victoria Hall in Wolverhampton, changing the skyline of the town.

Income Generation

Before the late 1980s little effort was put into organising, costing and measuring income-raising activities as part of the formal role of higher education. Research grants and teaching contracts with companies were useful supplements but funding was overwhelmingly in the hands of the state. Work might be done outside of the organisation without a clear profit gain. Staff might even be allowed to do outside work for themselves, as a perk of the job, although those actually involved in this were few. The casual approach is reflected in the lack of data for the earlier years. The first serious national survey at the end of the 1980s indentified several sources of income generation – donations, research grants, service teaching for outside organisations and the beginnings of 'spin off companies'. But it also showed the imbalance between institutions. 90% of such income went to the then university sector and only 10% to the polytechnic and soon to be new university sector, whose external income came primarily from the service teaching side. Within the then existing university sector too a mere five universities had 40% of the research income which was also heavily concentrated in certain areas of science and technology.

But from this point national policy put increasing pressure on universities to adopt what was seen as a more business like and commercial approach and not least in 'income generation'. One aim was for the state to save money by encouraging universities to find other sources of funding. Another was to try to encourage a closer link with 'business' – part of the service model of higher education. Beyond this the policy climate was one based on the idea of commercialisation, markets and market competition were good things, not least at a time when markets appeared to be booming. Even state funding would benefit from being organised in a quasi market way. But markets are notoriously prone to monopoly distortion and some also claimed that there was a hidden agenda to use these forms to allow or even intensify the concentration of resources amongst the few rather than the many – a point made rather more decorously by the various associations of universities, not least the Million+ group of which Wolverhampton was a member.

University status for Wolverhampton, therefore, more or less coincided with a new drive to make income generation much more central to the life of a university. Its share of funding rose, as did its status. Overseen by a member of the University executive, new positions were developed to gain, manage and deliver research grants and contracts, service teaching contacts, profits from intellectual property, holiday lets of halls of residence, conference organisation and spin off companies. Wolverhampton, like all

[7] *2012 Student Property Knight Frank*, Knight Frank London LLP, 2012; E.Hammond, 'Student housing is top property asset', *Financial Times*, November 4 2012.

The Commercial University

The recent expansion of higher education in Britain took place at a time when policy makers and politicians looked to the private sector and its values for models of how 'public services' should be run. The commercialisation and managerialisation of universities was also evident. Indeed universities have come to have some element of multi-national businesses as they move across the globe. One American study of the 1990s talked of a new Academic Capitalism and in Britain the ironic terms Education PLC and HiEdBizUK have been used. One vision of the future of higher education builds on these trends and looks towards a commercial university model motivated by and for profit.

In Britain, moves in this direction arise in three ways. One is the creation of fully private, commercial universities alongside existing ones like Wolverhampton. Examples of this exist but they have been marginal in the UK system and this does not seem set to change. The second has been to allow the take over, within the exiting structures, of universities and parts of their activity by major private sector service companies with a strong education face. Not the least of these are companies like Pearson which describes itself as a 'global media and education group' owning textbook publishers, Penguin books, the Financial Times newspaper as well as the examining board Edexcel.

For these companies the pseudo markets of the state, and education in particular, provide an attractive arena where high profit, or what economists call rent seeking, is possible.

The third possibility is that universities, or their 'executives', already to a degree freed from 'the public sector', might take this freedom one step further by converting into for-profit (or what is sometimes called 'social profit') organisations.

The peculiarity of debates about such possible futures is that since 2008 they have taken place against a background of massive private sector failure as the advanced world, and Britain in particular, has experienced unprecedented economic difficulties in which the financial system has only been kept afloat by massive state action, saving in the process huge swathes of the 'private sector'.

There is clearly, therefore, an argument about the practicalities of these models and their viability. But arguments for the commercial university also raise sharp debates about the meaning and nature of higher education and these are at the centre of controversies in British universities as this history is written.

universities, ceased to be just one thing and became a cluster of 'businesses', each with its own brass plate on the main building.

These developments have posed problems and created frictions. The inequalities between institutions apparent at the end of the 1980s have been perpetuated. The larger part of the potential income goes to the few. Within universities the potentially volatile income stream creates issues of stability, not least for staff whose posts are seen as 'externally funded'. External funding is supposed to create a net surplus but its costings are often a problem and, to the extent that it needs a big support structure, the real gain may be limited. For staff too 'income generation' brought a new language of entrepreneurialism which has clashed with other values. It has also created new hierarchies. Doing work off the books as a 'perk' is now more closely policed as institutions bring work in-house. New structures have also been developed internally to reward those who might, by good fortune, be in a currently commercially valuable or research intensive area.

Regional and National Development

In 1997 the Dearing Report (formally the National Committee of Inquiry into Higher Education) suggested that universities should be 'a significant force in the regional economy, support research and consultancy and attract inward investment, provide employment and meet labour market needs and foster entrepreneurship among students and staff'.[8]

This appears a formidable challenge but there was nothing new in this idea. In 1921 it was said 'today it is universally accepted that progress and development are dependent upon scientific knowledge and research'.[9] Colleges and universities had always had, if only implicitly, a regional economic role and from the start Wolverhampton and its forerunner colleges had seen themselves very much as part of Black Country and the wider West Midlands and its neighbouring areas. But the new rhetoric was important. It flowed from the view of both national policymakers and the European Union that the state could do little to manage demand to create growth and jobs. Instead the emphasis had to be on encouraging organisations and individuals to be more flexible and competitive. Knowledge was now an organisational and a national asset and workers, human capital. Universities combined huge amounts of this knowledge and human capital and therefore had to have a proactive regional role to mobilise to be, 'engaged' and 'entrepreneurial'. To encourage this, funding streams were developed, some of which were formula based and others bid based.

The sense that this role needed to be formalised also arose from the changing nature of higher education institutions. We have seen that in the Technical College era most members of staff and students were part-time, working on more technical qualifications. The local linkages were therefore natural and organic. The local role of business interests was reflected in representation on governing bodies. Local firms were also encouraged to support activity through financial aid, the giving of prizes and donations of equipment. Machinery in the engineering and science workshops at one stage was even given an affectionate nickname from the name of the company being thanked on the brass plate. Patchy developments of advisory committees took place. In 1950 a report noted the existence of committees advising on building, engineering, transport, the retail sector, pharmacy and looked forward to a committee on management studies. But as the scale of higher education grew, so staff and students became more full-time and the courses of study broadened and, to an extent changed their function.

[8] *National Committee of Inquiry into Higher Education, London, 1997, ch. 4.*
[9] *Wolverhampton Education Committee, Programme 1921-1922 Technical School, 1921, p. 8*

The World Beyond the Open Doors

Local linkages had therefore to be more orchestrated. No less, with the loss of significant parts of the regional manufacturing base and the shift to services, many of the employers who had had closer links in earlier decades either disappeared, moved out, or became more national and even globalised with their headquarters elsewhere. For two years from 1976 Nick Hedges visited local industrial workplaces to photograph the workers who made all our lives easier, doing the hard jobs producing goods we depended on. Within years of this project all but one of the works he photographed had closed. The research and innovation intensity of regional firms changed too as did their capacity to absorb knowledge and new ideas and to work with local universities. Even the most enthusiastic supporters of university regionalism had therefore to recognise that it was often easier to proclaim their ambitions than realise them.

The formalisation of the linkages in the last decades make them easier to track compared to the less formal links of the past. But this then risks a misleading contrast in terms of an understanding of their relative frequency, depth and quality. A report of the National Foundry College in the 1950s, for example, lists dozens of speakers coming in and works trips out across the country. But in a new era things had to

Collecting the last week's wages before redundancy at Birchley Rolling Mills

Work in the blast furnace, British Steel, Bilston

Machinist at Lee Howl
© Nick Hedges

162

be done in a different way. In 1993 the University began to work to create a Science Park in Wolverhampton as part of a joint venture with Wolverhampton City Council. In 2012 it became the University of Wolverhampton Science Park Ltd. Such initiatives were part of an approach to local and regional development encouraged from the centre with finances from the European Union and the British Government's 'city challenge programme'.

The Science Park developed through several stages and includes developing technical and creative industries groupings. By 2012 it was home to 100 businesses, mostly small. In 2006 it was complemented by an 'e-innovation centre' at the Telford campus which provided space for 36 incubator start ups. The University also developed a 'business solutions service' to assist local companies and Wolverhampton was prominent in taking advantage of knowledge transfer programmes, established by the UK government, to support postgraduates to work within companies to develop new products and processes.

Valuable though these initiatives are, the difficulty has been that bigger economic processes have tended to accentuate regional inequalities in the last decades. The faith of successive governments that 'market forces' would produce greater equality (on any dimension) has not been rewarded with evidence of real reductions in gaps. At the turn of the new century the Black Country has been one of only three sub-regions of the UK to face a population decline and what is called the 'output gap' – the difference between the actual output of the region and the national average is over £2.5 billion. In 2003, the local economic think tank, looked forward to 2033, imagining that 'in 2015, the University of Wolverhampton became the Black Country University (BCU) clear recognition of the value of the Black Country brand'.[10] The University of Wolverhampton has, as we have seen, always informally been 'the university of the Black Country, even when its core component was a technical college. But for this to happen formally it will require a reversal of policies that have accentuated the regional gaps. Not least dealing with the forces that have created a national economy where London and the South East now dominate to a greater extent than capital city regions do in most other advanced economies.

The most important local role of the university in economic terms is the indirect one. One aspect of this is the contribution made to the development and expansion of a pool of talent in the labour force. The share of people in the labour force with a degree has risen from a mere 6% in 1980 to 31% in 2011. We can estimate that over the decades well over 100,000 have graduated from Wolverhampton and its forerunners with degree level qualifications, as well as many tens of thousands with other higher education qualifications. The national postgraduate share in the labour force has also risen from 4% in 1996 to 11% in 2011, an increase to which Wolverhampton as a modern university again has made a proportional contribution. Contrary to claims

[10] Black Country Consortium, The Black Country Study, Oldbury, 2006; Black Country Consortium, Looking Forward: The Black Country in 2033, Oldbury, 2003.

that there is no need for so many people with degrees, the demand for graduates continues to grow. Three quarters of all job growth after 2000 was for jobs classified as associate professional and technical occupations, professional occupations and managerial. Moreover despite claims that the crisis that began in 2008 would hit these groups hard, graduate unemployment proved lower than in more traditional parts of the labour force. This is not to say that every graduate gets the job that they want – up to 25% may end up working in non-graduate jobs but 75% do not and this share shows no sign of declining. Higher education courses have also helped to meet more specific needs – training engineers, teachers of all types, nurses, enabling people to continue to take advantage of continuous professional development (and beyond as the population over 65 will rise from 17% in 2010 to 25% in 2035). In fact even in narrow economic terms a strong case can be made that there are too few graduates. In 2000 the UK had the 3rd highest numbers graduating amongst advanced countries but by 2008 its position had fallen to 15th and it had one of the lowest shares of resources devoted to tertiary education.

With higher education comes the possibility of better and more secure employment. The standard calculation at the start of the twenty-first century was that the average salary of a graduate was over £27,000 compared to £18,000 for a non-graduate. Of course there are costs of going to a university but the net lifetime premium of a graduate was still said to be £100,000. The wage differentials of those with post graduate qualifications appear to have risen from 5% in 1996 to 10% in 2011.

Those who have gained qualifications have always had a greater possibility of geographical mobility and even local graduates can move on and out of the area. London has always been a huge magnet but in the middle of the twentieth century the attraction of the West Midlands was considerable so possibly there was a net inflow of graduates. One of the problems that the Black Country has seen in recent decades is the opposite – lower graduate retention than many would like. Without a major local university this problem would be much worse. At the level of the national economy it has been estimated that a 1% increase in graduates may result in a 0.4-0.6% increase in output. It seems likely that this operates on a regional level too. In the case of an institution like Wolverhampton its ability to offer higher education to a wider section of the population means that it can have an impact on a scale quite different to the socially exclusive institutions – if it is allowed to and if its students are given the recognition that they deserve.

Since the 1970s, alongside the expansion of higher education and the abolition of the formal divides between institutions, the levels of inequality of wealth and income in Britain have grown and social mobility has declined. Indeed the UK is now one of the most unequal societies in the advanced world and one where it is hardest for those at the bottom to 'get on'. Educational inequalities both reflect and perpetuate this, including inequalities of resourcing, status and esteem in the university sector. Once, this was explicit. In 1921 the President of the Institute of Automobile Engineers told the audience 'how glad he was to see Wolverhampton classes for the education of a craftsman in his craft, not out of it'.[11] Today we talk a different language of opportunity but the focus on equity and social justice in policy statements has had a 'symbolic and rhetorical – non performative' element says one prominent expert. People are still categorised by policymakers as 'gifted and talented, struggling or just average'.[12] And people talk of universities too in terms of different missions defined in part by who they recruit – the research intensive, the

[11] Express and Star, 30 September 1921.
[12] S.Ball, The Education Debate, London, 2008, p. 180, 170.

teaching and the training.
Education cannot make up for inequalities whose impact is felt even before birth and reflected in low birth weights and variations in infant mortality. But it should not confuse background and status with ability. We should not allow being born to the 'right parents', going to the 'right school' and then the 'right' university to get the 'right job' to be seen as anything other than a process moulded by society. If we fail to appreciate this then we become blinded not only to the way that these processes work but the evidence that they do not need to be there at all.

Research in 2010 showed that only 1% of Wolverhampton students had been privately educated – the lowest share in the UK system.[13] Ironically the exact number of privately educated in the statistics for Wolverhampton was the same as the exact number of entrants to Oxford or Cambridge who had received free school meals. Does this neat inversion of numbers really tell us about the distribution of human ability or the distribution of division and snobbery? Caroline Gipps told an interesting story as she retired from being Vice-Chancellor at Wolverhampton in 2011. She had been to a launch of a government 'Social Mobility Strategy' and chatted to 'a senior staff member' in one of the great global accountancy firms based in London:

> *He said that they took on 1,300 graduates a year, even in the recession. When I asked what sort of universities they came from the response was 'A 2.1 from a Russell Group university, plus the Duke of Edinburgh award, and they've usually rowed the Atlantic twice.' So, I asked whether they might widen this in the interests of social mobility and the response was that they might accept a 2.1 from another type of university but they would still have to have the Duke of Edinburgh award, and probably have rowed the Atlantic once.*[14]

Here we see rolled up in one the idea that ability goes with the opportunities that only a few can have. We can also see how it might work to the systematic disadvantage of those from more humble backgrounds who come to universities like Wolverhampton and then graduate into the jobs market.

But reader pause for a moment. Discretion led her not to name the firm but poetic justice demands that it be the top global accountancy firm that year, namely PricewaterhouseCooper. Why? Its UK Board at that point had 12 members. Two we will exclude as they were educated in the US and Ireland. The remaining ten were UK educated and of them seven came from the Russell Group universities – reflecting the dominant element in all UK social mobility studies. Three did not have this super-élite background. One had been to Brunel University and one to the then Newcastle Polytechnic – now Northumbria University. That left one other, the Chairman of PwC with its 8,500 partners and 163,000 staff operating in over 150 countries around the world. He was Ian Powell who was born in Sedgley in the Black Country and who holds a BA (Hons) degree in Economics from the then Wolverhampton Polytechnic, now the University of Wolverhampton.

The economic contribution of a university has other aspects too. A university has been called an 'anchor institution' for a city and a region. This anchor role is especially important in those areas where

[13] Sutton Trust, *Responding to the new landscape for university access*, 2010 (December)
[14] C.Gipps, *Who Goes to University? And why it matters*, Wolverhampton, June 2011.

From Comprehensive Schools to Comprehensive Universities?

Comprehensive schooling developed from the 1950s as a result of a shared concern to break down the 'social apartheid' of English schooling to allow the possibility for all children to develop their talents in a more equal environment. It proved an unstoppable force. Primary schools are comprehensive by nature but in 1965 only 8.5% of children were in comprehensive secondary schools. By 1981 83% were in comprehensive secondary schools.

Mass comprehensive schooling could lead on to mass comprehensive universities, said Robin Pedley in the 1970s. Stopping at 16 or 18 was like building a motorway for half a journey. Access to higher education should not just be for an élite minority. Universities should not select but be open to all who had qualifications or the will to learn. Nor should the social apartheid of schools be broken down only to reproduce it at a higher level. 'For "grammar schools" now read "universities"', said Pedley, 'for "secondary moderns" read "colleges of further education" and for "creamed sub-comprehensives" which have to live alongside selective grammar schools, read "polytechnics" and "colleges of higher education"'.

But a system of comprehensive universities would also have to be different from the existing ones. Universities would have to be local in the same way that schools were meant to be. They would have to have the same capacities and resources. Above all, since they were concerned with educating adults, they would have to overcome the division between education, community and work, a way that opened up new individual and collective possibilities.

Such visions are always initially that of a minority. This minority could be found outside of the universities, some inside and some supporters of the new polytechnics. The next decades were to show that higher education could become a mass force and that learning could be thought of in lifelong terms. Just as the battle for schooling shifted from a fight for 'secondary education for all' to a debate over what forms secondary education should take, so the same is happening in higher education. Higher education is now mass higher education although still not fully open. The debates are increasingly about the best forms to enable it to be available as a basic right and whether it will break down or re-enforce social and economic barriers.

Courtyard at the Chubb Building – now the Light House

also support the local Grand Theatre and cinemas. In the 1980s too the Polytechnic supported the development of the Light House – a multi-media training, business and cinema complex now located in an iconic, renovated nineteenth century industrial building.

Students too help create another type of anchor. Union minibuses were available to community organisations out of term time, they could use the Union building for crèches and functions. Students helped and still help existing community groups. This is partly a political act.

the dynamism of the private sector is weak. This is not least because universities have other indirect effects – economists call them spillovers – in improving the attraction of an area. Personal and organisational location decisions can be affected by the presence of a university and its hidden influences. The quality and depth of local social networks is greater. A university can even play an economic role in enhancing the cultural and tourist base of a region. We have seen the close early association between the School of Art and the civic Art Gallery. When the Ironbridge Gorge Museum complex was planned (winning Word Heritage status in 1986 because of its unique role in the industrial revolution 'a major turning point in human society') staff from the then college and polytechnic were involved in its creation. A generation on the work they have done in understanding the Black Country and its development was one of the streams feeding into the development of the Black Country Museum in 1978.

The presence of an important school of art has been important for the local cultural economy since the late nineteenth century. The College gave rise to a tradition of in-house theatre which still flourishes in the Arena Theatre and Walsall Performance Hub. Staff and students

> *By getting involved in life outside the Polytechnic you can effectively publicise what students and students' unions are all about, and hopefully help to destroy the long-standing image of students as layabouts and wasters. Any sympathy for our case is a bonus especially under a government who openly wishes to destroy students' unions and cut higher education. Being seen doing three-legged pub crawls for Rag Week is not enough and to be quite frank these events do more harm for our image than good despite the obvious benefits. In addition to this sort of action more direct involvement is really of greater benefit to the community.[15]*

There was a problem 'how to harness the best asset' the time and energy of lots of people. This has been addressed by the University as a whole, with organisational capacity put into a matching system of

[15] Poly Passport Students Union Handbook 1983/84, p.78

'Active Volunteers' and individual projects. Students are encouraged to volunteer to gain credits on some modules and to gain useful experience by working with a wide range of over 100 local voluntary and community groups. A Law Advice Centre has been opened to provide free legal advice, by law students, for local people, supplementing overstretched charities. Victim Support are training students to give free and confidential help to anyone affected by crime, in drop-in surgeries in the Students' Union building, four days a week.

Beyond all of this a university can also be seen as a 'good corporate citizen', leading by example. This would be easier if a university could float above the world but it cannot. It is part of society as it is and marked by its imperfections but, a university is an organisation whose proclaimed goal is to engage critically. We have seen, for example, that employment conditions in the university have tended to be better than those in the region as a whole. Even so, higher education institutions have also had a large number of low paid staff. In 2013, Wolverhampton was one of the first organisations in the region to support the 'living wage' campaign for its lowest paid staff, giving them an hourly rate 10% above the minimum wage. In doing so the University, said the Vice-Chancellor, Geoff Layer, was taking 'a strong moral and ethical stance' which the UNISON trade union hoped would 'encourage other local employers to follow suit'. Being a good employer and corporate citizen has also involved a limited interest in outsourcing. At some points some services have been outsourced but in general this has not been a road taken. Outsourcing often thrives on low pay. It also misses the importance of the work that all staff contribute to the whole University. Giving a lead also means addressing the issue of sustainability both in terms of teaching and research and the everyday practices of the institutions.

Beyond this the University can show a lead in terms of community engagement.

Education and Human Potential

It is possible to reduce all of the 'good' impacts of a university to an economic calculation. Kindness can contribute to sustainability and save money. The in-house catering, caretaking or security worker who takes time to talk to a bewildered and homesick student increases retention levels. But the argument that the university should aspire to the best goes beyond this kind of calculation. It connects to the wider role that education has enabled us to overcome the individual and collective limits of the present and to encourage us to work together to help build a better future. To be true to itself a university has to practise what it preaches and show to others in its own actions why the values it tries to nurture matter.

Education is about increasing all-round human potential – individual and collective, local and global. In early 2013, Paul Mason, one of Britain's top economics journalists, gave his inaugural lecture as a visiting professor at Wolverhampton. He began by saying how honoured he was to come from:

"

the world that I come from, the world of news reporting which is all about action, tight deadlines and experience to the world of ideas. I know that modern universities are very vocationally oriented and this one in particular… But it is a world of ideas. When I was at university, more than 30 years ago now, what I remember most is the privilege of being in a world of ideas and

> *you want them to be as pure ideas and as big ideas as possible. I want to say that specifically to the undergraduates – make no apologies for demanding that from your university as well.*

These big ideas include those that involve the purpose of a university in an age when the doors are opening ever wider. An essay by two authors, one of whom left a Russell group university to become a Deputy Vice-Chancellor of a modern university like Wolverhampton, talks of the importance of a 'critical approach which looks at the wider social, political and economic context beyond the institution'. The big question is how, whatever we teach, we might engage with the world using the idea that we are all co-producers of the knowledge and world we live in. There is a need, they say, 'to reconstruct the student as producer; undergraduate students working in collaboration with academics to create work of social importance that is full of academic content and value, while at the same time reinvigorating the university beyond the logic of market economics'.[16] Sometimes this happens already – it then becomes education at its best but we need to find ways to make it happen more often – not behind closed doors but with the doors wide open.

For this we also need a vision of a more democratic life. This is not just about voting in the occasional election although that is important. In 1937 Lady Simon wrapped this argument in the liberal imperial sentiments of the time, telling the Wolverhampton prize day audience that:

> *This enormously big question of running an Empire is thrown at us without any preparation... I should like to suggest to you it is more important to run a country properly than an industry, and that it needs as much skill in choosing a member of Parliament as carrying out work in industry. Might you not spend some of your time on making yourself technically more efficient for your job and as a citizen of this country?*[17]

There is a deeper democracy, a democracy as a way of life. But if we are to have this it means a democracy within a university that links the professors and the porters, all staff and students as part of a common enterprise. This means acknowledging that a university cannot succeed if any of their different contributions are missing. It is also a democracy that links a university to its local community not only in the sense that the university must go out to the community but the community must also come in. Another of the paradoxes of expansion has been its managerial and technocratic form. This has opened up democratic deficits within institutions and between them and their local communities where local government has been in the eyes of many 'hollowed out' in favour of a centralised power in London.

In the 1980s the local community links of polytechnics through the local education authorities were increasingly problematic. One Polytechnic document explained that the LEA had 'statutory responsibility for the polytechnic, and for its finance – the Poly has no bank account, for instance'. At this point only 2.5% of the income was coming from the local authority. Even so, 'few wanted to divorce polytechnics completely from LEAs'.[18]

---

[16] M.Neary & J.Winn, 'The student as producer: reinventing the student experience in higher education' in L.Bell, M.Neary & H, Stevenson, The Future of Higher Education, London, 2009.
[17] Express and Star 12 November 1937
[18] 'What the poly costs' University Archive (nd 1986?)

Really Useful Knowledge

Running through our story of nearly two hundred years of developing higher education in Wolverhampton and beyond has been the debate about education itself – how much of it there should be, who should get it, what form it should have and what purpose it should serve?

When the first mechanics institutes were formed in the 1820s another organisation was created called 'the Society for the Diffusion of Useful Knowledge'. Its aim was to help people gain a self education but in a 'useful' knowledge that would fit them to the world as it existed. For the radicals, education had to do more – dismayed by the world that they saw around them and, as workers, experiencing its worst points at first hand – they were inspired by a hope of radical political change which looked forward to a different world and also looked forward to a different education. This would be built around what they called 'really useful knowledge' not limited by the higher orders and the demands of the day.

We cannot know how this debate played out in Wolverhampton in the 1820s. The evidence seems to suggest in this town that the focus was more on 'useful education' than 'really useful education' though more radical traditions were deeper rooted nearby. But the debate has not gone away.

It has continued to run through educational theory for two centuries and it runs through the history of institutions like Wolverhampton. One of the peculiarities of the debate in Britain has been that the Labour Party has both led radical change and limited it – sometimes being more conservative than the Conservative Party. In 1968 Eric Robinson talked of a divide between the idea of an educated elite 'who live through their work' and the mass who 'try to live in spite of their work'. He then complained that 'the ideal that everybody should find self-expression through his economic activity in this society is obviously unacceptable to the left which thus finds itself positively committed to a class structure in education'. Three decades on, others make the same complaint including Geoff Layer, 'there is still a particular view of universities in Labour Party policy which inhibits being radical through assuming hierarchies and élites'.

In 1832 one of the radical newspapers that was smuggled into the emerging Black Country was called the Poor Man's Guardian. It spoke of a 'knowledge to make you free'. In this vision of education, people might come together in a joint enterprise to explore why society was as it was, why they were as they were, and how things could be changed. It is still a vision to inspire.

On the eve of a new era The Polytechnic chose this image for its magazine – The Coat of Arms of the Wolverhampton Borough – with devices noting the founding of the free school and local industry

Yet this is what happened so this formal, tenuous link to a wider democracy of local government was lost. The result is that Wolverhampton, like other universities, is in the local community and to a larger extent again for the local community but it is not, in a traditional democratic sense, 'of the local community'. It is not alone in this – the democratic deficit is wide. But this does not mean that it cannot and should not be closed. How far it can be sustained into the future and what alterative forms may challenge the present 'autonomy' is unclear but this does not make the issue any less important.

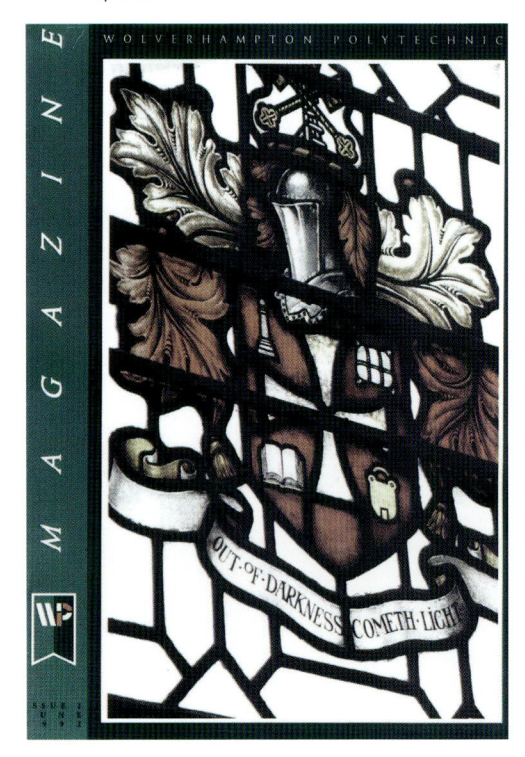

International Ripples

These debates are of more than parochial interest. The Black Country, Wolverhampton itself, and its colleges have always had a place in a bigger world. As with so much else its story is full of twists.

George Africanus was brought to the town in the late eighteenth century as a young slave, a gift for a businessman Benjamin Molyneux. He was freed and is today claimed as Britain's first black businessman. The chains on the slave ships were often made locally as were the chains on the Royal Navy ships that enforced the abolition of the slave trade. But so too were the chains on the ships that helped to expand the British Empire.

These contradictions were reflected within the area too. Slave abolitionism was part of the political life of Victorian England and debates on it figured in the Black Country newspapers read in the libraries and in the discussions and cultural life of the time. Empire too was a part of life and not just on the maps on the walls. At the end of the nineteenth century for those wanting to get on, the colonies might provide an avenue. One of these was Charles Morgan Webb who was to become perhaps the most famous 'son' of the Free Library and Technical College in the inter-war years. Webb went out to India, helped with the first census in Burma and then the establishment of the University of Rangoon where he was Vice-Chancellor for a short time. The university quickly became a hotbed of student nationalism and the fight for independence and Webb had to try to deal with student strikes for which he was in part rewarded with a knighthood. In these struggles a future generation of Burmese politicians began to cut their teeth and in their steps would follow a United Nations' Secretary General and the father of Aung San Suu Kyi.

Decolonisation led to new relations with what was now called 'the third world'. Aid, and within it educational help, became part of what would later be called 'soft diplomacy' – assistance that was an uneasy combination of self-interest and altruism. Technical assistance was one of the more valuable aspects of the aid that was given and especially

The World Beyond the Open Doors

technical assistance in agriculture and rural development since, at this stage the majority of the world's population was still rural. The Wolverhampton Technical Teachers' College had established an overseas technical assistance unit in the 1970s and between 1975 and 1997 technical trainer courses were run two or three times a year which trained over 700 people from different parts of the world.

Staff also developed a tradition of travelling – at first largely in Africa, but then beyond, to deliver technical training courses, initially with an agricultural focus but then broadening to incorporate a wider environmental and sustainability brief. This tradition continues today in the self financing Centre for International Development and Training (CIDT), which tries to facilitate 'people-centred, sustainable development across the globe'.

Such ripples exist in other parts of the University too. In glass, for example, the School of Art & Design has built up strong links with institutions in the rapidly developing China of the turn of the twenty-first century. Chinese academics came to Wolverhampton and returned along what some called 'a silica road' to develop glass education there. This goes beyond emulation to try to reconnect with their own traditions and relate them with what they had learned at Wolverhampton in more challenging and authentic fusions.[19]

It is with the many international students who have come to Wolverhampton that the ripples are potentially the greatest. Today these students bring in a large income both nationally and locally. In an age seemingly dominated by financial services it is salutatory to find that the value of UK higher education exports is greater than that provided by the financial sector. For a University like Wolverhampton international earnings, from over 2,000 international students bring in some £20 million pounds – over 10% of the revenue.

Global higher education is still only available to the few, though the extent to which this is the case is often misunderstood. Although the whole world seems to be speaking English it does not. India has a population of some 1.2 billion. English is an official language but it is learned as a second language by all but a tiny number. Less than 5%, perhaps only 1-2% have it to a high enough level to study to degree level in the English language. The same applies to many other parts of the world where English is a second language. No less important is the general poverty in the majority in countries like India, Sri Lanka, Nigeria and even the fast developing China. Those who come to study or study in franchise institutions are from a very narrow slice of their country's population. Others come from very different worlds like students from Saudi Arabia on government scholarships and bursaries that can even extend to private healthcare.

Whatever their background, these students bring to Wolverhampton their different experiences helping to create a more international space. Its potential is still insufficiently appreciated, hemmed in as it is, by national concerns about overseas students and immigration. While some English-educated staff struggle to say a few foreign words most of the overseas students are bilingual. Some know several languages. It can embarrassing for a member of staff to be confronted, for example, by a student fluent in English, French and German who when asked if he speaks any more languages says modestly, 'well my first language is my local 'dialect' but that is different from the 'dialect' that my wife speaks'.

Some of these students stay as local 'brain gain', even to the University as researchers and lecturers. But these students also can take something back when they leave. The specific skills, that they have learned may play an important role in

[19] K.Cummings, 'Born in Industry: The First 150 Years of Glass Education in Stourbridge, England', Glass (New York, N.Y.), Spring 2005, no. 98, pp. 40-45; Stuart Garfoot, Glass Routes: from Wolverhampton to China, University of Wolverhampton: CADRE Publications, 2008; M.Colin, 'Glass Routes: From Wolverhampton to China', Crafts, November/December 2008, no. 215, pp.74-75.

the societies to which they return but so too will the ethos that they take back. It is all the more important then that while they are here they see this ethos being developed in the best and most democratic ways possible.

On the Right Side of History?

History moves. It does not always move as fast as we want and sometimes it can appear for a time to go back on itself. But it does move and being on 'the right side of history' matters. Some readers may detect a hint of the influence of Karl Marx in this argument, They may, therefore, be surprised to find that 'On the right side of history' is also the title of the contribution of a Conservative Minister of Higher Education, David Willetts, to a volume celebrating 21 years of new universities. For Willetts too the expansion of higher education, its unification, and the work done in new universities has been on the right side of history.

> *I still come across curmudgeons who call for the old wall between different higher education institutions to be re-erected, but this is based on a fundamental misunderstanding of the shape and complexity of modern higher education. Just as it is now impossible to see exactly where the Berlin Wall went, it is unthinkable to imagine ever cleaving our higher education sector in two again.*[20]

This does not mean that history is ever finished or perfect. It advances, as we have tried to show, 'with contradictions' that combine old and new in fortunate and not so fortunate ways. There is still a world to win in higher education no less than elsewhere. One part of this is to eliminate the social divisions determining that what was called in 1963 'half our future' still do not get the chance to go into tertiary education. Another is then to confront the extent to which 'the class system is alive and well in English higher education' and the way that 'an elitist system of rankings based on perception and not reality' feeds off and into wider social divisions.[21] A third is to find ways of reaching William Lovett's vision of education as 'a universal entitlement for advancing the dignity of man and for gladdening his existence' through finding new forms to challenge the divisions that continue to mark both society and education. These are not separate tasks.

In writing this history we have tried to capture both how far we have come and how far we have to go. Our aim has not been to tell the story of who did what to whom. We have also not wanted to claim too much. This is the story of one modern university amongst many. In a sense it could be the story of any of them. But each has its own locality, its own past and its own features so it is also the story of one of them, Wolverhampton, in the heartlands, as we say in our title.

If history is a journey, then knowing where you have come from is important. Wolverhampton, like many universities, has, on occasion, had a cavalier attitude to its past even allowing part of the markers of its history to disappear. Only belatedly has it committed significant resources to create a formal alumni network. There has always been an informal network as some students from past courses, years and even shared halls of residence have kept in touch and held reunions. The advent of the internet and its social networking sites like 'Friends Reunited' and 'Facebook' has made this easier. People are recording their links not

---

[20] David Willetts, 'On the right side of history', in Million+, Breaking with Tradition, London, 2013, p. 27.
[21] Million+, Breaking with Tradition, London, 2013, p. 6.

only to the University, but the Polytechnics and the technical, art, education and nursing colleges that the unified institution emerged from.

The point of good history is not nostalgia. No less than a scientist seeking out a new drug, an engineer looking to help improve machinery or build better buildings, or an artist seeking to capture what words find hard to express, people who write history should have ambitions too. You seek to explore the past in order to understand the present so that you can act to make the future. Having told the story of what we have thought of as 'a busy and productive place', one that can trace itself back to the 1820s when new revolutionary industrial and political forms were being created, we should not be limited in the future by any lack of ambition and courage.

Index

A

Africanus, George........................171

Amis, Kingsley...............................38

Apprenticeship.............4, 23, 34, 51

B

Binary system........................... 32-46

Birkbeck College...............................8

Birmingham....................5, 6, 11, 24, 27, 69, 73, 84, 134, 143

Birmingham University.....11, 84, 155

Black Country...........5-9, 11, 18-19, 31, 37, 39, 62, 68-70, 72, 75, 78-79, 82, 103, 137, 157-159, 161-67, 170-171

Black Country Museum...............167

Bradbury, Malcolm..........................38

Brecht, Bertold...............................91

British Economy................................

    Nineteenth century.....................7

    Inter war years..........................18

    Long Boom...24-28, 31, 157-158

    1980s onwards...39-40, 158-168

Brooks, John..................................92

Bureaucratisation..................... 93-94

Burt, Cyril.......................................75

C

Cambridge University.........6, 61, 70, 80, 165

Chamberlain, Joseph...................155

Chartists..8

Chell, George......15, 18, 69, 91, 104

Civil Service.....................................6

Coates, Dr J.D..............................15

Commercial University.................160

Committee of Polytechnic Directors..35

Committee of Vice Chancellors......60

Comprehensive University......32, 166

Co-production.......................68, 169

Conservative Party and governments 39, 46, 53, 60, 61, 170

Council for National Academic Awards 28, 36, 40, 88

Credentials and credentialism....2, 45

Credit accumulation.......................41

Crosland, Anthony..........................32

Cummings, Keith...........................37

D

Dickens, Charles.............................5

Diploma in Higher Education....41, 76

Disease..7

Dudley..............7, 14, 23, 24, 36, 39, 57, 156, 157

Dudley, Earls of.................7, 14, 156

Dudley Teacher Training College........ 14, 16,18, 23, 36, 57, 104, 120, 126, 127, 126, 131, 133, 135, 151

E

Education..

    and class and inequality........2-4, 6-7, 9, 11, 13-15, 25, 28, 37, 42-43, 51, 67-70, 75-77, 79-80, 82, 101-103, 164-165, 173

    and compulsion....................3, 23

176

and democracy 8, 169-171

and ethnicity.........37, 67, 72, 77, 79, 82, 101-102, 113

and gender.............8, 14, 16, 19, 23, 37, 43, 49, 51-52, 67, 69-70, 71, 73-74, 77, 79, 84, 93, 96, 102

and intelligence debates   68-69, 75, 164

and purpose....8, 40-41, 168-171

and religion...........................4, 68

Primary..........................3-5, 9-10, 15, 16, 27, 31, 57, 67, 68-69, 102

Secondary........6, 15, 25, 75, 166

Tertiary/Higher...2, 3, 5, 15, 25, 28, 31-32, 34, 37-40, 42, 43, 45, 47, 50, 52-53, 57, 60-61, 67-88, 91-92, 101, 124, 157-160, 163-174

Elliot, John...9

Empire......................... 169, 171-172

Epton, Roger 60

F

Fisher, Dr W.E.......19, 71, 91, 95, 104

Fowler, Gerry 42

Fowler, Henry 8, 9

G

Gabo 145

Gee, Maggie..................................38

George Lloyd.................................18

Gipps, Caroline......................92, 165

Government Acts, Reports etc ....

1870 Forster's Act 4, 9

1889 Technical Instruction Act ..11

1902 Education Act............10, 15

1944 Education Act............25, 75

1962 Education Act..................76

1988 Education Reform Act 43

1992 Further and Higher Education Act 43

Select Committee on Arts and Manufactures (1835)................11

Taunton Commission (1868) 6

McNair Report (1944) 26

Addison Committee (1960).......76

Robbins Report (1963) ...5, 27, 31

Platt Report (1964) 52

Judge Report (1985).................52

Dearing Report 1997 161

Government finance for education ...3

Graduate earnings.......................163

Graduate employment......... 163-164

Graduation 84-86

Graham, Sir James.........................4

H

Hardy, Thomas 10

Harrison, Michael...............35, 79, 92

Hedges, Nick.......................113, 162

Heritage...5

Higher Education Funding Council 50

Higher Education Shop..................77

Higher National Diploma 39, 41, 43

Himley Hall 28, 36, 126, 156

Hodson, Barabra........................104

Holgate-Wright, Sheila. 73-74, 77, 83

I

Imperial College London 61

Indian Workers Association..........113

Inequality *(See Education and class)*

Ironbridge Gorge Museum............167

J

Jeffs, Steve....................................104

Jacobson, Howard 38, 101, 156

K

Kelly Family......................................78

Knowledge transfer 161-163

L

Labour Market.................................34

Labour Party...............11, 32, 42. 53, 155, 170

Lawrence, D.H. 69

Layer, Geoff 57, 62, 92, 168, 170

League tables..........................60, 61

Lewis, Jackie................................158

Lim, Pauline..................................104

Literacy 8

Local Authorities... 16, 25, 35, 42-43, 94, 99, 102-103, 108, 115, 169

Lodge, David 38

London School of Economics.........61

Lovett William 8, 173

Lowe, Robert.................................. 4

M

Machin, Steve................................82

Manchester University 70

Major, John.....................................46

Malone, Gareth............................144

Maria Grey Training College 24

Mason, Sir Josiah 11

Mason, Paul 168

Mason, Stuart...............................104

Matterson, Alan 5

Mature students 15, 32, 37, 41, 49, 77-79, 115, 125, 133

Maurice, F.D. 8

Mayakovsky, Vladimir...................145

Mechanics' Institutes 8, 12, 170

Migration ....

    Internal 7

    International 25, 72-73

Millington, Mil........................57, 101

Million+ group................................60

Miners 78

Modularisation..............................111

N

National Advisory Board for Higher Education 42

National Funding Council...............43

National Foundry College........ 26, 71, 131, 162

National Health Service..................52

National Union of Students 43, 113

National Union of Teachers 16

178

National Union of Women Workers 18

Neo-liberalism 40, 53

Newman, Cardinal J.H.................101

Nightingale, Florence 84

Nursing education 49, 51-52, 84, 96, 106, 127, 174

O

Open University 41, 67

Oxford University 6, 70, 80, 165

P

Part-time students... ...4, 9-10, 15, 23, 27, 32, 37, 39, 41, 43, 48-49, 61-70, 73, 76, 83, 93, 98, 115, 133, 157, 161

Pedley, Robin 166

Postgraduate education 38-39, 60-61, 67, 88, 93-94, 96, 163, 168

Portwood, Derek 36

Powell, Enoch...............................113

Powell, Ian....................................165

Priestley, J. B...........................19, 23

Professionalisation...............2, 34, 95

Q

Quality Assurance Agency 50

R

Redundancies 36, 57, 108

Research Assessment 61

Robinson, Eric 42, 170

Rugby School 6

Runciman, Walter 14

Russell Group................................60

S

Sandwich courses 28, 37, 39, 41-42, 76

Scott, Robert 28, 35, 91, 92, 126

Schools ....

    Public 6, 16, 165

    Elementary/ Board/Primary 3-5, 9-10, 15, 16, 27, 31, 57, 67, 68-69, 102

    Grammar.........6, 15, 25, 75, 166

    Secondary Modern..........75, 166

Seabrooke, George 35, 92

Serrant-Green, Laura.....................96

Sharpe, Tom...................................38

Simon, Lady 72, 169

Society for the Preservation of Ancient Buildings 17

Staffordshire 8, 11, 15, 17, 20, 28, 70

Stourbridge 12, 37

Students... 3, 12-15, 19, 21, 27, 32, 34, 36-42, 47-49, 51-52, 55-73, 92, 95-96, 99, 101-102, 112-152, 155, 157-158, 161, 164, 165, 167-169, 172-173

Student finance 57, 76, 79

T

Tawney, R.H. 3, 18

Taylor, Laurie.......................... 99-100

Teacher Education...... 14-15, 16, 23, 27-28, 35-36

Telford 5, 39, 54- 55, 57, 107, 127, 133, 156-157, 163

Thatcher, Margaret 39

Trades Unions ... 11, 18, 57, 105-108

U

Universities UK 60

University Grants Committee ...32, 43

University College, London 61

University of Wolverhampton

    Academics 96-99

    Administration 99-101

    Archives 152

    Campus development............49, 57, 81, 156-157

    Catering 119-122, 124

    CIDT.....................................172

    Communications 145-146

    Community engagement..167-168

    Computing 94, 123-124

    Economic impact.......... 157-166

    Facilities and staff...91, 100-101, 111, 151-152

    Income generation........ 159-161

    Library .. 50, 57, 83, 94, 123-131

    Music 143-144

    Overseas links.......61-62, 76-77, 171-173

    Parking.................................151

    Research.........18, 26, 31, 42, 56, 60-61, 93-96, 101-102, 108, 111, 124, 159, 161-162, 164, 168, 172

    Social life 134-140

    Sports 142

    Staff status and pay...... 101-105

    Student accommodation 131-134, 158-159

    Students' and Teachers' Union 112-14, 115

    Student Union 112-119, 134-137, 147-150, 167-168

    Student welfare 147-150

    Theatre......................... 137-140

    Transport 150-151

UCU 105-107

UNISON 105-107

Useful knowledge 170

W

Wallis, George 11-12

Walsall 5, 36

War ....

    WW 1 ....11, 18, 51, 71

    WW 2 ....23-24, 51, 71, 73-74

Webb, Charles Morgan................171

Wells, H.G. 67

West Midlands........ 5, 25, 27-28, 39, 107, 143, 157, 161, 164

West Midlands College of Education.. 27-28, 35-37

Wheeler, Sir Charles 23

Whiskey Money 11

White, Keith....................................93

Willetts, David..............................173

Willis, Paul 75

Willis, William 155

Wolverhampton Art Gallery 13-14, 113, 167

Wolverhampton Art School 11-14, 18, 72, 93, 99

Wolverhampton Council...15, 17, 134, 156

Wolverhampton Day Training College 27, 36

Wolverhampton Free Library 9-11, 15, 18, 99

Wolverhampton Grand Theatre 18, 76, 87, 159, 167

Wolverhampton Municipal Technical College 11

Wolverhampton Polytechnic (see also University).... 5, 28, 31-42, 45-46, 56, 58, 60-62, 67, 76-79, 82-83, 88, 92, 93, 94-96, 99-100, 102-104, 106-107, 113, 115, 121, 124-127, 131, 133, 136, 143, 148, 151, 156-9, 165, 167, 169

Wolverhampton Town/City..5-9, 11-12, 15, 19-20, 23, 25, 27-28, 32, 34, 39, 72, 111, 113, 134, 143, 156-59, 163, 168

Wolverhampton Science Park..56, 163

Wolverhampton, Science, Technical and Commercial School 10, 15

Wolverhampton and Staffordshire Technical College......... 15-28, 93, 99

Wolverhampton Technical Teachers' College 27, 36, 98, 133, 172

Wren, Sir Christopher 17

Wulfrun College of Education...25, 127

Wynne, Rev. Geoff 148

Y

Young, Percy M 74, 143-144

The Designer

Our thanks go to graphic designer **Kulbir Entwistle**, who designed the layout of the book. She works in Marketing and Communications at the University. Kulbir graduated from the School of Art & Design of the former Wolverhampton Polytechnic in 1991.

The Photographers

Our thanks also go to all the photographers who have taken pictures of the Colleges, Polytechnic and University over the years. They have left a wonderful record allowing us to select images to tell this story.

Nick Hedges has retired as the Head of Photography at the University. His work can be found in collections at the Birmingham City Archive and on his website:
www.workinglife.org.uk

Dr Aidan Byrne works in the University departments of English and Media, whilst also recording the lively acts of dissent and protest of its staff and students.

Other acknowledgements

We are grateful to staff at the University Print Services Unit, who have patiently digitised documents from the Archives enabling many of the images in this book to appear.

We would also like to acknowledge input from the University copywriters, who helped with proofreading.

Printed by Lion-FPG Ltd **www.lionfpg.co.uk**

> The text paper used for this publication was carbon balanced, and saved 1051 kgs carbon and preserved 88.28 sq m of endangered land.

21 and proud